CATHOLICS IN APARTHEID SOCIETY

edited by Andrew Prior

DAVID PHILIP : CAPE TOWN AND LONDON

First published in 1982 by David Philip, Publisher (Pty) Ltd,
217 Werdmuller Centre, Claremont, Cape Town, 7700 South Africa

Distributed in the United Kingdom and Europe by Global Book
Resources Ltd, 109 Great Russell Street, London WC1B 3NA

ISBN 0 908396 72 4

© David Philip, Publisher 1982

Printed and bound by The Citadel Press, Polaris Road, Lansdowne,
Cape Province, South Africa

CONTENTS

FOREWORD

Conflict between church and state is a perennial feature of church history. This conflict is heightened when states exercise power in areas which the church considers to be its domain; it is stilled when the church is effectively silenced by state authorities or when the church becomes a compliant instrument of the state.

In recent years different regions have, for differing reasons, seen an intensification of such conflict. In eastern Europe the church has fought to retain its autonomy in the face of the totalitarian reconstruction of society; in Latin America it has opposed the use of state power to further the advantage of a privileged élite; and in South Africa the opposition of certain churches to the state's racial policy has shown signs of becoming more intransigent. Much has been written on the churches in eastern Europe and Latin America; less on the churches in South Africa. This volume is aimed at examining the crucial areas of church-state conflict in South Africa and revealing some of their consequences. Such light as this examination can shed will, it is hoped, assist in the struggle against racism and inequality that is being waged in this part of the world.

During the fall term of 1980, the Yale-Wesleyan Southern African Research Program at Yale University generously provided me with an associate fellowship which enabled me to complete the preparation of the manuscript; Augustine Shutte kindly assisted with the editorial work; and Patrick Giddy helped to edit the paper of Bishop Zwane after his tragic death in a motor accident in August, 1980.
Andrew Prior
Cape Town, June 1982

NOTES ON CONTRIBUTORS

Andrew Prior lectures in political science at the University of Cape Town. He studied theology, philosophy, and politics at the Universities of Fribourg, Stellenbosch, and Kent at Canterbury. During part of 1980 he was a Visiting Fellow at Yale University. Among his publications are *Revolution and Philosophy* (Cape Town, 1972) and, with Leonard Thompson, *South African Politics* (Cape Town, 1982).

Bernard Connor is a member of the Southern African province of the Dominican order. He is promotor of studies for the order in Southern Africa, editor of *Grace and Truth*, member of the South African Catholic Bishops' Conference Commission for Justice and Peace, and visiting lecturer in moral theology at St Joseph's Scholasticate, Cedara, Natal.

John de Gruchy was chairman of the United Congregational Church of Southern Africa 1981-2, and is head of the Department of Religious Studies at the University of Cape Town. He is the author of *The Church Struggle in South Africa* (Cape Town, 1979), and editor of the *Journal of Theology for Southern Africa*.

Brigid Flanagan is a secretary on various commissions of the South African Catholic Bishops' Conference. She is a member of the Holy Family congregation. As Assistant General of this congregation from 1963 to 1975, she came into contact with educational systems in Africa, Asia, Latin America and Europe.

Adrian Hastings is Reader in Religious Studies at the University of Aberdeen, Scotland and was seconded in 1982 for two years as Professor of Religious Studies at the University of Zimbabwe. Ordained priest in Rome in 1955, he worked for twelve years in various parts of Africa. Among his books are *Christian Marriage in Africa* (London, 1973), *Wiriyamu* (London, 1974), and *A History of African Christianity 1950-1975* (Cambridge, 1979).

Denis Hurley was consecrated bishop in 1947, and became Archbishop of Durban in 1951. He played a leading part in the deliberations of the Second Vatican Council. He has written extensively on religious, philosophical and social matters, and is a former president of the South African Institute of Race Relations.

Ken Jubber lectures in sociology at the University of Cape Town. He has published various articles on religious sects in South Africa.

James Kiernan is Associate Professor of Social Anthropology at the University of Natal. He was awarded a Ph.D. by the University of Manchester for a study of religious separatism in South Africa. He has written extensively on separatist movements in South Africa.

Albert Nolan is the Provincial of the Dominican Province of Southern Africa, and national chaplain for the Young Christian Students. He is the author of *Jesus before Christianity* (Cape Town, 1976).

Jabulani Nxumalo is a member of the Missionary Oblates of Mary Immaculate, and teaches theology at St Joseph's Scholasticate, Cedara, Natal. He studied in Roma, Lesotho, and at the Gregorian University in Rome.

Trevor Verryn is a canon in the Church of the Province of South Africa (Anglican). He was the founder and for nine years director of the Ecumenical Research Unit in Pretoria, and now lectures in the science of religion at the University of South Africa.

Mandlenkhosi Zwane studied theology at St Peter's Seminary, Hammanskraal, and was consecrated bishop of Manzini, Swaziland, in 1976. In August, 1980, he was killed in a motor accident.

INTRODUCTION

Andrew Prior

The unique character of South African society has created unique problems for the Catholic church. How does an international church, which accepts the inherent equality of all men, survive in a society in which systematic inequalities are government policy? What modifications must the non-racial church make in its practices, to survive in a country in which official racism affects virtually every facet of people's lives? What stance does the church adopt towards the intensifying conflict as increasing numbers of racially oppressed rise up in protest against their bondage? And with whom does the multi-racial church identify in this inter-racial conflict?

All of these problems are rooted in the history of South African catholicism. The Catholic church was allowed to practise openly in South Africa in the early part of the nineteenth century at a time when the seeds of conflict had already been widely sown. Competition between the colonial British and resident Dutch caused these seeds to flourish and made the land-hungry trek-boers move northwards and eastwards. The black kingdoms resisted the threat to their lands and bloody wars ensued. The boers dismembered the black kingdoms, took possession of their lands, and black society became a dependent adjunct to white society. The settler war of 1899–1903 between the boers and British over ownership of Transvaal gold was a prelude to later settler alliances and the gradual incorporation of all whites into a common political society. If the Catholic church played any part in this process it was that of a distant observer, concerned with ministering to the spiritual and educational needs of those European settlers who were catholics.

The second phase of white conquest and black subordination was completed during the twentieth century. Legislation prohibited blacks from owning land in all areas except relatively small reserves, and taxes and land-scarcity forced them to seek work in the burgeoning industrial and mining cities. Lack of political and trade union rights, inadequate training and education, and industrial colour bars forced this group to collapse into a dispossessed class living on the periphery of an increasingly affluent and powerful white society.

Unequal treatment before the law combined with customary segregation to drive a wedge between black and white. The Catholic church was an early victim to this division—black and white catholics lived and worshipped separately and only a predominantly white episcopate and clergy prevented the emergence of two separate churches.

During this period the Catholic church became more actively involved in proselytising among the black population. Starting with schools, clinics and hospitals in the reserves, the immigrant brothers, nuns and priests then turned their attention to the 'locations' and urban slums surrounding the cities, where white schooling, hospitalisation, and social services supplied by state revenues far surpassed the poor quality facilities in the black townships. Often based in white parishes, the 'mission priests' were so successful in 'converting' socially uprooted blacks that by 1980 the black catholics outnumbered white catholics by at least six to one.

This massive influx of blacks into the previously white church did not ripple the tranquil waters of white catholicism. Relatively few blacks entered the priesthood, and those who did ministered to black parishes. Even fewer became bishops and when they did it was in the 'reserves' or the surrounding countries of Lesotho or Swaziland. Black and white churches were separated—not by law but by custom; white church officials ministered to blacks, but no blacks were placed in authority over whites. In this starkly contrasting world of white affluence and black poverty, the church still proclaimed that it was an institution which believed in (even if it did not in fact practise) equality of treatment for all. Insofar as it did not explicitly champion the cause of black advancement, it was because it shared the common liberal belief that industrialisation and the spread of education would, in time, right the wrongs of society and blacks would eventually be incorporated, on a just basis, into white society.

The swift run of national and international events was to test these optimistic beliefs severely. By the end of the second world war anti-racist and anti-colonialist ideologies were in the ascendant. The racist beliefs and practices of the colonial powers were losing their appearance of legitimacy and the new age of the break-up of colonial empires was beginning to dawn. South Africa was not isolated in these developments, and demands from blacks for an elimination of racism became more vociferous.

Ironically, the rise of black South African nationalism paralleled the rise of white Afrikaner nationalism. Playing on the racist fears of Afrikaners, the National Party took control of the government in 1948. Its political objective was straightforward: to prevent the emergence of an open, egalitarian, non-racial South Africa through the legal entrenching of racial divisions, and the systematic exclusion of blacks from political rights. To achieve this it passed legislation which suppressed political opponents, removed voting rights from persons of mixed race, prohibited inter-racial marriage, separated amenities, including churches, residential areas, schools and universities, and broke up families by tightening up on the laws which prohibited blacks from moving freely from the 'reserves' (later termed 'bantustans', 'homelands', or 'national states') to the cities in search of work.

The catholic bishops met the news of a National Party victory with incredulity. With many others of the time, they thought that the anti-racist rhetoric would be tempered by the realities of industrialisation and the need for economic integration into a common society. At worst, they considered the National Party to be an evanescent phenomenon which would be voted out of power at the 1952 elections. They were wrong on both counts. The National Party forged ahead to counteract the revolutionary changes being brought about by modernisation, and harmonised its racist beliefs and practices with an ebullient capitalism. The National Party was re-elected to power in 1952 with an increased majority. Since then, it has gained strength in virtually every election, and its racist policies have revolutionised the country.

The catholic bishops were at first reluctant to confront the government. The harsher features of racist legislation and state intervention in catholic schooling changed this. In 1950 the bishops issued the first of many statements deploring these state policies. Mild and conciliatory though this statement was, it tempered in no respect whatsoever the government's intention to implement its plan for the country.

The current of national and international events was flowing rapidly to change the mood of black-white relations in South Africa. White racism was no longer acceptable to the international community, and its proponents were moving into a state of siege. Spurred on by the mood of the times South African blacks rose up against their oppression. At Sharpeville in 1960, over sixty of a large crowd of Africans, most of them women and children, who had come to protest against the pass laws, were gunned down by the police. In the aftermath African political movements were banned, government repression was stepped up, and the armed revolutionary answer to the white regime became a real possibility.

During the 1960s the increasing assertiveness of blacks, directed partly by the 'black consciousness' ideology, was felt in the Catholic church. Blacks began to question the ability of the white leaders of a largely black church adequately to represent their interests. At the beginning of the 1970s black catholic priests formed their own caucus, and black students of the National Catholic Federation of Students, traditionally a racially integrated group, broke away to link with the black student organisation, the South African Students Organisation.

The defiant mood of South African blacks was further fuelled by the collapse of the Portuguese African empire in 1974, the coming of independence to Mozambique and Angola, the stepping up of the Zimbabwean civil war, and the 1976 Soweto uprising of black youth.

At the beginning of the 1980s the South African church finds itself caught up in the serious tensions of the time: conflicting ideologies, divisions within its own body, the demands for self-reform, and its opposition to a government with whom it has an increasingly uneasy relationship.

A wide range of contributors—social scientists, theologians, and churchmen—examine these issues in this book. It is divided into three parts. The *first* provides a broad overview of South African catholicism, the nature of the society of which it is a part, the church's teaching on social matters, and its involvement in South African society. The *second* looks at specific issues concerning South African catholicism: calvinism, education, separatism, black catholics, and the relationship between black and white priests. The *third* looks critically at the South African Catholic church, and makes projections for future developments. The book concludes with the statements of the bishops on these matters, and provides a useful reference to official church teaching. The success of this project will be measured by the degree to which it correctly analyses, constructively criticises, and provides guidelines for understanding and solving some of the problems facing the South African Catholic church.

1 THE POLITICAL AND SOCIAL CONTEXT

Albert Nolan

The second Vatican council has encouraged catholics to analyse the situation in which they live so that they will be able to see clearly what their religious response to their society ought to be. This article aims to provide such an understanding by analysing selected key features of South African society, the dominant ideology which justifies and structures it, the resistance to this ideology, South Africa's place in the world community, and the practical consequences of all of these for the South African Catholic church.

Analysis is a basis for understanding. To analyse something is to break it down into its component parts. In social analysis we try to uncover the structures or dynamics of society. Different people will give different analyses or explanations of the society in which they live. Their assumptions, interests and concerns give them a variety of perspectives on the same social reality. It is important, then, before starting, to declare one's assumptions, interests and concerns. The assumption in this article is the one at the heart of christian social teaching, that people are more important than things—any 'things': money, possessions, property, power, status, race or ideas. The concern is for the sufferings of people, and the interest is centred on the needs of people. That is the starting point and perspective of our social analysis.

THE DOMINANT IDEOLOGY

In order to avoid misunderstanding I would like to begin by outlining what I understand by the word *ideology*. An ideology is a set of ideas about what society should be like. But it is called an ideology only when the set of ideas is adhered to uncritically, dogmatically, and with a great deal of emotion rather than as a result of some kind of objective reasoning based upon facts. In other words, the set of ideas usually becomes a set of myths and prejudices that

*This is a modified version of two articles that originally appeared in the South African Dominican journal *Grace and Truth* (1982/1 and 1982/2).

are used to justify or rationalise what we would want our society to be like. The dominant ideology in a country is the one according to which the country is ruled and governed. It is the basis of government policy and practice.

The dominant ideology in South Africa today can be broken down into four component parts or sub-ideologies: the racial ideology, the capitalist ideology, the ideology of Afrikaner nationalism and the ideology of national security ('total strategy'). These are not really different and separate ideologies but it is useful to distinguish them as different ideo-sets or sub-ideologies, and then to look into each one, to discover how they are related and to see how they form one structure or system—the dominant ideology.

Racism

In South Africa this ideology has been called *segregation, trusteeship, apartheid, separate development, multi-nationalism* and *ethnicity*. It has obviously undergone some changes and adaptions over the years but there is no denying that it has been and still is a form of discrimination against people of colour who are believed to be inferior, less developed, less civilised, unintelligent, slow thinkers, lazy, irresponsible and dangerous. And for these reasons it is argued that they ought to be separated as much as possible from white people. This racial ideology has been the cause of a very great deal of suffering for a very great number of people.

However the point of an analysis is not to condemn but to understand. Thus the questions we need to ask are: What are the historical origins of this racial ideology? Where and how did it arise and what circumstances enabled it to continue and to be gradually altered? In short we must look at two things: its *origins* and its *development*.

Origins

Racial prejudice was part and parcel of all European colonialism. In Africa, Asia and the Americas, people of colour were treated as inferior and used as slaves or servants. However this does not account for the specific form of rigid and institutionalised separation that arose only in South Africa. Elsewhere there was always a certain measure of mixing, and people who became 'educated' and 'civilised' were often assimilated and treated as equal. This did begin to happen in the early days of the Cape colony, but something different happened in the interior.

The Voortrekkers who travelled to and gradually settled in the northern Cape, the Orange Free State, the Transvaal and part of

Natal developed another kind of society—a society that can best be described as *semi-feudal*.

Feudalism is a pre-capitalist form of society. It is based upon a subsistence economy with bargaining and small local trading rather than commerce and industry. It divides society into *lords* and *serfs* and it bases this division upon ancestry. One is born into the aristocracy or into serfdom. There is no way that anyone can move up or down from the one 'estate' to the other. The 'estate' into which one is born is seen as the will of God who decides where one will be born.

However lords and serfs form one community. They have mutual responsibilities. The serf must work for and obey his feudal lord and, because *noblesse oblige*, the feudal lord must protect and care for his serfs. He is the parent or guardian and his serfs are like children.

This was the kind of pre-capitalist society developed by the Voortrekkers. The Voortrekker was not an employer, he was a kind of feudal lord or aristocrat and people of colour were not at first employees or labourers, they were serfs—at least after the emancipation of slaves. Ancestry in this case was racial. The race into which one was born was seen as the will of God. It determined one's place in the community forever. White blood gave one the feudal authority of guardianship over people of a different race or ancestry. All power, all decision-making and any kind of voting or franchise would be in the hands of the aristocracy. It was totally unthinkable that serfs should share power or have a vote. This belief underlay the principle asserted in the constitution of the Transvaal Republic that there would be no equality between white and black in church or state.

This was the origin of the particular form of racialism that we find in South Africa. With the help of calvinism, and especially the calvinist doctrines of predestination and election, racialism developed into an ideology with a strong religious backing. Calvinism itself was not the origin of the racial ideology. Calvinists in other parts of the world are no more and no less racialist than other christians. In fact, calvinists who do not come from the economic and social background of Afrikaner semi-feudalism, like calvinists in the Netherlands and the United States or English-speaking calvinists in South Africa (presbyterians), all dispute this racial interpretation of Calvin and the bible. It was in the economic and social circumstances of the Great Trek that the Old Testament idea of a chosen people came to be applied to the white aristocracy while the black serfs were seen as the cursed sons of Ham or simply as the biblical heathens. And it was only in these same circumstances that divine predestination could be interpreted as God's will to separate the races and to give one race the authority of guardianship over another so that marriages across the colour-line could be seen as a sin against the divinely established order of things. Calvinism does not explain the racial ideology but it certainly gave it a strength and a coherence that it would not otherwise have had.*

Developments

In normal circumstances one would have expected this kind of racial ideology to disappear as the pre-capitalist economy of the northern Afrikaners gradually gave way to a commercial, mining and industrial form of capitalism. This is what happened in Europe and elsewhere, but somehow it did not happen in South Africa. Racialism not only persisted but it gradually came to triumph over the more 'liberal' ideas of British capitalism. Even after the Afrikaner defeat in the Anglo-Boer War, which was in many ways a clash between the semi-feudal ideas of the Boer and the capitalist aspirations of the Briton, it was the racialism of the Afrikaner that came to dominate the scene. Why did racialism persist even after the Afrikaner himself had entered fully into the capitalism system?

Before we try to answer this question we shall have to take a closer look at the nature, needs and interests of capitalism in South Africa.

Capitalism

The capitalism of high finance, mining and industry was introduced into South Africa after the discovery of diamonds and gold during the second half of the nineteenth century. A new wave of white settlers came to South Africa simply to get rich.

Capitalism divides society in two basic classes: the middle class (bourgeoisie) and the working class (proletariat). The basis of the division is not ancestry or race but money and ownership. This division is therefore not fixed. People can move from one class to another. The middle-class owner and employer, unlike the feudal lord, has no responsibility for his employees. The understanding is: they work for him, he pays them a wage for their work. The new white settlers were soon divided into these two classes: owners and workers.

*For a fuller discussion of calvinism and racism, see John de Gruchy's article *Catholics in a Calvinist Country* below, pp 67–82.

The basic motivation in capitalism is the desire for money and its aim is the maximisation of *profits*. One of the main interests of the capitalist then is cheap labour. The white workers from Europe were not cheap labour. They were accustomed to have rights, trade unions and good wages. They were skilled workers, and the mine magnates needed their skills, but they also needed many unskilled workers who would not be able to demand high wages. It would otherwise have been impossible to maximise profits. This is where the racial ideology turned out to be extremely useful.

The racial ideology deprived blacks of all rights, especially the right to vote, and in general it enabled the blacks to be treated differently. This meant that hundreds of thousands of them could be employed as cheap labour without any danger of their organising trade unions, strikes and election campaigns against the capitalists. The only problem was how to entice black people to come and work on the mines. At this period they were on the land either as farmers themselves or as serfs to white farmers. They managed to subsist in this way and had no desire to go and work for wages in the mines.

The first strategy of the mine-owners was to get the government to tax the black people on the land and to demand that the tax be paid in cash. This would force them to seek employment. A series of tax laws (hut tax, poll tax, labour tax) brought a fair number of blacks to the mines—but not enough. The next step was the Land Act of 1913. This Act divided all the land into land that could only be owned or rented by whites and land that could only be owned or rented by blacks. The latter amounted to less than ten per cent of the land, and the result was that the tens of thousands of blacks who lost the land they had previously owned or rented flocked to the mines to find employment. Racial discrimination had thus helped the capitalists to create a cheap, unskilled labour force.

Racialism helped the capitalists in another way too. It divided the working class. It prevented black and white workers from getting together to demand equal rights or a better deal for all the workers.

Finally racialism was also of benefit to the white workers. They wanted high wages and protection from too much competition from blacks who might take over their trades and skills. Race was a convenient way of achieving this and still is today. A worker who can have many privileges and much protection because of his white skin will quickly adopt a racial ideology. To this day they will say that what they want to maintain is their 'standard of living'.

The interests of white workers, of course, did not always coincide with the interests of the mine-owners. For example, after the First World War when the mines could only make a big profit by cutting down on white wages and giving some semi-skilled jobs to blacks at lower wages, the white workers went on strike. The 1922 white worker strike was ended by the Smuts government with considerable violence—Benoni and Germiston were bombed and there was fighting in the streets of Johannesburg. One hundred and fifty-three white workers were killed and five hundred wounded. Racialism had now become a deeply entrenched attitude of the white working class.

Afrikaner nationalism
Nationalism is a way of uniting people who have somewhat different interests. The history of white nationalism in South Africa is the history of the attempts to unite Boer and Briton, and the white working class and the white bourgeoisie. The Act of Union and the South African Party of Botha and Smuts did not fully succeed in uniting Boer and Briton and simply failed to unite the white working and middle classes, as the events of 1922 demonstrated. The 1933 coalition government of Smuts's South African Party and Hertzog's National Party succeeded in uniting the white working class among themselves and with a certain number of the white middle class. But even this did not create a viable white South African nationalism. Among other things there were too few common national symbols like language, culture and religion, and too few common economic interests. It was in this context that an uncompromising Afrikaner nationalism was developed. It was able to create a strong bonding between certain whites not only on the basis of a common history, a common cultural heritage, a common interpretation of calvinism and a common racial ideology, but also on the basis of a common economic interest of competition with the economically superior English. A very important part of the rise of Afrikaner nationalism was the pooling of resources between the Afrikaner middle and working classes, both of whom were economically worse off than their English-speaking counterparts. Out of all this was forged a very strong bond of nationalism. But it was a form of nationalism that defined itself over against the English population and the British Empire, and also the black, 'Coloured' and Indian populations. Racialism had become a form of nationalism.

The new economic and social circumstances meant that the old feudal way of understanding racialism had to be adapted. This led to the 'homelands' policy, the policy of separate nationalisms and separate cultures. It could no longer be argued that blacks had no rights because they were serfs, so it was argued that they had no rights because they belonged to other 'nations' in separate 'homelands'. They could be given rights in areas that were outside the maximum profit areas of mining, industry and commercial farming. The black man became a migrant labourer instead of a serf. The ideology was formulated by the Afrikaner but it was extremely profitable to all white capitalists. Unlike other capitalists in the rest of the world, the white South African capitalist would not be responsible for contributing in tax to the education and upbringing of his black employees' young and the care of their aged. This would be done by their 'homeland' governments. The capitalist would be responsible for the expenses of his workers only during their active working years.

In recent times, however, the needs of capitalism have changed, and this has led to further adaptations in the racial and nationalist ideologies. It is a constant refrain in company reports that there is an urgent need for many more skilled workers: artisans, technicians, clerks and middle managers. Unless this need is met, they say, there will be a slower rate of economic growth, or perhaps no growth at all, and this would curtail profits. But now the only way of meeting this need rapidly is to enlist the aid of the black population.

The solution of the English and Afrikaans enlightened ('verligtes') is to divide apartheid into *petty apartheid* (separate amenities and job reservation) and *grand apartheid* (the 'homelands' policy and the migrant labour system), and then gradually to phase out the former while keeping the latter. On the one hand, they feel that this is the only way to get more skilled workers and to create a lower middle class of satisfied blacks which will prevent unrest and have a vested interest in the system. On the other hand, unskilled workers will have to remain migrant workers with a 'homeland' elsewhere in order to keep down labour costs and to avoid majority rule.

But this adaptation is not easy to achieve, as the prime minister P. W. Botha has discovered. The phasing out of petty apartheid is not in the interest of the conservatives ('verkramptes') because they are largely the lower-middle-class whites whose jobs may be threatened under such a dispensation, and commercial farmers who do not need skilled workers.

The white population is now divided. The National party is somewhere in the middle trying desperately to hold together the 'not-too-verlig' and the 'not-too-verkramp', while the 'more-verlig' join the Progressive Federal Party and the 'more-verkramp' join the Herstigte Nasionale Party, the new Conservative Party, or groups even further to the right.

This has put great strains on the whole ideology of nationalism as it has previously been conceived, and especially on Afrikaner nationalism. Both English and Afrikaans capitalists and academics have more in common with one another than they have with the English or Afrikaans working class or lower middle class. They can no longer be united around a common culture or language or religion because of their different economic interests, their different ways of maintaining their economic privileges or 'standards of living'. However, a new and somewhat different form of white nationalism is now developing—the national security state.

The national security state (NSS)

This is a relatively new form of totalitarian nationalism. It has some similarities with fascism, nazism and the totalitarian communist states. But it also differs from all of these, and exists to some degree in many other countries, for example Brazil, Argentina, Uruguay, Paraguay, Chile, Taiwan, South Korea, the Philippines and Israel. In fact it originated in Brazil less than twenty years ago. The set of ideas that forms this particular ideology is as follows:

1 *The state* is supreme and absolute. It must control and determine everything in the life of the nation. It cannot be controlled, dictated to or influenced by anything outside of itself, not even the church.

2 *The enemy* of the state is seen as communism. According to the geopolitics of this ideology, the world is divided into two camps, west and east. The west is the free world and the east is the one and only enemy; thus everything and anything that appears to threaten the supremacy of the state is labelled 'communism'. The state is threatened not only by external enemies (Russia and the other 'communist' countries) but also by internal enemies—in fact, every citizen of the state is a potential enemy because every citizen is potentially a 'communist'.

3 Consequently, the state is understood to be facing a *total onslaught*. It can be attacked and undermined militarily, economically, politically, culturally and pyschologically.

4 The state is also involved in a *total war*. There is no peace and the state cannot act as if it were at peace. There is a continuous war and the state must develop a *total strategy* to combat the enemy. This strategy is called total because it includes a military, economic, political, cultural and psychological strategy. No area of life can be excluded from this war and its strategy.

5 The highest aim or goal of the state, therefore, is its *security* and *survival*. Every and any means can be justified if it is deemed necessary for state security. And everything and anything that threatens the security of the state must be eliminated and destroyed.

The NSS does not see its highest aim as the welfare or service of the people, but as the survival and security of the state. The security in question is not that of the people but of the state. Hence the phrase *state security*.

6 Because any means at all can be used to ensure the security of the state, we find most of the following phenomena in every national security state in the world today: a strong army; security or secret police; riot police; detention without trial; the banning of people, organisations and meetings; telephone tapping and the opening of mail; censorship of all mass media; official secrecy about prisons; interrogation and torture; road blocks and the searching of persons and homes; the use of informers and spies; people beaten up, attacked with tear gas or shot; people dying in prison or 'committing suicide'; a propaganda campaign through all the mass media and overseas.

The original Afrikaner nationalism is in the process of being transformed into a national security ideology. It should be noticed that over the past fifteen years or so much new legislation has been not about apartheid but about security. In the last two general elections the slogans of the National Party have invoked not apartheid (the HNP has taken that over) but 'security' and 'survival'. This ideological language became more explicit when P. W. Botha became prime minister. P. W. Botha as minister of Defence had been much influenced by Generals like Magnus Malan, who has now himself become minister of Defence and Security. There is now also a National Security Council which includes members of the military, and which can veto any decision of any other government department. Other NSSs have a similar council.

What are the circumstances giving rise to this way of thinking? The ideology has arisen not so much in the first world of Europe and North America but in the more developed third world countries.

In these countries, where there is a relatively small wealthy élite
and a large number of peasants, workers, or unemployed, the
ruling class has wanted to remain capitalist while the majority of
the people has wanted changes that would tend towards socialism.
When the majority of the people in a country is dissatisfied,
dictatorial methods and totalitarian ideologies have to be used to
maintain the status quo. Liberal democracy is a luxury which
these third world states have felt they could not afford if the capitalist status quo was to be maintained. Thus they have become
either military dictatorships or oligarchies elected by a franchise
that excludes most of the dissatisfied people. They have developed
ideologies like that of the NSS to justify their methods of preven-
ting any real change.

The growing dissatisfaction of the majority of South Africans
caused the military strategists and some of the politicians to realise
that the only way to maintain the racial and capitalist status quo
was by developing a NSS ideology. Some of those who identify
with the capitalist or nationalist ideologies do not realise this and
therefore criticise the security measures taken by the state. Hence,
although the NSS ideology is at the service of these ideologies,
there is sometimes a measure of tension between them.

* * *

We can now see how closely related and inter-linked these sub-
ideologies are. There are tensions between the 'verkramptes', who
want to maintain the traditional racial ideology, and 'verligtes',
who want to adapt to the needs of capitalism or 'free enterprise',
and also between those who understand why strict security measures are necessary and those who do not fully understand this.
But in the last resort the ideologies are one and united. Together
they form the context within which the Catholic church in South
Africa functions.

THE OPPOSITION

This analysis begins with a distinction between those who oppose
the system from within the system, and those who opposite it
from without. The first group are 'collaborators' because they co-
operate with the system at least to the extent of accepting a place
within its structures as a platform from which to oppose it. The
second group are 'non-collaborators' because they refuse to co-
operate in any way and do not wish to occupy any place within

the structures of the system.

The first group may be 'reformists' if they want to correct, amend, and improve the system. The second may be 'revolutionaries', not because they neccesarily want to overthrow the government with violence, but because they want to replace the system with a new and different system. Here there are two different concepts of change. Variations on both types of opposition can be found in South Africa.

Collaborative opposition

The first name that comes to mind here is that of Gatsha Buthelezi, leader of the Inkatha movement. His opposition is collaborative because he has accepted a government-created platform as a 'homeland' leader, and is using it to oppose the government. All the 'homeland' leaders are in this position, although most of the others offer the government little or no opposition. On the whole they have adopted the South African system in almost every respect except for social apartheid. The so-called 'independent homelands' like Transkei, Ciskei and Venda have security measures that are as harsh as, if not harsher than, those of South Africa itself. And all the homelands are part of the same capitalist system. Buthelezi stands out because of his refusal to accept 'independence' for his 'homeland'.

Those who have accepted the structures offered by the government to 'Coloureds' and Indians are in much the same position as the 'homeland' leaders. There is the now defunct Coloured Persons Representative Council, and the South African Indian Council that is limping badly owing to lack of support from South African Indians. The latest attempt to find a place for 'Coloureds' and Indians has been the creation of the President's Council. There have been certain mild attempts from these quarters to reform the system. But so far nothing has been achieved and when the 'Coloured' Labour Party tried too hard their platform within the system was simply eliminated.

Mention should also be made of the community councils in the black townships and of the growing black middle class. Their aim is also reform through collaborative opposition.

To complete the picture, the Progressive Federal Party should be listed here. They are part of the white parliamentary system, but they do oppose some aspects of the system and they stand for one man one vote and a national convention to formulate a new constitution. This would indeed create new possibilities for South

Africa. However it is highly unlikely that they will ever gain a majority in an all-white parliament.

Non-collaborative opposition
The best way to understand the dimensions and the variations of this kind of opposition today is to trace its history in South Africa.

The beginnings of the African National Congress (ANC)
Leaving aside some minor protests and moral indignation in earlier years, one could say that the history of black resistance began with the peace treaty between the British and the Boer Republics after the Anglo-Boer War. Blacks felt that they had been betrayed by the British, upon whom they had relied for more rights, especially a nation-wide franchise. While whites met to plan the Union of South Africa, blacks met in congresses to formulate petitions against *their exclusion from this Union*. They sent their petitions to the white leaders and to Britain, and they even sent a delegation to London. Their petitions were ignored.

The ANC was founded in 1912. It was the black response to the all-white Act of Union in 1910. Its members were lawyers, teachers, ministers of religion and traditional chiefs—almost all products of missionary education. At first they called themselves the South African Native National Congress, but the name was soon changed.

The aim of Union, as seen by the ANC, was to unify Boer and Briton against black South Africans. The aim of the ANC was *to unify black and white* by absorbing blacks into the white society and government. This remained the goal of all ANC activities until the 'Africanism' of the 1940s. Moreover the activities of the ANC in these early years was confined to meetings and written petitions and protests. Gradually these developed into acts of passive resistance and civil disobedience like strikes, demonstrations and boycotts and later still they organised the Defiance Campaign and the burning of passes.

The successive white governments, however, became more and more intransigent, gradually depriving blacks, 'Coloureds' and Indians of the few privileges that they had had in the Cape and Natal, while at the same time crushing all forms of passive resistance.

The Pan-Africanist Congress (PAC) breakaway
The ANC resistance experienced ups and downs and developed through alliances and breakaways. There were two main tendencies:

the one towards *unity* and the other towards *Africanism*. The first aimed to develop a broad front of solidarity between all resistance groups whether educated middle class or trade union working class, whether Indian, 'Coloured', or black or white. This led to several different alliances including an alliance with the mostly white Communist Party. The other aimed toward 'Africanism', which was introduced into the ANC by the Youth League in 1940. It was espoused by such men as Mandela, Sisulu, Sobukwe and Lembede. Lembede, a catholic lawyer, was the philosopher of Africanism. He developed an African view of man and society, and argued that Africans should not be absorbed into white society *but should be liberated from it*. This gave the ANC a new aim, but it also tended to jeopardise the alliances and broad front of unity with those who were not African.

Lembede, Mandela and Tembo were able to hold these two tendencies together, and the ANC still manages to do this today. But others like Sisulu, Sobukwe and Leballo felt it necessary to break away. They founded the PAC as an exclusively African and anti-communist movement.

The banning of the ANC and the PAC

1960 was a turning point. The PAC started a campaign against pass laws. The ANC joined in. Masses of people marched to police stations and threw down their passes. The police used force to disperse them in Langa, Nyanga and particularly in Sharpeville, where over 60 were killed and 180 wounded. A state of emergency was declared, many were arrested and the ANC and PAC were banned.

For the ANC this was the last straw. They went underground, re-organised outside the country and decided to give up their previous insistence that only non-violent means should be used. Non-violent resistance had always been met by violent repression. The white man seemed to understand only violence. They decided that peaceful means alone would never succeed against this kind of government. Thus began the armed struggle.

Black consciousness

For about ten years after the banning of the ANC and the PAC and the exile or imprisonment of all their leaders, there was a lull in the non-collaborative opposition in South Africa. Armed struggle remained an idea rather than a reality. Then at the beginning of the 1970s a new mood and a new initiative began. It was known as 'black consciousness' and its central figure was Steve Biko. To a certain extent it was inspired by the black consciousness or black power movements in North America, but it was given a genuine South African flavour.

The main aim of the movement was to restore the black person's pride and dignity and his confidence in himself. In many cases this had been destroyed, not only by apartheid and the defeats of the past, but also by paternalistic white liberals who often took the initiative for black people.

Black consciousness was therefore an exclusively black movement. It spawned all sorts of organisations open only to blacks. The movement reached its height in 1976 with the student uprising in Soweto. In October 1977 the government tried to obliterate it by banning all its many organisations and by banning or imprisoning most of its leaders and collaborators. Steve Biko died in prison.

The resurgence of the ANC

This time there was no lull. The banning of black consciousness organisations was at least one of the factors that led to the phenomenal revival both inside and outside South African of the ANC and its armed wing, *Umkhonto we Sizwe*. Indications of this new phase in the resistance include the ever-increasing acts of sabotage, attacks on police stations and even army camps, the increased support for the ANC outside South Africa and its marked rise in popularity inside the country. This has led some analysts to predict a comfortable victory for the ANC if a 'one man one vote' election were to take place today.

Several factors have contributed to the rise in popularity of the ANC. Among them are the following:

1 The success of other liberation movements and liberation armies in Southern Africa (the MPLA in Angola, Frelimo in Mozambique, Zanu in Zimbabwe, and the expected victory of Swapo in Namibia) has given the ANC a similar sort of image and credibility in the eyes of many South African blacks.

2 After 1976, when the government crushed the non-violent resistance, including the black consciousness organisations, many young people fled the country and joined the ANC. And many of those who stayed behind now feel too that armed struggle is the only realistic means to liberation.

3 Another factor is the fading of the black consciousness movement. Many of its adherents began to see that the fundamental

problem is not race but class, not prejudice but money—or rather economic exploitation. Having regained their pride and dignity they could look back on the days of black consciousness as a phase that had now been superseded. The new phase in the struggle is characterised by non-racialism and co-operation with whites. The ANC has always maintained a non-racialist stand. Today black consciousness survives as an alternative only in the small group known as the Azanian People's Organisation.

4 Closely linked to this is the fading of the PAC within and outside South Africa. With internal divisions, leadership problems, the superseding of black consciousness and Africanism by a mood of non-racialism, the PAC has lost most of its power and influence outside the country and has all but disappeared off the scene inside.

5 Another factor is the recent change of focus from students to workers, from school boycotts to trade union activity and strikes. The worker struggle and resistance in the form of strikes has a long history in South Africa. It is not possible to detail that long history here, but much of it has been associated with the ANC. While it is very difficult to know how much of the extraordinary growth in 'labour unrest' in recent years is linked directly or indirectly to the ANC, black workers do tend to look to the ANC and its flag as symbols of future liberation.

6 The broadness of ANC policy and especially of the Freedom Charter (adopted by a large gathering of people of all races in Kliptown in 1955) is another factor operating in its favour. The ANC presents itself as an alliance of all 'progressive' forces including the small South African Communist Party. The Freedom Charter calls for an extension of the franchise to all South Africans, the de-racialisation of the legal system, the extension of liberal freedoms to all in the country, and a partial nationalisation of the major organs of wealth production.

7 The ANC has gained in international prestige by signing the Geneva Convention. This includes the undertaking to avoid attacking or harming non-combatant civilians and an agreement to take prisoners rather than to kill opposing combatants. South Africa has not signed.

All of these factors taken together convince many South Africans that the ANC is the only feasible alternative to the present system.

However, many blacks and most whites reject the ANC. They do so for several reasons: the South African government has successfully labelled it a 'terrorist' movement; its association with communism or the USSR; its non-racial nationalism rather than black nationalism; its headquarters are outside South Africa; its internal divisions; it is not sufficiently marxist. This does not include that large group that withdraws from politics from fear or indifference.

* * *

What conclusions can we draw from the above analysis? Without attempting any judgments about what should or should not be done we can at least recognise the dimensions of the conflict in South Africa. We live in a thoroughly revolutionary situation. The government calls it a 'total onslaught' or 'total war' and responds with its 'total strategy', but the true dimensions of the conflict are more soberly summed up by Mr Harald Pakendorf, the editor of the pro-government Afrikaans newspaper *Die Vaderland*. He says that the National Party and the African National Congress were formed with the same purpose—to rule South Africa:

> Until now we [the Afrikaners] have won, because we have had a dispensation in our favour in which we have decided who may vote. . . . The tables are now turned—we fought for our freedom, now they are fighting for their freedom. We could support them in their struggle in terms of our history, except that they are fighting against us for their freedom. That is the bitter irony. We, the first freedom-fighters, the militant anti-colonialists of the century, have become the oppressors.*

The future is not easy to predict, but we can be sure that revolutionary activities ranging from guerrilla warfare (rural and urban) to strikes, boycotts and riots will increase year by year. On the one hand the state with its security measures and military apparatus seems to be invincible and on the other hand the opposition has become more confident and defiant. The struggle could go on for a very long time. Moreover, there are other factors involved, like the strategic position of South Africa in the world and the attitudes of other nations to South Africa. We must now look at these other factors.

THE INTERNATIONAL PERSPECTIVE

A strategic nation
South Africa has become one of the most powerful nations in the world. It is now a highly industrialised and highly urbanised

___

* Quoted in *Ecunews*, 2/1982, pp. 23–4.

country. It is richer in minerals than any other Western nation, and it has a high proportion of the minerals that are of strategic necessity for the survival of western capitalism. Moreover the Cape route is of strategic importance in the balance of power between Russia and America. There is a growing feeling among many western nations that they are far more dependent upon South Africa than South Africa is upon them.

The constellation of states
A very important element in the 'total strategy' is the so-called Constellation of South African States. This concept includes the 'homeland' states, Namibia, Lesotho, Botswana, Swaziland, Zimbabwe, Zambia and Malawi. It is said that they should become inter-dependent economically, but in fact what South Africa has in mind is the control of all its neighbours by making them more economically dependent upon South Africa. In other words, the surrounding nations would become dependent on South Africa as the third world is dependent upon the first world. This is sometimes called 'neo-colonialism' or 'economic imperialism'.

The 'frontline states' have met to plan their response to this strategy, but they are all so economically dependent on South Africa that it will not be easy to resist it. And even if they did succeed, the closer neighbours have no chance of becoming economically independent of South Africa. This will therefore be a very important factor in the future power struggle.

The fourth block
There has been talk in recent years of forming a 'fourth block' in the world. It would be an alliance of the national security states. South Africa would be one of the most important, if not the most important, partner in this block. South Africa is very busy forging closer links with Chile and Taiwan (the only two nations who accepted an invitation to the 1981 Republic Day festivities) as well as the Argentine, Paraguay and Uruguay, and has a strategic alliance with the only 'nuclear' nation in the block so far: Israel.

All these nations have begun to feel that the west has become too soft on communism and that a much harder line is necessary. The USA under Reagan now agrees with them and is trying to prevent possible breaches with the national security states and especially with South Africa. South Africa almost seems to be in a position to snub the USA while the USA feels it cannot snub South Africa.

THE PRACTICAL CONSEQUENCES

The purpose of this analysis is not to speculate about national and international politics. It is to understand the social forces that determine the lives of the people in South Africa to whom the christian message is communicated. Thus the real issue here is the practical consequences that the dominant ideology has on the daily lives of the people—all the people, black and white, rich and poor.

Urbanisation

Urbanisation as such is not a consequence of the dominant ideology in South Africa, but the usual problems and sufferings of urbanisation are made far worse by the South African system of group areas, pass laws, job reservation, separate amenities and migrant labour.

Urbanisation breaks down traditional community values and customs and throws people into a world of anonymous individualism, competition and the survival of the fittest. When this is combined with separation from one's family, it becomes extremely unsettling, and leads very easily to the collapse of a person's moral framework. The big city then exploits this collapse for profit by providing people with outlets for pleasure.

Poverty and wealth

The dominant ideology with its strong capitalist tendency and its discrimination against people of colour produces a situation in which the rich get richer and the poor poorer. There is no limit to the personal accumulation of wealth by the rich in South Africa. On the other hand, with the rising cost of living, ever-increasing thousands of unemployed, a worsening housing shortage and the rapid growth in population, the poor are growing in number and are becoming poorer. This poverty is hidden from the eyes of the rich and the fairly well-off by group areas, separate homelands, or re-settlement areas.

Health

Poverty leads to disease, malnutrition and starvation. The mortality rate for black children is very high and hospitals are hopelessly overcrowded and often very far from where the poor live. Some of us have seen the appalling conditions in many black hospitals. The dominant ideology with its concern for white superiority, high profits and state security does not give their improvement a high priority.

Ignorance

The policy of separation tends to keep the races ignorant of one another and to kindle myths and prejudices about one another. This is made far worse by censorship and the intense campaign of propaganda through all the media, so that fewer and fewer people have any real understanding or even information about what is happening in their own country. Even education, especially with its programmes of 'youth preparedness', has become a form of propaganda. Military training or national service is now almost a kind of brainwashing, so that white youth today support the dominant ideology even more vigorously and violently than their parents do.

The lack of education, or very poor education, among black people leads to another, more straightforward, kind of ignorance. The situation in most black schools is one of bad teaching, inadequate facilities and corruption. Moreover the values that are so effectively promoted by capitalist advertising brings with them an ever-increasing destruction of moral values, let alone gospel values.

Ignorance of religion is also increasing and the separation of religion from politics leads to confusion about the true meaning of the christian faith. This is exacerbated by the association of christianity with the dominant ideology. Not surprisingly, politicised young blacks find it difficult to take christianity seriously.

Ignorance and confusion are amongst the most frightening consequences of the present system in South Africa. But in spite of this there is occurring a very deep and honest questioning which has the potential of leading to a deeper understanding of man, society, values and the christian faith.

Fear

Fear is the overriding emotion in South African society. Much of what is said and done by rich and poor, black and white is based upon fear. Whites fear blacks and many of today's racial prejudices are based upon an unfounded fear of black 'savagery'.

Blacks, too, are fearful of whites. They fear those upon whom their very livelihood and continued existence depends. They fear the police and the army whom they see as merciless enemy. Blacks live in constant fear of being punished, beaten, imprisoned, endorsed out, losing their jobs, their houses and the little freedom they might possess. And as if this were not enough, they are also 'terrorised' by gangsters in the crime-ridden urban townships. They live in a perpetual state of insecurity.

Alienation

Everything in the system promotes alienation. People are separated from one another by group areas and other forms of discrimination. Husbands are separated from their wives and children. Individuals are separated or alienated from one another by competition and individualism. People treat one another as objects to be exploited or as dispensable labour units. The value-system of, and the pursuit of, wealth, status, luxuries, pleasure and possessions alienates people both from their true selves and from one another.

This means that almost everyone in the society is frustrated. Both black and white feel powerless, helpless and insecure. And this in turn leads to every imaginable form of escapism: alcohol, drugs, passive forms of entertainment, sport and religion. Sport and religion need not be forms of escapism but in the disturbed and frustrated society in which we live, everything and anything can be used (or abused) as a way of forgetting or distracting oneself from the unbearable realities of life. Religion, as we know, can so easily be used as a form of opium.

Violence

Last, but not least, the intransigence of the dominant ideology has created a horrifyingly violent society. First there is the institutionalised violence of the police and the army and especially of the security police and the riot police. As they become more and more desperate at not being able to contain the anger of so many dissatisfied black people, so do they resort more and more to violent aggression. As the blacks become more and more disillusioned and frustrated, so do they turn more and more to violent resistance.

Moreover the general state of alienation, frustration, fear and insecurity makes almost everyone want to take up a gun and shoot those they fear. In the townships this also leads to more and more violent crime until the whole community gets caught up in forms of violence that blunt sensitivity to the sufferings of others and the normal respect for life. This whole tragic spiral of violence is made even worse by films that capitalise on the unconscious desire for violence of a frustrated society.

What we have here in South Africa then is not simply a group of people with racial prejudices. We have a totalitarian system that governs every aspect of the lives of all the people. The people, all the people, are victims of a system that has gradually developed in the particular historical circumstances of our country. There is no point in imputing blame to this one or that one, to this group or that group. We are all in this boat together with varying degrees of advantage or disadvantage, privilege or suffering, and with varying degrees of awareness of what is really happening to us.

This is the society in which the South African Catholic church is placed. What is the meaning of evangelisation for such a country? How can the Catholic church make a contribution towards the evolution of a new society? My hope is that this analysis might help to find answers to these questions, order priorities and make plans.

2 CATHOLIC SOCIAL TEACHING AND IDEOLOGY

Denis Hurley

One cannot speak of the Catholic church and ideologies in Southern Africa without setting the theme in its historical context. The ideologies that prevail or struggle to prevail in the subcontinent, nationalism, racism, capitalism, socialism and communism, all grew up in the Western world as the old christendom was dissolving. Christendom had reigned as the culture of the west for close on a thousand years. Its dominant values had been religious and all its human dimensions—social, political, economic and cultural—had been subsumed, in greater or lesser degree, under the tutelage of the sacred.

The tensions and contradictions in christendom came to a head in the Reformation. Christian culture was split down the middle and christian vitality wore itself out in bitter theological controversy and religious warfare. The reaction took the form of the emergence in the eighteenth century, under the banner of the 'Enlightenment', of a new culture dominated by human values intent on casting off their christian tutelage and asserting their independent identity: reason, freedom, science, technology, democracy. These were the values of the new, self-reliant humanism discarding, at times violently, at other times quietly, its christian origins. The age of secularism had begun.

We pick up the story at the beginning of the nineteenth century with a threefold revolution in progress: the industrial revolution that had begun fifty years earlier and had found in Adam Smith (1723–1790) the prophet of a free economy that was to prove so disastrous for workers, as capitalism developed without a conscience; a scientific revolution that was to alter the pattern of western thought; and a political revolution spreading the ideas of democracy derived from France and the newly independent United States of America, and of nationalism, the ideology of supreme loyalty to the nation state.

The Catholic church was going to find it difficult to come to terms with this three-fold revolution, for three reasons principally: first, because what was happening, dramatically exemplified by the French Revolution, seemed to have been born out of opposition to things catholic; secondly, because authority in the Catholic church had built up its reflexes over something like fifteen centuries and it was not going to adjust easily to the new democratic western world coming into existence; thirdly, because christianity as a whole was being questioned, not just this or that aspect of christian teaching or practice, but the whole thing. Secularism, an outlook that can manage without God, was building a new culture in the place of christendom. It took a long time for christian leaders to understand this. They kept appealing to the christian conscience, unaware that it was on the way out. They kept struggling to preserve christendom, unaware that it had dissolved. The Catholic church did not really come to terms with all this until the Second Vatican Council (1962-1965). It is still struggling to find an effective way of evangelising a world characterised by humanistic values originally nurtured in its own bosom and now, after a rebellious adolescence, demanding the recognition due to their maturity. An important chapter in the saga of how the Catholic church has reached this point in its history is the story of its social doctrine.

Catholic social doctrine found its first systematic formulation in the encyclical *Rerum Novarum* of Pope Leo XIII, published in May 1891. Its theme was the worker who had suffered so much during almost a century and a half of industrialisation. For seventy years after *Rerum Novarum* catholic social teaching concentrated almost exclusively on the social and intellectual turmoil caused by liberal capitalism and reactions to it. Then, with Pope John XXIII and the Second Vatican Council, it broadened out to embrace the world and all its problems.

This article consists of two parts and a conclusion. The first part provides a brief review of the development of catholic social teaching under two headings: *The church and the worker* and *The church and the world*. The second part contains a brief summary of current ideologies and the Church's attitude to them.

THE DEVELOPMENT OF CATHOLIC SOCIAL TEACHING

The church and the worker

The first-born ideology of secularism was liberal capitalism. The dawning faith in freedom of the eighteenth century came at a most convenient time for the successful promoters of the industrial revolution. They subscribed to it enthusiastically. There should be no outside interference with the economy. The free market must settle its own affairs, including wage contracts between employers and workers. The result might be cruelly long hours for men, women and children; starvation wages; widespread unemployment and subhuman standards of food, clothing and shelter. This was the price that had to be paid for freedom, a price well worth it in the view of many new factory owners.

The reaction was not long in coming, aimed at the social control of those 'dark satanic mills' that were reducing workers to slaves of industry. It came to be known as socialism. There were some professed christians among the early socialists but, by and large, the generation after the Napoleonic wars was more for anarchy and revolution than brotherly love.

This thinking lacked coherence until there burst on the scene in the revolutionary year of 1848 the *Communist Manifesto* of Karl Marx and Friedrich Engels. Here was a powerful amalgam of two dynamic forces, the force of anger at the blatant injustices of capitalism and the force of an idea that gave the anger a coherent intellectual and moral thrust.

The idea was the materialist conception of history. According to this conception, history is made of struggles for power and in the ultimate analysis the struggles are over who controls the means of production. Every stage of development produces an establishment or organisation to exercise this control, but, as development forges ahead, tension arises between the old organisation and the new stage of development. The tension takes the form of class struggle and is resolved by revolution, not necessarily violent revolution. As Marx saw the situation in the middle of the nineteenth century it was ripening for the proletarian revolution to overthrow liberal capitalism.

During the last quarter of the nineteenth century the marxist brand of socialism was triumphant in most of Europe. It had the advantage of giving to its adherents a clearcut conviction that history was on their side and that they represented the unstoppable forces of reality rolling irresistibly towards a predestined goal: the triumph of the proletariat. The revolution was just around the corner. But there was a split in the interpretation of 'revolution'. Some were for the conquest and use of existing state structures, whereas Marx had reached the conviction that the bourgeois state was incapable of conversion and should be eliminated to make way for a new transitional structure called the 'dictatorship of the proletariat'.

While socialism was developing to this point, christian thinkers and activists were trying, but without comparable success, to formulate a christian solution to the problem raised by the industrial revolution. In England the activities of christian socialists gave a fillip to the co-operative movement and tried to promote ideas of profit-sharing and co-partnership between owners and workers. In the latter years of his life Cardinal Manning vigorously espoused the workers' cause. In the United States a similar task was undertaken by Cardinal Gibbon and Archbishop Ireland.

In France the delicate beginnings of christian democracy with popular appeal were wiped out in the revolutionary year of 1848. When social concern revived after 1870 it did so at first among upper-class traditionalists who favoured the 'corporatist' solution to social problems, the solution propounded by Karl von Vogelsang in Austria. A 'corporation' as he envisaged it was an association of all involved in a common economic undertaking, employers and workers together, with the employers by implication exerting the major influence and managing the project on paternalistic lines.

At about this time too catholic concern for social issues began to emerge in Italy and Spain, mainly in intellectual circles. German catholics tackled the problem with greater vigour. The approach was generally paternalistic and corporatist but it was characterised by German practicality and organisational ability. Concern for workers quickly became a priority in the German catholic revival of the nineteenth century. Radiating from Cologne, Father Adolf Kolping (1813–1865) founded his society of young journeymen in the new industrial areas of Germany and the Bishop of Mainz, William Emmanuel von Ketteler (1811–1877), though a traditionalist himself, took the lead in advocating the workers' cause and promoting a christian social outlook among German catholics to the extent that the social laws promulgated after his death were called 'Ketteler's Laws' and Leo XIII referred to him as 'my predecessor'.

It was against this background that Pope Leo XIII published his encyclical *Rerum Novarum* in 1891. After vindicating his right as chief pastor to speak on social and economic matters he entered the capitalist-socialist debate by rejecting both these secular solutions to the industrial problem and put the blame for both aberrations on secularism's abandonment of religion. The only true solution, he claimed, lay in a return to christian faith and the practice of christian love and justice. Against socialism Leo argued for private property as a demand of the natural law. Against liberal capitalism he called for an observance of the social responsibilities of private ownership and for firm state action to protect the poor and the weak. This set the tone for all subsequent catholic social teaching with its appeal to the moral teaching of the gospel addressing itself to the conscience of employers, employees and state representatives. In the matter of wages Leo accepted the practice of free agreements but emphasised that free agreements are subject to the principle of justice that requires 'that remuneration ought to be sufficient to support a frugal and well-behaved wage-earner'. Let employers and workers make their free agreements but there is a level beneath which wages must not sink. This binds the conscience of the employer. The best protection for the worker and the best way of promoting his welfare is to be found in associations, in working-men's unions. Leo envisaged these as being deeply imbued with a religious spirit and concerned to promote the worker and his welfare while recognising the legitimate rights and interests of employers who should also work through associations inspired by christian principles. Basically for Leo the social sickness was a problem of human relations that needed a good dose of christianity and commonsense and could do without market idolatry and agnostic ideology.

All that was lacking to Leo's prophetic call was a receptive audience. On two scores receptivity was poor: first because Leo was talking in catholic terms in a catholic context whereas in catholic parts of the world secularism was already widespread; secondly, because few catholics, whether lay or clerical or even episcopal, were attuned to the message. However, the 'social catholics' went to work with publications, commentaries on the encyclical, 'social weeks' and all the apparatus of promotion they could muster. They were a small but vigorous and vocal segment of the church trying bravely to disperse the incomprehension and apathy of an ecclesiastical tradition that could not see what all this had to do with religion.

Probably the most important development after *Rerum Novarum* was the launching of the christian trade union movement in continental Europe, for this at last involved the catholic worker in his own salvation. Inevitably, there were problems and quarrels. Corporatism contended with trade unionism, the neutral union with the christian union, the union involved in party politics with the union not so involved. Slowly, hesitantly, contentiously the catholic social movement gained momentum and after the convulsion of the 1914–1918 war was ready for new growth.

In 1922, Pope Pius XI was elected to the chair of Peter to preside over this new growth. The greatest war in history had almost ruined Europe. Atheistic communism had taken over Russia. Adolf Hitler was launching the Nazis in Germany and Mussolini was to march on Rome later that same year. The new pope turned to 'catholic action' as a means of re-christianising society and rolling back the tide of secularism. 'Catholic action' owed its existence to the call of Leo XIII to the laity to help in the preservation and promotion of christian values in society. Pope Pius X (1903–1914) had reinforced the appeal and had begun to refer to the part to be played by the laity by the new term 'catholic action'. Any organised effort aimed at influencing society in a christian way could be called 'catholic action'. Pope Pius XI took up the idea and promoted it vigorously. In certain countries a specific structure emerged known as Catholic Action, having branches at parish level for men and women, boys and girls and co-ordinating structures at diocesan and national level. The main activity of each branch was christian social formation, usually on a theoretical level. The structure never took on in English-speaking countries, which retained their cluster of lay associations, sometimes co-ordinated and sometimes not. These were catholic action with a small 'a'. In South Africa the Catholic African Union (later known as Catholic Africa Organisation), founded by the Mariannhill Fathers B. Huss and E. Hanisch in 1927, had some of the characteristics of structured Catholic Action though it was more closely modelled on the German 'verein'.

Catholic Action was both a training school and an organ of action, and was to be firmly under the control and guidance of the hierarchy. Pope Pius XI defined it as 'the participation of the laity in the apostolate of the hierarchy'. To belong to Catholic Action an organisation had to be officially mandated by the hierarchy. In regard to certain forms of activity, for which hierarchical control and close identification with church structures were undesirable, it was envisaged that laity trained in Catholic Action would move out to create their own catholic-inspired organisations and operate on their own responsibility. This would apply, for instance, to political parties, trade unions, employers' associations and other professional bodies. In practice, it would not always be easy to draw the line between hierarchically controlled Catholic Action and social or political action taken by laymen on their own responsibility. After the second world war Pope Pius XII (1939–1958) did not scruple to throw his Catholic Action brigades behind the Christian Democratic election campaign in Italy to ward off the communist 'danger'. In the vision of his predecessor Catholic Action was to produce the committed catholic laity that would promote and put into practice catholic social teaching.

Halfway through his pontificate Pope Pius XI felt that after forty years of *Rerum Novarum* the time was ripe for a further strong papal directive on catholic social action. It was all the more necessary because of the severe economic crisis afflicting the world since the collapse of the American stock exchange in October 1929. The pope published *Quadragesimo Anno* in May 1931. Its purpose was to reassert and vindicate the basic teaching of *Rerum Novarum* and to bring the applications up to date.

In this encyclical Pope Pius XI deals once again with the papal right to teach in social matters, with the right to private property and its individual and social dimensions, with the role of the state in social and economic matters, with the relationship between capital and labour, the emancipation of the proletariat, the payment of just wages, and the reconstruction of the social order by a collaboration between social groups and classes and by the restoration of a guiding principle for economic life, namely, social justice inspired by social love. Worker participation in the ownership and management of industry is advocated and catholic interest in corporatism is revived by a strong recommendation of a system of collaboration between employers and workers within the same industry. The capital/labour division continues to be acceptable but capitalistic excesses are castigated as only Pius XI knew how to castigate. The controllers of money and credit are his main target. The evolution in socialism is noted. The communist form is vigorously rejected while it is recognised that there is a moderate form of socialism which has toned down the old belief in class warfare and the abolition of private property and, in some cases, has reached the point when 'its opinions sometimes closely approach the just demands of christian social reformers' (113). In spite of this, Pope Pius XI will have no truck with socialism for, in his view, socialism is at heart agnostic and concerns itself only with material well-being (120).

Among the various means of re-christianising society and making justice and love meaningful virtues in economic life, Pope Pius XI makes a certain significant reference. 'Undoubtedly,' he writes, 'the first and immediate apostles of the working men must themselves be working men, while the apostles of the industrial and commercial world should themselves be employers and merchants.' (141)

The man who had given him this idea, the 'milieu' idea, was the

Belgian priest, Father Joseph Cardijn. With this man we come to one of the most vital and promising developments of the 1920s, a development that quietly revolutionised vast areas of the church's evangelising effort and style. Joseph Cardijn was an educational genius. The two poles of his remarkable new vision in the matter of social education were 'the milieu' and 'the experiential'. In the case of 'the experiential' he based his approach on helping people to discover for themselves. The method by which the discovery has to be made is in a small manageable group, noticing facts, reporting on them, reflecting on them in the light of the gospel and acting on the conclusions reached: 'see, judge and act'. The *social milieu* that absorbed Cardijn's attention was that of young industrial workers. In 1924 he founded the Young Christian Workers.

It was soon realised that Cardijn's insistence on milieu and on the method of personal discovery in groups, starting from life experience, was applicable not only to young industrial workers but to groups of all ages and all milieux. He had elaborated a universal method for catholic social formation. It was taken up by students, agricultural workers, white-collar workers, employers' associations and became a standard method of lay formation. The movements that adopted his principles were called 'specialised Catholic Action' in contrast with those that followed the old, more traditional lines without reference to milieu, which were termed 'general Catholic Action'.

Some forty years after the launching of the Young Christian Workers, the 'see, judge and act' programme was advocated by Pope John XXIII in his encyclical *Mater et Magistra* (60) and canonised by the Second Vatican Council in its decree on the Apostolate of the Laity (29). By that time it had already profoundly influenced catechetics and was about to become the inspiration of the 'liberation theology' of Latin America and its 'basic community' movement. It can be said to have revolutionised a great deal of the pastoral life of the church. These successes of the Cardijn method still lay in the future when Pope Pius XI wrote *Quadragesimo Anno* and advocated the milieu principle, the 'apostolate of like to like'.

In 1931 the conflict between capital and labour was still the main and practically the only social problem for the church. Other social problems had not yet surfaced in her corporate consciousness nor, consequently, in her official teaching. Little, if any, attention was given to the subjugation of conquered peoples and to colonial exploitation. Mussolini's attack on Ethiopia in 1935 evoked hardly any papal reaction. Competing European nationalisms had led to the holocaust of the First World War, yet the catholic conscience had not as yet begun a serious reflection on the issue, despite the condemnation by Pope Pius XI in his inaugural encyclical of exaggerated patriotism and narrow nationalism. On two further occasions Pius XI was to join issue with narrow nationalism, first in the case of France when in 1931 he condemned *Action Française* and later, in the case of Germany, when in 1937 he issued the encyclical *Mit Brennender Sorge* on the condition of the church in Germany. Under Hitler, German nationalism had become an apotheosis of Aryan racism. The pope dealt with it severely in his 1937 encyclical five days before another encyclical gave a similar treatment to atheistic communism.

Pope Pius XI died in February 1939. He had played a great pastoral part in the struggle for christian social order but he had not yet thrown off certain characteristics of the old mentality: catholicism had to work in isolation and was particularly wary of anything not explicitly christian; attacks on religion were more reprehensible than attacks on human rights; the clergy were the only official church workers, and the laity, though indispensable in the overall effort, were only auxiliaries. Historical conditioning dies hard. The spirit of christendom still lingered on.

The church and the world

Pope Pius XII, elected on 2nd March 1939, saw out, albeit unintentionally, the last vestiges of the old mentality. Already under Pius XI a new vision had been stirring. Spurred by the growing emphasis on the laity, catholic thinkers had begun to delve more deeply into matters that were of vital concern to lay people: work, for example, and marriage, and the knotty problem of how temporal concerns generally relate to the eternal. France had taken the lead, with Jacques Maritain and his christian humanism, Emmanuel Mounier and his personalism and, behind the scenes, Pierre Teilhard de Chardin with a vision he had been forbidden to publish, a vision that had been leaking out here and there through lectures and copies of notes that were circulating in the network, a daring vision that gave the temporal a direct orientation to the goal of salvation, brought faith and science into a scintillating embrace and saw Christ not only as redeemer but also as the Omega of cosmic evolution.

Pius XII's personal contribution to catholic social teaching was not great, though he continued to emphasise the established themes in his multitudinous addresses, and in a Christmas radio message in 1942 became the first pope to formulate a list of human rights.

He approved and encouraged two world congresses of the lay apostolate in 1951 and 1957 respectively. The new term 'lay apostolate', though still somewhat hazy in meaning, indicated a development in understanding of the apostolic role of the laity beyond the limitations imposed by the way that Catholic Action had been conceived. The truth began to emerge that the laity had a mission not merely in virtue of a hierarchical mandate but in virtue of their own baptism.

The ever-increasing emphasis on the responsibility of the laity was bound to result sooner or later in a painful tension between the exercise of this responsibility and the limits placed upon it by the hierarchy. In the later years of Pope Pius XII Catholic Action entered its crisis of authority in several countries, particularly in France.

Along with this crisis came the acute realisation that catholics could not work in the world to 'consecrate' it without mixing with a variety of fellow-workers who did not share their faith but did share their hunger for justice and often appeared to be more experienced and more effective in the pursuit of their ideal. Catholics had to associate with communists and socialists as often enough they had associated with them in concentration camps and resistance movements during the second world war.

The crisis of authority and the anti-isolationist trend were not the only problems. In the country that still maintained the lead in progressive catholic thought the realisation dawned rather traumatically that France could scarcely be called a 'christian country' any more. As far as the vast body of industrial workers was concerned, communists and socialists dominated the scene and the experiment with priest-workers showed how difficult it was for even the most dedicated among them not to be absorbed by the milieu. It became more and more difficult for militant social catholics to believe in the conquering power of christian love and to turn a deaf ear to the siren call of the marxist analysis of class conflict.

After six decades and more of catholic social teaching the church was still making little impact on a secularised western world and its social problems. Something more dramatic had to be done. Despite all indications to the contrary the successor of Pius XII, the septuagenarian John XXIII, became the man to do it. Within the space of four and a half years Pope John published two great encyclicals and convened the Second Vatican Council.

Mater en Magistra was published in April 1961 to mark the seventieth anniversary of *Rerum Novarum*. It continued the steady line of papal teaching on social questions, emphasising the fundamental moral issues, the balance that must be sought between the personal and social dimensions of property and economic activity and the rights and duties of the state. It refers to the phenomenon of 'socialisation', 'the progressive multiplication of relations in society with different forms of life and activity and juridical institutionalisation' (8). It accepts socialisation as a good thing provided it allows space for an individual's personal growth.

The encyclical gives strong encouragement to worker participation in industrial management and pays a great deal of attention to 'macro-economics', that is, the relations between various sectors of the economy and between nations differing in economic development. It refers to catholic social doctrine based on truth, justice and love as 'an integral part of the christian conception of life' (57) and recommends the Cardijn method of 'see, judge and act' (60).

Pope John had moved catholic social teaching into a wider sphere than that merely of employer-worker tensions. The 'macro' dimensions are taken up and enlarged still further by *Pacem in Terris* published in April 1963 as the last testament of a dying pope. The purpose of this encyclical is to foster good order in human society by emphasising and clarifying the laws written in the heart of man, laws governing the relationship of men among themselves, between citizens and the state, between state and state and, finally, between all individuals and all states in a world community.

Between individuals there must be respect for human rights and performance of corresponding duties. Pope John takes over the list of rights of Pius XII and enlarges on it and calls for social order based on truth, justice, love and freedom. The same moral values must govern relations between individual citizens and the state and also those between one state and another. Pope John has much to say about a variety of themes that come under each heading and as he goes from theme to theme one has the sense of a crescendo mounting to the climax of his call in the last part of the encyclical for a 'public authority having world-wide power and endowed with the proper means for the efficacious pursuit of its objective which is the universal common good in concrete form'. He praises the United Nations Organisation and its Universal Declaration of

Human Rights and earnestly wishes 'that the United Nations Organisation—in its structure and its means—may become ever more equal to the magnitude and nobility of its task'. In a concluding pastoral exhortation (Part V) he writes the epitaph of catholic isolationism by laying down practical directives for co-operation between catholics and those who do not share their faith and even profess what to catholics is a false philosophy.

Even before *Pacem in Terris* was written Pope John had taken a giant stride towards dissolving catholic isolationism and bringing the Catholic church into close and meaningful communication with a world alienated from the old christendom by half a millenium of western European history and its encounter with other histories and other cultures. He had taken the step of convening the Second Vatican Council and of launching its first session in October 1962. After that session, on the suggestion of Cardinal Suenens, it had been agreed that one of the themes of the Council would be the relations between the church and the world. Discussion of this theme led, two years after Pope John's death, to the promulgation of *Gaudium et Spes*, the Council's pastoral constitution on *The Church in the Modern World*.

This constitution formalised perhaps the greatest transformation the church had experienced since the Council of Jerusalem in AD 49. The Council of Jerusalem gave formal expression to the liberation of the church from its Jewish context. *Gaudium et Spes* gave formal expression to the church's acceptance of 'the world' as an integral part of God's plan for his Kingdom. For 1900 years the church had been ill at ease in its assessment of the world, appreciating it as the work of God's creation but apprehensive of the evil that lurked in it. The very term 'world' was ambiguous in the gospel, in catechesis and in the theology of the priesthood and the religious life. For religious there was a certain satisfaction in having 'renounced the world', and priests were exhorted to be 'in the world but not of it'. Theology had little idea of how *this* world was related to the true and lasting values of the *next*. At best this world looked like a testing ground where christians proved whether or not they were worthy of eternal happiness. Apart from this, what they actually did in the world was of scant importance. The thing that counted was the 'right intention'.

Volumes remain to be written on the long history of christian dualism. For the Catholic church *Gaudium et Spes* wound it up with a sensational evaluation of the world's intrinsic importance to the building of the Kingdom. A couple of sentences reflect a little of the old ambiguity: 'Earthly progress must be carefully distinguished from the growth of the Kingdom. Nevertheless, to the extent that the former can contribute to the better ordering of human society, it is of vital concern to the Kingdom of God.' (39) But there is no ambiguity about statements like this: 'For after we have obeyed the Lord, and in His Spirit nurtured on earth the values of human dignity, brotherhood and freedom, and indeed all the good fruits of our nature and enterprise, we will find them again, but freed of stain, burnished and transfigured. This will be so when Christ hands over to the Father a Kingdom eternal and universal: a Kingdom of truth and life, of holiness and grace, of justice, love, and peace. On this earth that Kingdom is already present in mystery. When the Lord returns, it will be brought into full flower.' (39)

The church's involvement in social problems, her reaction to secularism, her call to the laity to play their part, and theological reflection on the experience had brought about in a few decades this revolution in catholic thought. Possibly the four principal architects of the revolution were Jospeh Cardijn with his practical pedagogy, Teilhard de Chardin whose principal works were published posthumously in the years immediately preceding the Council, Pope John XXIII whose saintly instinct told him that only a Council could bring church and world together, and Cardinal Suenens who suggested putting the world on the agenda.

Besides dealing with the basic problem of relations between the church and the world, *Gaudium et Spes* discusses a wide spectrum of other issues: the dignity of the human person, atheism, the community of man, marriage and the family, culture, socio-economic life, politics, peace and war and the promotion of a community of nations.

In regard to all these themes, *Gaudium et Spes* indicates the role of the church as an animating and spiritualising force bringing the truth and power of Christ to heal and complete, to balance and perfect all that man is and all that he does so that, in co-operation with other forms of human involvement, the church may play her vital and indispensable role in the building of the Kingdom.

Basically the practical conclusion of *Gaudium et Spes* is that christians must love the world in which they live, must love its human involvements and human achievements, must perceive the problems that arise, must come to grips with them concretely and vividly, and bring what they can of the love of Christ to the situations they encounter.

This is where a colossal call is made on the laity. More than bishops, priests and religious they are involved in the complexities of worldly situations and must be ready to give their christian witness. In this they are not auxiliaries, they are frontline troops, they carry the church and the power of Christ with them wherever they go. They are indispensable evangelisers in their own right—by right of their baptism and confirmation. This is the clear message of Vatican II in *Gaudium et Spes*, *Lumen Gentium* and the decree on *The Apostolate of the Laity*.

Vatican II was a watershed in the history of the Catholic church. We leave on the far side of the watershed a church gazing heavenwards, wrapped in her isolation and identified with her bishops, priests and religious. On this side of the watershed we are swept along in a somewhat turbulent church, still gazing heavenwards but taking in as well the terrestrial scene, shedding her isolation and recognising that the bulk of herself is made up of the laity.

Since Vatican II there have been further important statements on catholic social teaching enlarging the scope of social morality and applying to it specific situations. Pope Paul VI did this for 'the development of peoples' in his encyclical of March 1967, *Populorum Progressio*, and for a variety of social issues in his apostolic letter of May 1971, *Octogesima Adveniens*, on the eightieth anniversary of *Rerum Novarum*. In November 1971 a document emanating from the Synod of Bishops was published under the title *Justice in the World*, from which this oft-quoted passage is drawn: 'Action on behalf of justice and participation in the transformation of the world fully appear to us as a constitutive dimension of the preaching of the Gospel, or, in other words, of the church's mission for the redemption of the human race and its liberation from every oppressive situation.'

In September 1981 Pope John Paul II returned to the theme of his work with his encyclical *Laborem Exercens*, marking the ninetieth anniversary of Pope Leo's *Rerum Novarum*. He used this opportunity to apply his now celebrated Christian humanist outlook to work and to the relations that work creates between people. In all that work is and means and achieves, the most important element is the person working, who through work grows within himself and contributes to the growth of mankind and the development of the Kingdom of God. The person working is infinitely more precious than all the capital invested and the profit realised.

Throughout all this development of a theology of social relations runs the golden thread of an appeal to conscience. Steering an independent course between conflicting ideologies with their appeals to less profound human values, the social teaching of the church insists that the real problem is in the heart of man and that that is where the remedy must be applied. The love inspired by Christ must be 'social' love. It must be strong enough to transcend the barriers of class, nation, race and every other social grouping. Moving into this kind of love, this dimension of christian living, requires not just a routine effort on the part of christians and of the church as a whole. It requires a radical conversion, the conversion referred to by Pope John Paul II in *Redemptor Hominis* (16), something in the world of love comparable to Marx's revolution.

THE CATHOLIC CHURCH AND IDEOLOGY

Liberal capitalism

We have already noted that the first ideology to emerge in the secularistic world was liberal capitalism. Though greatly modified since the principle of a completely free and unfettered economy was promoted in the first century of the industrial revolution, capitalism still retains a good deal of its unchristian concern with the profit motive regardless of the consequences. Moreover, liberal capitalism easily becomes illiberal in its willingness to accept the protection of a Hitler, a Mussolini or a Franco in the face of socialist and communist threats, and ends up as totalitarian as the system it came into being opposing. In Latin America an alliance with the military caste has produced the National Security State. Some maintain this is the trend in South Africa too. The great corporations known as the 'multi-nationals' are a principal target of criticism, and are blamed for sucking up the resources and destroying the enterprises of the countries they exploit with scant concern for the local population. The multi-nationals' response is that they bring life and dynamism to stagnant economies.

The consistent attitude of papal social teaching from Leo XIII down to John Paul II has been that private property is a worthwhile institution, that free enterprise is a good thing, but that they must not disregard their social responsibilities. Pope Leo XIII laid this down clearly in *Rerum Novarum*, invoking the thirteenth-century theologian Thomas Aquinas, in whose view 'Man should not consider his outward possessions as his own, but as common to all, so as to share them without hesitation when others are in need. Whence the apostle says, Command the rich of this world . . . to offer with no stint, to apportion largely.' In *Quadragesimo Anno* Pius XI repeated this teaching and strongly recom-

mended the participation of workers in the ownership and management of businesses (65). Pius XII, in a broadcast message in 1941
celebrating the fiftieth anniversary of *Rerum Novarum*, insisted
that private property can be justified only if and when it fulfils its
social purposes. *Mater et Magistra* (15-16) takes up the theme and
so does *Gaudium et Spes* (68-69).

Disregard for the social dimensions of private property and free
enterprise have been severely castigated by the popes time and time
again. In *Rerum Novarum* Leo XIII wrote of the 'hard-heartedness
of employers and the greed of unchecked competition', of 'rapa-
cious usury' and of 'a small number of very rich men' being able
'to lay upon the teeming masses of the labouring poor a yoke little
better than that of slavery itself'.

Pope Pius XI uses stronger language in *Quadragesimo Anno*
(105-106), and in *Populorum Progressio* Pope Paul VI hammers a
system 'which considers profit as the key motive for economic
progress, competition as the supreme law of economics, and private
ownership of the means of production as an absolute right that has
no limits and carries no corresponding social obligation'. (26)

In raising their voices against these abuses the popes go on believing in the value of conscience. Naivety? Utopia? They are con-
vinced that employers can be brought to overcome the tyranny of
the profit motive and act in terms of concern for their fellow men.
The church will have to work hard to prove them right.

In the South African economy there is a fairly large public sector,
but the reigning economic orthodoxy is liberal capitalism. Since
coming to terms with the white trade unions and more or less co-
opting them into the system, capitalism has had things very much
its own way. Colonial conquest and the colour bar have made it
easy to convert vast numbers of a dispossessed black population
into an industrial proletariat. Among the whites, worker solidarity
has yielded in a most unmarxmanlike way to racial solidarity. As a
result politicised blacks tend to identify liberal capitalism with
white domination and to apply pure class rhetoric to a complex
race-class situation.

Socialism and communism

As we have seen, the followers of Marx in the nineteenth century
soon split into two streams, the radical stream that came to be
called communism and the moderate stream that retained the name
of social democracy. Leading communists soon discarded Marx's
ambiguity about revolution and opted for the violent type with

Lenin, Trotsky, Stalin and Mao Tse-tung advocating their various strategies. The communist parties of Italy, France and Spain have opted for the ballot box while still maintaining that this does not make them social democrats. There are also neo-marxists who see more hope for marxist dynamism among intellectuals than among workers. Finally, some christians, while treasuring their religious faith, feel they can accept some aspects of marxism which they contend are not directly linked with historical materialism.

If the communist scene is complex the overall socialist scene is much more so. For 'socialism' embraces not only the various interpretations of communism that claim Marx as their source but also other systems which for pragmatic rather than ideological reasons want to see capitalism controlled. One extreme of pragmatic socialism believes with Marx that all or most of the means of production should be socialised. Other forms of socialism advocate state ownership of some enterprises or state control through legislation and parastatal agencies. State welfare is also often included under the umbrella of socialism and also the promotion of trade unions, worker participation, co-operatives and credit unions within a free enterprise system. Many countries that have felt the influence of a strong social democratic party have ended up with a pragmatic form of socialism, combining public ownership of some aspects of the economy with free enterprise in others, a vigorous trade union movement and a comprehensive system of social security. Recently, African socialism has been much spoken of. The concept is not yet fully developed but essentially it connotes a variety of socialist provisions inspired by the African community tradition.

So socialism can mean many things from out-and-out marxism to having a 'social conscience'. The conclusion is that before getting into a discussion about marxism, communism or socialism one should always ask: what kind?

In regard to the catholic reaction, the denial of God in the overall marxist view makes it obviously incompatible with christianity. The accepted catholic view is that this denial necessarily implies a false view of morality. Morality, instead of having a divine origin has a human, even a materialistic one, with the result that whatever promotes man's materialistic and social growth as interpreted by Marx is good ethics. From this implication arises the tragic irony of marxism: that the colossal indignation aroused in Marx by the exploitation of the poor should have inspired in him a philosophy whose ethics in catholic eyes can condone any horror. The church was not surprised by Stalin. He might have gone beyond what Marx intended and foresaw in the matter of terror but if Marx could draw his right and wrong from a materialist reading of history, why not Stalin?

In regard to the milder forms of ideological socialism derived from Marx, until the death of Pope Pius XII in 1958 they were generally seen as instances of secular philosophy advocating the social ownership of property. As such they were out of bounds to catholics on two scores: their irreligious outlook and their attack on private property, which papal teaching saw as something associated with man by natural law and essential to his freedom and dignity. Curiously enough, Leo XIII's criticism of socialism in *Rerum Novarum* is aimed not so much at its secularism as its attack on private property. Whereas forty years later Pope Pius XI in *Quadragesimo Anno*, while recognising that socialism had changed a lot and in some instances was almost indistinguishable from catholic social doctrine, rejected it still because of its hostility to the christian faith (117).

With pragmatic socialism the church has really had no quarrel. In fact, they have shared the same conclusions about free enterprise, limited state ownership, trade unionism and social security. Moreover, by the time that Pope John XXIII came to the papal throne attitudes had changed a good deal and catholics and socialists had begun to find one another and to engage in dialogue. In *Pacem in Terris* Pope John wrote his guidelines for catholic collaboration with those who do not share their philosophy (Part V).

This was interpreted by some as acceptance also of the dialogue with marxism that had been going on in certain quarters for ten years and more and which had induced the more daring spirits to see a compatibility between christian faith and some or all of the following points of marxism: the marxist analysis of socio-economic situations, the condemning of liberal capitalism, the belief in the inevitability of class conflict and in the social ownership of the means of production.

In *Octogesima Adveniens* Pope Paul VI uttered a caution against even the most innocent-looking aspects of marxism: 'While, through the concrete existing form of marxism, one can distinguish these various aspects and the questions they pose for the reflection and activity of christians, it would be illusory and dangerous to reach a point of forgetting the intimate link which radically binds them together, to accept the elements of marxist analysis without recognising their relationships with ideology, and to enter into the practice of class struggle and its marxist interpretations, while failing to note the kind of totalitarian and violent society to which this process leads.' (34)

Nationalism and racism

It could be argued that the strongest instinct in man is the community instinct, for history proves how easily people can be persuaded that a particular community is a value for which everything else should be sacrificed, be that community one of nation or race or class or religion. The strength of a community is due in great measure to the culture or sub-culture which it develops, a complex of interlocking interests, involvements, loyalties and forms of expression usually marked by a high degree of vitality and tenacity.

Race and nation have a variety of connotations. Roughly speaking race has a biological connotation in the sense that it is associated with the larger groupings into which humanity divided in the course of its evolution—caucasian, negroid, mongolian. Nation has a political connotation with strong cultural associations and not infrequently a biological background. Nation and race down the ages have commanded immense instinctive loyalties that have come into conflict with tragic frequency and ferocity.

What was instinctive in nation and race became conscious of itself in western Europe from the eighteenth century onwards. With the diminution of the awareness of God and of a broad christian culture, broad but divided, the way was clear for new community loyalties.

National loyalties came into their own as monarchies were toppled or weakened and emphasis was laid on the people as the depository of political power. France led the way, closely followed by Germany and Italy, with Britain and then others developing a powerful imperial dimension to nationalism. Each nation was inclined to see itself as superior to all others and endowed with a divine destiny. These divine destinies clashed in two horrendous world wars and western Europe slipped chastened and weakened into the geopolitical background.

Conscious western racism developed at the same time. It found a powerful ally in the cultural dynamism and the scientific and technological superiority of the west, which enabled western nations to colonise the greater part of the earth. This partial and transient superiority appeared in the eyes of western europeans as something normal, natural and permanent. Over-simplified Darwinism saw the triumph of the west as a convincing illustration of the survival of the fittest. Writers like J. A. Gobineau (1816–1882) and H. S. Chamberlain (1855–1927) endeavoured to give western racism an intellectual justification. Nazism made a religion of it.

In reacting against western emperialism its victims instinctively appealed to biological and cultural loyalties to create the solidarity necessary for the struggle. There would be little justification, however, for calling such loyalties racist or national. They make scant claim to racial superiority and, generally speaking, especially in Africa, lack recognisable national identity.

In regard to catholic attitudes to nationalism and racism we have seen how they began to crystallise under Pius XI, mainly in reaction to nazism. A fuller development of these attitudes took place during the decades of ferment from that time to the 1960s, a period which, in the Catholic church as in other christian churches, produced a radically new outlook on the world and the church's role in the world. As far as the Catholic church is concerned, this new outlook came into full view with *Pacem in Terris* and the Second Vatican Council. Nationalism and racism are seen as issues that must be dealt with by christians in terms of justice and love, now expected to assume global proportions. The love and sharing that should be the hallmark of christian individuals and families must also become the norm for dealings between national and racial communities.

During the years of ferment, the racial issue was dealt with at local level by the hierarchies of countries where it was particularly conspicuous, like the United States, South Africa and Zimbabwe. In 1967 Paul VI's *Populorum Progressio* left no doubt about the official catholic attitude to nationalism and racism. 'These legitimate feelings [i.e. national loyalties] should be ennobled by that universal charity which embraces the entire human family. Nationalism isolates people from their true good. It would be especially harmful where the weakness of national economics demands rather the pooling of efforts, of knowledge and of funds, in order to implement programmes of development and to increase commercial and cultural exchanges (62). . . . Racism is still an obstacle to collaboration among disadvantaged nations and a cause of division and hatred within countries whenever individuals and families see the inviolable rights of the human person held in scorn, as they themselves are unjustly subjected to a regime of discrimination because of their race or their colour.' (63)

CONCLUSION

The appeal to the gospel of love and the right reason of the natural law which the Catholic church introduces into the current ideological battlefield scarcely brushes the surface of the turbulence which it is designed to calm and order. Possibly by the nature of things this apparent impotence of the church is inevitable. It is conceivable that we have just survived the first few hundred years of the emergence of a new cultural period in the evolution of man, destined to supplant and last as long as the ten thousand year period that began when mankind left the caves and embarked on the first agricultural revolution. Teilhard de Chardin (1959) quotes with approval the saying of his mentor Henri Breuil, 'We have only just cast off the last moorings which held us to that neolithic age.' Perhaps the church cannot be expected to exert moral influence over humanity in such a feverish sweat of change. Or perhaps the church has been a little slow to develop the means necessary to deal with the situation.

I am inclined to think that both factors are at work. Moving out of the neolithic into the scientific age is a great travail and, despite the guidance of the Holy Spirit, the church with its far-reaching but constricting human dimensions cannot be expected to cope easily and effectively. But she has also been a little slow to develop the means that she should be utilising in the crisis of change: a more satisfying vision of her role in the world, and more effective pastoral methods.

The problem about her role in the world stems, as I have already mentioned, from the difficulty she experienced in finding a really significant relationship between the temporal order and the eternal. Vatican II, drawing together the strands of the theological ferment of preceding decades, gave a good indication of this relation but much remains to be done in spelling out the details. In this matter Karl Marx in the nineteenth century had an enormous advantage over the church. For him the temporal order in its historical unfolding was the one and only reality, whereas for the church the temporal order was merely the stage on which eternity's dramas were being enacted. The communist's involvement in history was his ultimate concern; he was immediately and tangibly involved in building the future: the classless society. For the christian the history of the world did not seem to be going anywhere but to destruction. What counted was eternity. Now it is different—in principle. But much remains to be worked out in practice as to how the christian's involvement in the *temporal* world is helping to build the *eternal* Kingdom.

Closely related to this new vision of the church's role in the world is the question of communicating it. When Cardijn evolved his 'see, judge and act' method in the early twenties he laid the foundations for a pastoral revolution. The method has proved particularly valuable in relating faith to life and making the social experience of people the field for the exercise of an enlightened and practical faith. Despite this, the method is not yet commonplace in the church, not even, sad to say, in many seminaries where one would imagine it would constitute an essential form of pastoral training.

That part of the church which has taken it most seriously in its pastoral methodology is also today the most creative: Latin America. In saying this I am referring to the 'basic community' method which seems to be fostering an extraordinary vitality in many parts of Latin America, particularly Brazil. Basic communities bring groups of people together to pray, to read the gospel, to reflect on life and to relate gospel to life. The christianity of *Gaudium et Spes* seems to be coming to life in this ferment of community exchange and action.

Admittedly, the basic communities are succeeding almost exclusively among the poor. In their case there is a powerful motivation for seeking an improvement of their way of life inspired and supported by a shared and vivid faith. A similar approach, though more difficult, is not impossible among christians at other levels of society, as many lay movements demonstrate. But the approach needs to become general, a commonplace of pastoral action and of lay formation and endeavour.

The commitment to the world, the realisation that the church is for the world because it is for man has opened up before our eyes an immense field for the practice of christian love, but a field dotted with a million obstacles: the attitudes and structures that are the product of history, of culture, of community conflicts and social conditioning. We know a little more now about the magnitude of the christian task in this world, in which whatever good we do to it and to one another we will find again in eternity, as *Gaudium et Spes* (39) says, 'freed of stain, burnished and transfigured'.

References

Aquinas, St Thomas. *Summa Theologica* II–II, Question 66, Article 2.

De Chardin, P. Teilhard. *The Phenomenon of Man* (London, 1959), p. 214.

Pope Leo XIII. *Rerum Novarum*, The Condition of the Working Classes (1891).

Pope Pius XI. *Quadragesimo Anno*, The Social Order (1931).

— *Mit Brennender Sorge*, The Persecution of the Church in Germany (1937).

Pope John XXIII. *Mater et Magistra*, On Recent Developments of the Social Question in the Light of Christian Teaching (1961).

— *Pacem in Terris*, On Establishing Universal Peace in Truth, Justice, Charity and Liberty (1963).

Pope Paul VI. *Populorum Progressio*, On the Development of Peoples (1967).

— *Octogesima Adveniens*, On the Occasion of the Eightieth Anniversary of the Encyclical *Rerum Novarum* (1971).

Pope John Paul II. *Redemptor Hominis*, The Redeemer of Man (1979).

— *Laborem Exercens*, On Human Work (1981).

Second Vatican Council. *Gaudium et Spes,* The Pastoral Constitution of the Church in the Modern World, in *Documents of Vatican II*, ed. W. M. Abbott and J. Gallagher (London, 1965).

Synod of Bishops. *Justice in the World* (1971).

3   CHURCH, SALVATION, AND POLITICS

Jabulani Nxumalo

Eighty per cent of South African catholics are blacks, that is, the underprivileged and the politically oppressed. For these the church carries serious responsibilities. It cannot avoid facing their plight. But the questions are asked, 'Should the church be involved in politics? Is the church not a community of salvation which therefore should concern itself rather with religious matters?

In the debate about what stance the church should take in South African politics two concepts are often confused: 'politics' understood as 'party politics', and 'politics' understood as the general arrangement of life on which fundamental human relationships rest and from which party politics emerge. This issue was raised in 1977 at the trial of Fr Dominic Scholten in the Pretoria Supreme Court. He was being tried for allegedly possessing and mailing banned publications. The question was put to him by counsel for the defence: 'It is often said that the church should not concern itself with politics. What do you understand by this statement?'

The reply of Fr Scholten epitomises the teaching of the church on social matters. 'In no case it seems to me should the church involve itself with party political matters, but it should concern itself with human society.' This is a re-iteration of the sentiments of the Catholic bishops' pastoral letter of 1972. 'The first question we must ask ourselves . . . is whether the church is entering party politics. Our unequivocal answer is "No". We are simply showing greater concern for the demands of the gospel in social life. . . . It is necessary to distinguish between party political action and concern for justice in human relations which the church must promote under any political system. . . . Only the insincere or the mischievous could describe as political our defence of the poor in their essential rights to family life, work, a living wage and participation in public life. These are matters of primary justice, of rights written by God into human nature from the beginning, before political parties were born.'

This distinction between party political involvement and concern for fundamental human rights on the part of the church has not succeeded in defusing tension within the church itself. The struggle goes on. In 1977 the Catholic Defence League, a group of white right-wing catholics, accused the bishops of involving themselves in politics. The same accusation was made by the *Genoot van Afrikaanssprekende Katolieke* (the society of Afrikaans-speaking catholics), while the *Black Priests Solidarity Group* under the leadership of Fr Lebamang Sebidi pledged support for the bishops' decision to deracialise catholic schools, and for their 1977 stand on social justice.

The political responsibility of the South African church is directed towards those matters which affect man as man, and towards the fundamental and inalienable rights of man. This was clearly stated by Fr Scholten. 'If the moral code . . . is violated then the church can do nothing else than to take up its prophetic role by trying to put a finger on the wounds of this particular society. It can do this not by starting another political party or criticising only those on one side, but by trying to be fair to all and to take up a role as a reconciler in the society that has been violated—a healing role.' This means that the concern of the church is to defend persons against oppression and manipulation in relation to their incontestable rights. This type of politics transcends parties and forms of government and prevents the church from being impartial on matters of oppression of one group by another, or when people are deprived of their divinely given rights.

This partiality of the church has its foundation in the gospel and the attitude of Christ. The New Testament demonstrates how love is rejected by some who are invited by Christ to follow him. The story of the rich young man illustrates this. 'Jesus looked straight at him with love and said, "You need only one thing. Go and sell all you have and give the money to the poor, and you will have riches in heaven; then come and follow me!" When the man heard this, gloom spread over his face and he went away sad, because he was very rich.' In this sense the message of the gospel becomes partial and shows Christ's preference for the poor, the rightless and dispossessed.

If the church is engaged in political activity in this sense then the message of salvation cannot be reduced to the narrow intimacy of religious privacy. The church has to be involved for the common good of all men and it cannot abstain from engaging in criticism of certain political actions which violate fundamental rights.

In the case of South Africa the implementation of the apartheid ideology has affected and violated such rights and constitutes a challenge for the church. It is at this point that the church cannot avoid getting involved in South African politics.

IDEOLOGIES AND THE CHURCH

The Catholic church has always been critical of any ideology which pretends to offer salvation. The dominant South African ideologies are apartheid, black consciousness, and marxism. How does the church view these? The answer to this question can be drawn from what has been said above. The church is above any temporal ideology—it is the bearer of a message and not a system. When Cardinal Silva of Santiago was accused of meddling in politics he made this statement: 'We do something much deeper than political ideologies can reach; we are using our enormous potential in this otherwise violent world for love and understanding.' The church in South Africa has rejected the system of apartheid for a number of reasons: a group of people is discriminated against on the basis of colour; blacks do not have rights of movement; the policy of apartheid is implemented at the cost of large scale removals of blacks from 'white' areas; and blacks are victims of economic exploitation.

How does the church assess 'black consciousness', which seems to be an inverted form of apartheid? This ideology has become one of the main elements which influence blacks in their struggle for freedom, and the catholic bishops have agreed that many legitimate black aspirations are expressed through this movement. But it too is subject to the criticism of the church. 'If black consciousness were to be exclusive and deny the humanity of the white man, or if it taught hatred, then it would be wrong. But if it defends all humanity in defending the most misused humanity, intends to allow everyone his rights, and only works in separation to re-establish those who have been most disinherited, then it may be doing service to God and all men.'[1]

In this way the church strives to be free of all ideological captivity and to remain critical of any ideology or system. The right cannot claim the support of the church in maintaining the status quo, nor can the left in their revolutionary efforts. Christians are invited to humanise revolution by recalling its humane purposes. They save it by refusing to absolutise its claims. They know that power is not an absolute. Ideologies are formulated by man and are affected by human fallibility and sinfulness.

The church, therefore, does not seek to support any ideologies in South Africa. It seeks constantly, however, to challenge the fundamental basis of the policies on which political institutions rest.

SALVATION AND LIBERATION

The church, with her message of the gospel, promises man that salvation will make his life meaningful in this world. However, various other ideologies and belief systems promise salvation of a sort. Each claims to lead people to a better life and to bring liberation and peace. The different understandings of the word require us to spell out what we mean when using it. 'Popularly, what salvation is depends on what one needs. To the prisoner in his cell salvation may simply be an unlocked door. To the fading beauty, a new skin cream. To those who are hungry, a bowl of rice. To the Chinese communist, salvation is the plan for a new society put into practice. To the soldier in the front lines, the armistice. To the dying, the assurance of heaven.'[2]

Salvation is linked to liberation. To those who are oppressed liberation means freedom from domination and exploitation, and salvation means ultimate and final liberation. But salvation, as understood in the bible, is a gift which comes only from God and is not the product of human struggle.

The biblical meanings of salvation are varied. It can mean deliverance in the context of war. God intervenes so that his people are not overwhelmed and exterminated by the enemy. According to the prophet Isaiah, salvation is the state of social righteousness: this is demanded by God. It also means deliverance from an external enemy. But it also means deliverance from the enemy within, that is, from those who take advantage of the poor and exploit them. Finally, in the New Testament salvation is concerned with the soul and salvation from sin. But even this is not, of course, without historical and political implications.

Many attempts have recently been made to explain the notion of salvation in relation to the liberation of man. The Bangkok Conference (1973) and the Roman Catholic Bishops' Synod held in Rome (1974) tried to give a comprehensive explanation of the idea of salvation today.

The Bangkok Conference distinguished four social dimensions, four struggles in which salvation works:

1 for economic justice against exploitation of people by people;
2 for human dignity against political oppression;
3 for solidarity against alienation of person from person;
4 for hope against despair in personal life.

This can be complemented by the Bishops' Synod. A paper on salvation was issued, focusing on three main ideas:

1 the personal character of salvation brought about through the drive of the Holy Spirit;

2 the relativity and temporality of earthly goods, which do not suffice for salvation without communion with God;

3 salvation, in the fullest sense, is eschatological, that is to say, it comes from God, and leads man to God.

The Synod moved away from the popular understanding which sees salvation as a response to a call for relief from urgent needs in this world. Salvation, in the religious sense, is something more.

How do the different South African population groups understand salvation? The conflict-ridden history of the country shows that the various groups perceive their salvation in different ways.

SALVATION AND THE AFRIKANERS

At the turn of the century Afrikaners fought against a British imperialism which they saw as being intent upon their destruction. Even after the formation of Union in 1910 and the later recognition of Afrikaans as an official language, the Afrikaners felt themselves to be second-class citizens in their own land. They saw their liberation from this in the intensifying of group unity and a sense of identity, and the fostering of their own culture and traditions. In other words, this salvation would be initiated through an 'Afrikaner consciousness'. This movement continues today, but under a different form. Now that the Afrikaners have attained a position of political power they are using the ideologies of apartheid and 'separate development' to ensure their survival.

The Dutch Reformed church has been deeply involved in the Afrikaner movement. Some of their churchmen have developed a theology which justifies these efforts at self-preservation through the theory and practice of racial and ethnic differences between South Africans. For example, 'The universality of the people of God in which all believers are united as equals does not imply the effacement of differences between the races. . . . When a person becomes a believer and is incorporated in the People of God, it does not mean that he is sundered from his race. . . . Every race is taken up in the people of God as an organic race-entity.'[3]

A similar preoccupation is found in *Credo van 'n Afrikaner* by Andries Treurnicht, a minister in the Dutch Reformed church and a former cabinet minister. Here he spells out the ideals of an Afrikaner: to build up his people, to strengthen christian nationalism and not to allow the dissolution of his national identity.

This desire for salvation sprang from a feeling of persecution. But the desire to survive has been replaced by the desire to dominate. Ezekiel Mphahlele has traced the development of this through an examination of Afrikaans poetry. '[The Afrikaner poet Totius] built up in his poetry an image of his people as a persecuted race who, like the Israelites, travelled miles and miles of desert to look for Canaan and, in the process, to bring salvation to the [black] barbarians. Alas, that persecution complex has released a great number of excesses in Afrikaner domination.'[4]

The transforming of this struggle for liberation into a religious quest has bedevilled the Afrikaners' legitimate aspirations. They saw themselves as actors in a biblical drama and their history as God-willed and God-justified, and they turned this into an ideology which allowed them to dominate others. In the 1930s, when the Nazis were coming to power, Dietrich Bonhoeffer was critical of a similar outlook. 'One need only hold that something is God-willed and God-created for it to be vindicated forever: the division of man into nations, national struggles, war, class struggle, the exploitation of the weak by the strong, the cut-throat competition of economics.'[5]

SALVATION AND THE BLACKS

For a young black person from Soweto salvation means abolition of the pass laws, freedom of movement, free education, and majority or black rule in South Africa.

The need for black deliverance was clearly expressed at the memorial service at Kimberley on the fourth anniversary of the June 1976 uprising. Speaking for all blacks, the Revd Motshumi Maropong said, 'Our blood and sweat built this country. . . . We would like to take a rightful place in the free world. . . . The policies of this country are making us avowed enemies of this land. If calls for justice and freedom are not heeded, then all South Africans are in for a hard time. We want to share the happiness and joy of this land. This is the midnight hour for if we cannot live together we shall destroy each other. Change must come now before it is too late.'[6]

The salvation and liberation of blacks is something which must begin now through the change of political structures and a sharing in the material products and fruits of this country. Many feel that liberation will start when blacks 'accept themselves' as black people, and when they become a community that is united to fight daringly for their freedom.

There are some points of similarity between the blacks under Afrikaner rule, and the Afrikaners under British rule. However, blacks are not worried about their national or ethnic identity as the Afrikaner is. What they want is freedom and political control over the country of their birth. A black man born in a 'white area' wants the right to remain where he was born, and the right to own a home there. A migrant worker wants freedom to move to and from the place he works, and the freedom to live with his family where he works. He wants liberation from the permit system which controls his movements as he goes about seeking work, selling his labour.

How do blacks try to solve their problems? Some look to the government to initiate change. Others accept the 'independence' of their 'homelands' as designed by the government, in the hope that they will thus have a platform from which to negotiate with the government without any harassment. Others reject the idea of the balkanisation of the country through the creation of 'homelands'; they want to struggle for a united South Africa. Some feel that it is only through an armed struggle that liberation will be attained. Many of these are young people, and many have left the country and gone for military training outside South Africa.

THE CATHOLIC CHURCH, APARTHEID, AND THE BLACKS
The Catholic church is not an institution alongside or above our society. It is an institution within society with the important task of social criticism. Since 1950 it has been a very strong critic of the policy and legislation of the National Party government. The bishops' official statements have re-iterated the doctrine of the Catholic church on human dignity and human rights. It is a basic teaching that there ought to be no racial discrimination whatsoever in the church. But the bishops admit that the teaching is often at variance with the practice. In 1957 they stated that 'The practice of segregation, though officially not recognised in our churches, characterises nevertheless many of our church societies, our schools, seminaries, convents, hospitals, and the social life of our people. In the light of Christ's teaching this cannot be tolerated forever. The time has come to pursue more vigorously the change of heart and practice that the law of Christ demands. We are hypocrites if we condemn apartheid in South Africa and condone it in our institutions.'

In the light of this it is amazing to note that the bishops built a *black* national seminary at Hammanskraal in 1963, only fifty kilometres north of the *white* national seminary in Pretoria. Only those who were involved in this shameful project can reveal what was the reason behind compromising the principle upheld in the 1957 declaration. Twenty years had to pass before the bishops took the first step to demonstrate before the whole world that they were really prepared for conflict on the question of racial discrimination when they opened catholic schools to all race groups.

The 1977 'Declaration of Catholic Commitment on Social Justice' is a call to the whole church, the clergy and the laity, to struggle against apartheid. The Declaration emphasises renewal in the church so that it may become a true witness to the gospel. It calls for the church to examine its own practices and to 'eradicate all differentiation on purely racial grounds in the treatment of persons at presbyteries, convents, other institutions and private homes'. Liberation must be a task which commences within the church so that she is in a position of strength and righteousness to confront this society's unrighteous racial practices.

In this document the bishops resolve 'to speed up the promotion of black persons to the responsible functions and high posts in the church; to encourage them to accept such functions and responsibilities, so that the multi-cultural nature of the church in South Africa may be clearly recognised; and to provide the training necessary for this purpose.' If vigorously implemented this resolution can have far-reaching effects on the black people in the church. It can instil a sense of wholeness of person in those who feel the evil of being less than a person, in those people who are declared not to be citizens in their own country.

The appointment of blacks to senior positions in the church can be liberating for whites as well as blacks. It can be seen as a means of breaking away from an unacceptable social system, and also as a means of humanising a situation which has been created through the physical separation of black and white. It can also serve to bring about reconciliation between christians. Through such simple steps the church can witness to the reality of liberation and, ultimately, of salvation.

It should be obvious from what has been said above that the church should more readily use its resources in favour of the dispossessed poor. Parishes should see themselves as part of a larger corporate body, with responsibility to all sections of society, particularly to those who are poorest.

This leads us to the conclusion that the church's role is neither to support ideologies which lead people to revolution, nor those which passively accept the status quo. It has to bring about an alteration of man's understanding of his nature and his calling to salvation, which demands a restructuring of his relations with other men. The church is only subversive in the terms of the pastoral exhortation of Paul VI (*Evangelii Nuntiandi*): 'It is a question not only of preaching the gospel in ever wider geographic areas or to ever greater numbers of people, but also of affecting, and, as it were, upsetting, through the power of the gospel, mankind's criteria of judgement, determining values, points of interest, lines of thought, sources of inspiration and models of life, which are in contrast with the word of God and the plan of salvation.'

References
    1. Statement of Bishop P. F. J. Butelezi (1974). See Appendix.
    2. A. Sovik, *Salvation Today* (Minneapolis, 1973).
    3. C. W. H. Boshoff, 'Christianity and the Afrikaner', *Journal of Theology for Southern Africa* (September, 1977), p. 11
    4. E. Mphahlele, *The African Image* (New York, 1974), p. 132.
    5. D. Bonhoeffer, *No Rusty Swords* (London, 1965), p. 165.
    6. Quoted in *The Voice*, 18 June 1980, p. 3.

4   CATHOLIC BISHOPS AND APARTHEID

Trevor Verryn

In a country such as South Africa, with its strong calvinistic tradition and concomitant fear of popery, the catholic pioneers and their immediate successors felt no great urge to attract publicity by flaunting unpopular political opinions. The fact that most of the episcopate, and a large proportion of the priests and religious brothers and sisters have always been white expatriates, and in the country under sufferance, has further encouraged the leadership of the church to follow a course of prudence.

Before the National Party came to power in 1948 racist sentiments had existed for many years in South Africa, along with a certain amount of discriminatory legislation, and a much larger measure of discriminatory practice. The prevailing atmosphere, however, was one of apathy, and it was only the particularly dedicated opponent of racism who felt stirred to protest.

This changed after 1948 when, fuelled by a sure sense of divine mission and election, the National Party embarked on a systematic programme of discriminatory legislation. In 1952 this provoked the catholic bishops to issue the first of seven major statements on race relations. The 'Statement on Race Relations' of June 1952 is no clarion call to revolution. Urging 'prudence' and acknowledging that 'it is not easy for fallen man, even with the help of God's grace, to attain this ideal' of loving their 'Father in heaven and one another for his sake', it points out that South Africa has 'a particular difficulty in this regard'.

The bishops sketched the disadvantaged position of those to whom it referred as 'non-Europeans'. They had virtually no voice in the governing of the land and lacked equal opportunity in employment and social affairs. What was worse was the psychological counterpart of discriminatory law and custom—the stigma attached to skin colour. This aroused 'resentment, animosity and distrust' among its victims.

They pointed out that it was not the 'Europeans' alone who

were to blame for this state of affairs. The great 'majority of non-Europeans, and particularly the Africans, have not yet reached a state of development that would justify their integration into a homogeneous society with the European'. There were 'many' who, nevertheless, had already attained the cultural level deemed by the bishops to qualify them for full participation in the social, political and economic life of the country, and justice demanded that these should not be debarred.

The problem, as the bishops saw it, consisted of four elements: deep-rooted prejudice in 'Europeans'; resentment and distrust aggravated by bitter experience on the part of 'many non-Europeans'; disparity of cultural attainments according to 'Western standards'; and inter-tribal friction among Africans. The solution lay in 'prudent and careful planning', justice and charity. This sentiment was elaborated upon at some length, with reinforcement from scriptural texts.

A discussion of human rights followed, with a distinction being drawn between primary rights, which stemmed from man's nature as man—'the right to life, dignity, sustenance, worship, the integrity, use and normal development of faculties; to work and the fruit of work; to private ownership of property; to sojourn and movement; to marriage and the procreation and education of children; to association with one's fellowmen'—and secondary rights which varied according to the type of society and the qualifications it set for these rights, which included the right to vote in elections, to state-aided education, unemployment insurance, and old-age pensions.

Neither primary nor contingent rights might be abridged by the state, which existed for the people, and not vice versa. The state might control the exercise of rights for the common good. Its duty was to create conditions in which citizens might prosper in the exercise of their rights. Moreover the state could not bear this burden alone. Employers of labour and those who exerted great influence on the country's economy had also to see to it that people could live in 'at least frugal comfort'.

Rights involved duties, and the demand for rights had to be understood to include a readiness to accept the responsibilities involved.

The document concluded with a further admission that it would be difficult to put principles into practice in South Africa. The need for charity, justice and prudence was once again underlined, and the support of the prayers, goodwill and co-operation of those who desire to see justice and peace reign in the land was urged.

There is much in this cautious and paternalistic document which, thirty years later, would make some bishops blush and others shake with rage. But it needs to be evaluated against the backdrop of its age, when it could lay a modest claim to being at least in the rearguard of that small band of liberals which in those days were stigmatised as *kafferboeties*.

This was six years before Alan Paton's *Cry, the Beloved Country*, and eighteen months after the Christian Council of South Africa, the forerunner of the South African Council of Churches, had convened a major conference on 'The christian citizen in a multi-racial society'. The catholic bishops had not taken part in that deliberation, but it is possible that they were influenced by its report. Most other churches, except the three Afrikaans Reformed 'sister churches' had been represented, including two churches with entirely black memberships, and ten with a membership consisting only of white missionaries and an entirely black rank and file. The black christian voice, insofar as it existed in those days, was heard at the conference. The published report, which came with study and discussion material, was moderate in tone, and affirmed that all men were made in God's image, and had an essential unity; that individuals who had progressed from a 'primitive state to one more advanced' should be given rights and matching responsibilities; that the franchise should be extended to qualified blacks; that every child should be educated to the limit of his capabilities; and that man had the right to work in the sphere where his abilities could best contribute to the common good. This modest statement represented the advanced thought of protestants in 1949. No record existed of whether or not the catholic bishops took the statement into account in drawing up their own. In tone and philosophy the protestant and catholic documents are very similar. 'Guardianship', 'civilization', 'qualified franchise' and 'prudence' are among the common themes. Whether or not the one document influenced the other, it certainly is true that all churches except the Afrikaans Reformed were voicing similar sentiments.

For all their advocacy of gradualism and prudence, neither the bishops' statement of 1952, nor the Christian Council conference of 1949, left any discernible impression on the government: legislation designed to establish apartheid for all generations proceeded inexorably. Indeed, one might even speculate whether the statements left some politicians secretly relieved that the first four years of apartheid had provoked such temperate responses, and consequently emboldened the policy-makers to stretch out their hands to grasp more important booty—the mission schools. These institutions were no optional appendages to christian missionary endeavour. They were, in fact, the centre-piece of evangelistic strategy: the single truly effective instrument in winning converts.

In 1954 Dr H. F. Verwoerd announced his government's intention of taking over all mission schools which were in receipt of state aid. In some respects a case could have been made out for accepting, or even welcoming, this move. The state had for many years shouldered the financial and administrative burden of education for white children. Had it intended the take-over to be the first step towards providing equal education for all, it would not have encountered any opposition. In the event the 'Bantu Education' Bill provoked strenuous resistance which concentrated on three points in particular: the limiting of education to provide no more than that which could be exploited by blacks 'in accordance with their opportunities in life';* the organisation of all schools on ethnic lines; and the question of the right of mission schools to continue, with or without grants-in-aid. The new syllabus was bitterly opposed by most blacks, who saw in the compulsory use of the mother tongue up to standard six a serious handicap.

The catholic bishops, like all christian leaders except those of the Reformed churches, were profoundly distressed. Some churches tried to maintain their most cherished schools without subsidies; some closed them rather than hand them over; some, with heavy hearts, handed them over to the state, rather than throw teachers out of work and children out of school. The catholics were, at that time, running 688 subsidised schools (about 15% of the schools then open to blacks) and had, in addition, about 130 schools awaiting subsidy. The bishops decided to keep as many as possible of their schools in church hands and forgo subsidy. To this end they launched the Catholic Missions School Appeal Fund, and during 1955 raised R1 500 000. Local black communities helped pay teachers' salaries, and teachers themselves accepted wages lower than those in state schools. Since those days many of these church schools have been closed under Group Areas legislation, or for other reasons. By 1966, 472 schools remained in church hands, but by 1980 the number had fallen to about half that number.

The bishops issued a pastoral letter on 30 November 1954, in which they characterised the attitude of the church as that of a 'solicitous mother and the careful guardian of her children' who

*H. F. Verwoerd; Hansard, 5th session, 11th Parliament col. 1306.

had passed through the 'bitter verbal strife' of recent times 'with calm serenity and untiring charity', seeking only a solution which would be acceptable to the state, the church and the parents of the children affected by the proposed legislation. The Vaticanesque phraseology with which the document opened soon yielded to a crisper style, which dismissed the promise of 'some religious intruction' in the 'Bantu Education' schools as inadequate.

Then, in heavy type, it declared: 'To safisfy the demands of the Catholic church, it is necessary that all the teaching and the whole organisation of the school, its teachers and the whole spirit of their teaching be regulated by a truly christian spirit, under the direction and supervision of the church.' Popes Pius XI and Leo XIII were both cited, the one to define education as the preparation of man for the accomplishment of his life's task in a manner congruent with his 'sublime end' and to assert the right and duty of parents to ensure that their children are educated in this way; the other to elaborate on how christian piety should permeate all instruction.

The reluctance of the state to give church schools any financial aid, even if these adhere to the provisions of the Bantu Education Act, was noted. Then followed an appeal for catholic unity and sacrifice, for fervent prayer and generous support for the Catholic Mission Schools' Fund which would be created to keep the schools open.

There was, however, some discrepancy between what the bishops regarded as the most important reasons for retaining the schools (to form good catholics, and help them to attain their 'sublime end') and the most pressing concerns of the black parents and pupils (the attainment of as high a level of qualification as possible, in no way inferior to that of whites). Blacks believed that church schools would save them from the stigma of having followed the 'Bantu Education' syllabus. In the event the best that could be attained was the teaching of the hated syllabus by catholic rather than non-catholic teachers.

* * *

Apartheid, meanwhile, continued its remorseless progress, to be greeted at each fresh major step with ever more trenchant criticism in the bishops' pastoral letters. In 1957 the bishops proclaimed:

It is argued that only in this manner [of 'separate development', as apartheid was now termed] will these races be doing the will of God, lending themselves to the fulfilment of His providential designs. The contention sounds plausible as long as we overlook an important qualification, namely, that separate development is subordinate to white supremacy. The white man makes himself the agent of God's will and the interpreter of His providence in assigning the range and determining the bounds of non-white development. One trembles at the blasphemy of thus attributing to God the offences against charity and justice that are apartheid's necessary accompaniment.

Still the bishops urged patience, and an evolutionary approach, acknowledging the great cultural differences which are obstacles to immediate universal franchise and integration, but at the same time they warned of the rising tide of bitterness in the hearts of black people. The burden of affecting urgent reforms was now placed firmly on the shoulders of whites. They then addressed themselves to the practice of segregation in churches and church institutions, serving notice that all discriminatory customs had to be eliminated as soon as possible.

The tone of the bishops' pastoral letter of 1960 was more urgent still. They were 'gravely concerned' about the future, and cautioned that people who were long exasperated in their quest for legitimate rights might turn to violence if peaceful means fail. 'While we do not condone such acts,' they stated, 'we would demand that their root cause in the form of injustice and oppressive measures be removed.' The unity of mankind was affirmed. The dignity and rights of human beings were expressed in the clearest of terms, following the guidelines laid down by Pius XII: the role of the state was primarily that of custodian of these rights. The bishops drew attention to the commandment of love, the necessity of change, and called for a new vision of society with a franchise based on justice. Economic opportunities should be open to all, and there should be freedom of association regardless of colour. The Mixed Marriages Act, which prohibited inter-racial marriage, was singled out as a specific curtailing of a fundamental human right, as was the Group Areas Act which not only impaired freedom of association, but also lessened the right of ownership for individuals of certain groups. The letter concluded with an appeal to all people in Southern Africa to approach in a christian spirit the grave matters that had been raised. The bishops directed that sermons be preached on aspects covered by their letter so that consciences might be directed towards obedience to God's will and the coming of His kingdom. These were the last words of the bishops to the church by means of a pastoral letter before the Second Vatican Council.

When we look back from the 1980s on the pivotal years of *aggiornamento* between 1959 and 1965, and reflect on the vast transformation which occurred, we expect to find a fresh tone, perhaps even a new theology of church and state, to pervade the letters and policy of the bishops. In this respect their letter of 1962 is at first something of a disappointment. We need to remember, however, that at that point the Council had dealt with the subjects of Liturgy, Revelation and The Church. Only in 1965 would The Modern World come up for discussion. The pastoral letter issued early in 1962, therefore, reflects the sombre impressions of rising godlessness and social disorder which had evidently struck the bishops during time spent listening to papers on the subject of their fellow pastors' problems in 'post-christian' Europe. This led to a prolonged meditation on the church and the Holy Spirit, and the affirmation that the church would endure. There was a general exhortation to justice and charity, and the need to combat starvation, job reservation, compulsory migratory labour and oppression in general was briefly mentioned. The faithful were urged not to lose heart at the immensity and complexity of the task which confronted them, but to persevere in acts of kindness and 'gentle courtesies' in daily life.

* * *

The Second Vatican Council prompted the establishment of national councils of laity and of priests, and these began work in the late 1960s and early 1970s, considering in a fresh way the application of catholic morality to public life.

The passing of the Bantu Laws Amendment Bill in 1964 constituted a major 'invasion of human rights', depriving black citizens of a strict right to residence, movement or employment outside their 'Bantu' areas. This legislation provoked an immediate and sharp protest from the episcopate against the 'negation of social morality and christian thinking'. Significantly, the bishops' press statement specifically associated the Catholic church with the outcry of 'those other churches and christian bodies in the Republic' against the affront to human dignity which the bill represented. This deliberate ecumenical dimension, the product both of Vatican II and the grimness of the struggle in South Africa, has remained a feature of catholic social witness from that time. In July 1966, for instance, the bishops addressed a 'message to all', offering the 'honest assistance of the church in fostering that brotherhood of all men' and congratulating and thanking 'our fellow-christians of other communions who have inspired us by their witness'.

The avowed intention of this pastoral letter was to apply the insights of Vatican II, and particularly the Pastoral Constitution on the Church in the Modern World, to the situation in South Africa. Abundance and poverty, the interdependence of the human family, the natural right of free association, human rights, true patriotism, authority and discrimination all received attention. The bishops noted with gratitude that efforts had been made to raise the standard of living of the less developed groups in the country. There had been advances in housing, education, health and social welfare, but much still cried out for attention as far as the lot of the unskilled worker was concerned. Migratory labour was branded as unjust when it involved the enforced and lengthy separation of husband and wife, particularly where the arrangement could not be regarded as temporary.

Action followed. The bishops' conference established various full-time departments, including one devoted to Justice and Reconciliation. This department served to link the bishops' conference to diocesan commissions and local groups devoted to the social apostolate, and beyond to individuals who strove for justice and peace. The department aimed to keep in close touch with similar endeavours in other churches, and with the South African Council of Churches. It supported in various ways people who witnessed against oppression and discrimination, and published various documents to make catholics and others better informed as to what was at stake.

* * *

An important document published in 1974 was a statement on 'Black Consciousness' by Bishop P. F. J. Butelezi.* The document symbolises what might be called the 'new voice' of the catholic bishops. No longer do we have Irish or German expatriates making cautious applications of time-honoured guidelines, but 'sons of the soil', to use one of their own favourite phrases, speaking directly and urgently about the agonies and hopes of their own people.

In this new and more active phase of catholic leadership the concern for the 'social justice apostolate' was not confined to pronouncements in joint pastoral letters on aspects of human rights and dignity. The bishops also turned their attention to specific issues such as industrial relations, and 'development'. The bishops'

*See Appendix.

commission for 'Missions, Migration and Tourism' was, for example, charged with the publication and dissemination of a 'pastoral note' on migratory labour. This nine-page document was designed to be used by individuals and small groups as a guide to the study of the problem in Southern Africa, in order to spur local groups to action aimed both at the amelioration of the suffering caused by the system, as well as the eradication of the system itself. Aware of the fact that actual case studies of individuals who have been the victims of the system are more telling than masses of statistics, the compilers of the document included details of six actual cases, and urged readers to collect more as part of their response to the challenge posed by the system. Fr Finbar Synnott, secretary of the Justice and Reconciliation Department, noted in his annual report a year later that 'most white catholics and many clergy and religious' have been apathetic in their response to the call to do something about migrant labour. Bishops have been accused of interfering in politics, he observed, but they are 'driven to witness' on this issue 'by the terrible suffering of people under our laws and the scandal to the name of Christ given by christians conforming with injustice'.

'Development' has its own secretariat under the Bishops' Conference. The term includes an immense variety of activities all designed to equip and inspire the less privileged members of society to obtain a greater share in the good things of this country. Literacy campaigns, local co-operative projects, buying agencies, home crafts or sub-contracting into industry, technical and mechanical training, cooking, sewing, town hygiene and budgeting, and many other courses of instruction are offered. Those responsible for this aspect of the work of the church are well aware of the criticism that has been levelled against 'developmentalism' in Latin America, where the accusation is that it makes the best of a bad system, but fails to change the system. The development projects need, therefore, to be seen as but an aspect of the entire 'social apostolate' which the bishops have been seeking to foster. It is, moreover, possible to argue that the people cannot effect a change in society when they are abject. It is when conditions of life are improving that aspirations begin to grow. Developmental work can therefore claim a legitimate role in the struggle for a just society, particularly if a campaign is waged on other fronts as well.

Another area to which the bishops have given major attention is catechetics. The term, which in the recent past was usually taken to refer to the specific instruction of prospective converts to catholicism, is now accepted as including the regular and systematic education of all church members. Adults, who all their lives have been churchgoers, need catechesis, just as do young people or new members. The bishops' conference has established a department to promote catechesis, and an increasing number of religious Sisters and Brothers are receiving training under its auspices, and devoting their energies and talents to part-time or full-time work in this field. Reports on their work make it clear that the responsibility of christians for social justice receives its due emphasis in their programme. The effects of this new thrust in the training of church members has yet to be discerned in the life of the country. The eighteen individual catechists and twenty-two catechetical teams whose efforts form the substance of the 1977 report of the department indicated that, among the problems they were encountering, lack of awareness of the importance of catechetics, a sluggish response and low level of motivation among ordinary church members were causing considerable disappointment and delay.

1977 witnessed a climax in the bishops' drive for greater sociopolitical engagement in Southern Africa. In February of that year, at their plenary session, they made a solemn commitment to a programme to: (1) Change social attitudes and customs which were derogatory, insulting, discriminatory or in any other way offensive to the standards of christian social righteousness; bring various groups together in the schools, hospitals, church councils and other institutions of the church; (2) Advance blacks to responsible functions and high positions within the church; give fullest responsibility to church councils in black parishes which were served by white priests; (3) Re-assess the distribution of the personnel of the church so that the ministry would be concentrated where needs were greatest; appoint black priests to white parishes in order to break away from the prevailing social system; implement the principle of equal pay for equal work; promote more vigorously the training in social justice in the catechetical programme; support the just aspirations of the Black Consciousness movement; foster all possible development programmes; appoint full-time justice and reconciliation workers in each diocese; encourage clergy, religious and lay associations to undertake development work less exclusively within the church; encourage local community groups to initiate training and development programmes and the timely handing over to the local community groups of institutions, property and funds connected with these projects; (4) Give a more visible expression to the communalising of church funds; (5) Examine the feasibility of a Pastoral Consultation in which the large majority of participants would be black, in order to develop further a policy on church life and the apostolate in the present social context.

The bishops, noting the intensifying armed struggle along the borders of the country, discussed the topic of conscientious objection and defended the right of every individual to follow his conscience. The bishops urged the state to make provision for alternative forms of non-military national service, as is done in almost every other non-communist country in the world which has conscription.

This commitment and the statement on conscientious objection were published together with a 'statement on the current situation', which refers to the greater intensity which the struggle for liberty has assumed since the 'Soweto demonstrations' of June 1976. The bishops express their particularly grave misgivings at reliable reports of 'seemingly systematic beatings and unjustifiable shootings during disturbances and of cold-blooded torture of detained persons'; it is noted that these reports have been accompanied by many deaths of detained persons. The legislation which the government was proposing to indemnify police and security personnel who may have been guilty of unprovoked and disproportionate violence is condemned in 'the strongest possible terms', and the bishops note that 'the black people of the Republic have passed the point of no return'. No temporary suppression of violence, the bishops declare, will avert the civil war which must break out unless there is a just sharing of citizenship.

The stance that the bishops have come to adopt, the tone in which they express themselves, their very choice of words and phrases, the programmes they have launched and continue to foster, all reflect a change of attitude from that of the 50s and 60s. There is less paternalism, more humility, a greater concern for and a deliberate identification with the oppressed and their demand for freedom. From the mid-70s onwards there is a decrease in the use of the distinction between the natural world and the supernatural world. Church groups, one and all, are urged to view the practice of christianity no longer in terms of certain individual virtues and spiritual exercises which have a mainly supernatural referent and which prepare souls for heaven. The impact not only of Vatican II but also of the this-worldly emphasis of Latin American 'liberation theology' has become increasingly evident. However it is the papal encyclicals *Justitia et Pax*, *Populorum Progressio* and, supremely, *Pacem in Terris* that have been the chief sources of inspiration to the bishops in recent years, during which it would be fair to say that three new dimensions have been discovered in the meaning of the word *saeculum*, 'world'.

First, a new and profound appreciation of the essential relationship of all history to God has grown. 'History' involves society, culture, politics, economics and the forces at work in these. This is increasingly perceived as defining the arena of christian experience, witness and living, the place of encounter with God.

Secondly, man is viewed in a new light, as the one in whom world history, including the mighty story of the evolution of the universe, life and all things is 'recapitulated'. This invests man with great dignity and an exalted destiny, which requires that he be approached with a profound sense of wonder.

Thirdly, certain 'moments' or 'events' in history, such as the event of Israel, the event of Jesus and the event 'in his Spirit' (in other words, the church), can by faith be indicated as moments of a special 'history of salvation'.

There are practical consequences of these perspectives on the *saeculum*. One is that the world is no longer regarded as a mere backdrop or secondary item in the quest for another world. Nor is it seen as self-evidently good, or self-evidently evil, or even self-evidently neutral: it is in 'potential', evolving toward God for his glorification. Because of this the world must be approached in an attitude of 'critical loyalty'.

Another corollary is that man, the bearer of this 'critical loyalty', has a special responsibility as God's fellow-worker in 'perfecting' the world. Failure to follow this calling constitutes sin. Conversely, morally sound, righteous behaviour consists in interpreting reality and uncovering its potential, striving to bring history to its goal. But the totality of human possibilities is, and remains, a free gift of God, which is to say, grace. This unmerited gift is most clearly visible in Christ's crucifixion. Here both man's failure and the power of God's action stand revealed. Thus the growing community of new humanity, the church, must constantly remember the sinfulness of man and its own liability to fail, in order to remain alive to the graciousness of God and to keep alive that 'expectation' of his gratuitous favour in the future.

* * *

There can be no doubt that the bishops are determined to spare no effort to eradicate racial prejudice and discrimination. They regard the quest of the poor for liberty and dignity as well within that sphere of human striving which finds its summation in Christ. What is uncertain is whether they have correctly identified the problem they wish to solve. Is racial prejudice and discrimination the centre-piece? We are witnessing the confrontation between a classical calvinist theology of church and state, with its extremely pessimistic view of all human endeavours, and a modern catholic theology, with its optimistic affirmation of the human quest. But is economic exploitation, the unequal distribution of wealth and opportunity, in short, the growing class conflict (which happens to coincide with racial lines) not the real problem of Southern Africa?

There are signs that government policy makers view the situation from this perspective, and hope to avert the threatening class war by the rapid expansion of a black middle class. But there is still awaited from the catholic bishops thorough treatment of the problems of the ownership of resources, the means of production, class exploitation and conflict and related issues.

References

The full texts of all relevant pastoral letters are published in:

Pastoral Letters (Press Commission S.A.C.B.C., P. O. Box 941, Pretoria 0001).

Other important texts (obtainable from the same address) are:

Pastoral Note on Christian Responsibility in Migratory Labour Situations. Occasional papers series no. 4.

Justice and Reconciliation in South Africa, report by F. Synott, O. P. Pastoral Action series no. 5.

Development through tutorial and adult education seen as apostolic work. Pastoral Action series no. 8.

The Catechetical Situation in South Africa. Pastoral Action series no. 10.

Southern African Catholic Bishops' Statements (Catholic Institute for International Relations, 22 Coleman Fields, London, N1).

5 CATHOLICS IN A CALVINIST COUNTRY

John de Gruchy

It would almost seem as though Dutch Reformed Calvinist man and Catholic man in South Africa are two different creatures with different and irreconcilable ways of looking at man and the world.–Alan Paton.[1]

The Roman Catholic church in South Africa cannot properly be understood solely as part of a universal institution, or as an entity in itself; it has to be understood and examined in relation to its social and historical context. In this essay we shall consider it in relation to Afrikaner calvinism, a determinative component of South African society.[2] This will help us to appreciate better the social forces which have affected its life and witness in South Africa, and also provide us with a necessary background for considering its relation to the state.

Although Afrikaner calvinism is largely derived from calvinism proper it is important not to equate the two. There are varieties of calvinism, and these varieties are found within South Africa itself, of which Afrikaner calvinism is the dominant one.[3] Afrikaner calvinism is calvinism as shaped by the historical experience of Afrikanerdom; it is bound up with Afrikaner nationalism, ethnicity and identity. From the perspective of Afrikaner calvinism, catholicism as something international and non-racial is not just a threat to faith and sound doctrine, it is also a danger to Afrikanerdom as such. Indeed, the Catholic church is regarded with some suspicion as being a foreign body, answerable to the Vatican alone, and in contemporary perspective one that is liable to support revolution as certain segments of it are presently doing in Latin America and have done in Zimbabwe.[4]

Afrikaner calvinism is primarily transmitted through the Afrikaner churches. The size and strength of the Nederduitse Gereformeerde Kerk (the Dutch Reformed church) and its smaller sister churches, the Nederduitsch Hervormde Kerk and the Gereformeerde Kerk, have ensured that the calvinist creed should be dominant, even though it is not the one confessed by the majority of christians in South Africa. Virtually all the National Party members of parliament, and by far the majority of their supporters, belong to one of these churches. This is a salutary indication of Afrikaner calvinism's proximity to the corridors of power and influence.

We shall explore our theme in several ways. Firstly, we shall reflect on the nature and significance of Afrikaner calvinism; secondly, we shall examine the neo-calvinist world-view which has shaped the Afrikaner calvinist's approach to politics and social issues; thirdly, we shall consider the ways in which Afrikaner calvinism, and especially the Dutch Reformed church, has regarded Roman catholicism, and to what extent this may have influenced political policies; and, finally, we shall reflect on current tendencies, both ecumenical and political, which have emerged in South Africa since Vatican II. We shall then be in a position either to confirm or contest Alan Paton's evaluation that we are here dealing with two irreconcilable ways of looking at man and the world. Although not a Roman catholic, the Revd A. W. Eaton, editor of the Anglican newspaper *The Watchman*, wrote the following after the Conference on Christian Reconstruction held at Fort Hare in 1942. 'The issue that confronts us is between catholicism and calvinism. When we are capable of an understanding of these two faiths which form our dual ancestry we shall be equipped to see our more immediate problems in their true perspective.'[5] For the moment we will reserve our judgement on this analysis.

AFRIKANER CALVINISM

While the majority of South Africans are by no means calvinists, it is nevertheless true that Afrikaner calvinism permeates the fabric of South African society, and that understanding the former is helpful for understanding the latter.

Unlike the first Portuguese explorers of the Cape of Good Hope, who were Roman catholics, the first Dutch settlers at the Cape were almost all members of the established Reformed church of the Netherlands. This church was confessionally committed to the strict calvinist orthodoxy of the Synod of Dort (1618–1619). This does not mean that all the Dutch settlers belonging to this church were strict calvinists, but they were certainly protestant, and this they shared in common with the German lutherans and the French hugenots who settled amongst them. As such, the European settler community was not really representative of European society, or even of Dutch society of the time. It is true that some of the settlers were Roman catholics, but they were very few, and certainly not anything like the proportion at that time in Holland. This fact caused W. E. Brown to consider 'how far the history of South Africa might have been different, and whether the approach in these recent years to the critical problem of racial relationship might not have been different, if from the first the Dutch population in South Africa had been a true projection of the population in the Netherlands, with catholics a minority of at least a third among the boer farmers, numerous enough to establish a tradition in contrast to that which is in fact so deeply entrenched and which is grounded in calvinist theology.'[6]

Brown's hypothetical query raises several important issues related to our inquiry. Two questions are particularly pertinent. In the light of the track record of European catholic settlers in Africa (e.g. Mozambique and Angola) or Latin America, is there much ground for maintaining that they would necessarily have done much better than the Dutch calvinists? And, can we blame calvinist theology for the advent of apartheid and the problem of race relations in contemporary South Africa? The first question must be shelved for the moment, but the second is crucial to our discussion.

No church, creed or confession can be understood in isolation from its historical and cultural setting. Calvinism, and the Afrikaner churches in South Africa, are no exception. The character of Afrikaner calvinism has varied over the centuries since the Dutch first came to the Cape in the seventeenth century. The reasons are naturally complex, having to do with theological, ecclesiological, social and political developments both in Europe, especially in Holland, and in South Africa. Without in any way wishing to detract from the interaction between Afrikaner calvinism and sociopolitical events and pressures, we shall concentrate for the moment on the key theological developments particularly in the nineteenth century.

Under the impact of the eighteenth century Enlightenment, the 'established calvinism' of the Netherlands Reformed church, both in Holland and at the Cape, was deeply affected by rationalism. Certainly, and contrary to popular opinion, the ideas of the Enlightenment did not by-pass the settlement at the Cape though they did not reach very far into the interior.[7] As Irving Hexham has convincingly shown, Dutch calvinism at the Cape at the turn of the nineteenth century was not the 'pure calvinism' of the Synod of Dort (1618–19).[8]

The undermining of classical Dutch calvinism by Enlightenment ideas, ideas which were also creating social ferment and revolution, brought forth at least two significant responses which affected Afrikaner calvinism. The 'Reveil' movement in Holland sought to combat the inroads of rationalism in the Dutch church through the revival of Scriptural piety and holiness. One of those who was deeply influenced by the movement was the young Andrew Murray jnr, who studied theology in the Netherlands around the middle of the nineteenth century. On his return home to the Cape, and throughout his long and distinguished ministry within the Dutch Reformed church, Andrew Murray sought to shape Afrikaner calvinism along evangelical and pietistic lines. It was largely due to his influence that rationalist and liberal tendencies in the Cape church were defeated. It was also largely under his influence that the church became so deeply committed to mission and educational work.[9] But Murray's influence had other consequences as well. It tended to make those who were evangelically inclined apolitical, and it failed to provide an adequate theological basis for the Afrikaner people in their struggle for identity and power. This was provided by another development in Holland, namely, the rise of neo-calvinism under the leadership of Groen van Prinsterer and especially Abraham Kuyper.

Abraham Kuyper (1837–1920) not only atttempted to resuscitate the strict or hyper-calvinism of the Synod of Dort, he also inherited the leadership of the anti-revolutionary political party in Holland from its founder van Prinsterer. Having started off as a liberally inclined rationalist pastor, Kuyper was soon led to orthodox calvanism by the needs and the piety of his congregation. This, in turn, led to conflict between him and the established Netherlands Reformed church of which he was a minister. Eventually he broke from the church and was instrumental in forming the Gereformeerde Kerken, the parent church of the Gereformeerde Kerk in South Africa (the so-called 'Dopper Kerk'), a church which has had closer ties in recent years with the Afrikaner churches than the established church in the Netherlands.

Kuyper was also influenced by the political credo of van Prinsterer, which he regarded as not only relevant to the political crises facing Holland and Europe, but also one which related positively to calvinism and to the struggle for a free Reformed church in the Netherlands. Thus Kuyper became the theological and political leader of those calvinists in Holland who wished to counteract liberalism in the church and revolution in society. He attempted to inject what he regarded as the corrective of calvinism as a 'life-system' into political, social and ecclesiastical life. The extent of his influence and the size of his success may be measured from the fact that he eventually became prime minister of Holland.

During the latter part of the nineteenth century, and for much of the twentieth, Abraham Kuyper's neo-calvinism has had a decisive impact upon Dutch Reformed theology in South Africa, and, unlike Murray's evangelicalism, it has provided the theological basis for Afrikaner calvinism's advance into the political and social arena. Although his neo-calvinism has been more germane in some respects to the theology and convictions of the Gereformeerde Kerk centred on Potchefstroom, it has had a profound effect on the thought and the policies of the Dutch Reformed church as well.[10] At the same time, as we shall indicate below, some of Kuyper's insights have been distorted in the process to the detriment of the calvinist witness in South Africa.

CALVINISM AS 'LIFE-SYSTEM'

Abraham Kuyper begins his famous *Lectures on Calvinism*, given at Princeton University in 1898, by stressing that calvinism is not only a theological or ecclesiastical interpretation of christianity, but an all-embracing 'life-system'. Calvinism, he declares, 'puts its impress in and outside the church upon every department of human life'.[11] To quote him at some length:

Calvinism is rooted in a form of religion which was peculiarly its own, and from this specific religious consciousness there was developed first a peculiar theology, then a special church-order, and then a given form for political and social life, for the interpretation of the moral world-order, for the relation between nature and grace, between christianity and the world, between church and state, and finally for art and science; and amid all these life-utterances it remained always the self-same calvinism, in so far as simultaneously all these developments sprang from its deepest life-principle. Hence to this extent *it stands in line with those other great complexes of human life, known as paganism, islamism and romanism, by which we distinguish four entirely different worlds in the one collective world of human life.* And if, speaking precisely, you should co-ordinate christianity and not calvinism with paganism and islamism, it is nevertheless better to place calvinism in line with them, because it claims to embody the christian idea more purely and accurately than could romanism or lutheranism. . . . Hence of romanism only can it be said that it has embodied its life-thought in a world of conceptions and utterances entirely its own. *But by the side of romanism, and in opposition to it, calvinism made its appearance, not merely to create a different church form, but an entirely different form for human life, to furnish human society with a different method of existence, and to populate the world of the human heart with different ideals and conceptions.*[12]

In his treatment of calvinism and politics, Kuyper develops his distinctive idea of 'sphere-sovereignty', an idea which has been widely used and abused in Afrikaner calvinism. For Kuyper, God's sovereignty is exercised in the world through separate spheres, each of which stands in its own right under God. So Kuyper speaks of the sovereignty of God in the state, in society (which includes the family, education etc.), and in the church. Each of these spheres is directly reponsible to God, and they should not interfere in each other's arena. Because we are primarily concerned in this volume with issues of church and state, let us consider how Kuyper deals with these subjects in particular.

For Kuyper, the state is God's remedy for human disorder which has resulted from man's sin. Through his 'common grace' God exercises his authority for justice and order directly through the state. Kuyper's understanding of the state, however, is as opposed to the idea of state-sovereignty as developed in Germany as it is to popular-sovereignty as exemplified in France since 1789. He regarded both as usurping the sovereign authority of God. It is *God*'s authority *in* the state, not the sovereignty *of* the state which is at stake. For Kuyper, 'sphere-sovereignty' was not a theory which set the state free to do its own will, but one which set the state free from ecclesiastical tutelage to be responsible to God, and God alone. Moreover, 'sphere-sovereignty' was intended as a means to prevent State absolutism and corruption; indeed, Kuyper declared, 'We must watch against the danger which lurks for our personal liberty in the power of the state.'[13] The state has a limited role in society. It exists to maintain justice, to maintain the rights of the separate spheres, not to interfere in them, and to protect individuals and especially the weak against the power of others.

God's sovereignty in the church means that the church alone is responsible for the ordering of its faith and common life. The state has no right to interfere. The corollary to this is that the church *as an institution* should not interfere in the affairs of the state. God's Word must rule, 'but in the sphere of the state only through the conscience of the persons invested with authority'.[14] In other words, the church may well be, indeed should be involved in politics through its individual members, but not as a corporate body. If individual christians wish to form a political party, as Kuyper indeed did, that is something else. At this point Kuyper's understanding of church and state relations is not the same as Calvin's,[15] but not unlike the position adopted by Vatican II.[16]

Kuyper's concept of calvinism as a 'life-system' and his teaching on 'sphere-sovereignty' have had a profound effect on Afrikaner calvinist thinking and policy in South Africa, and have thereby also influenced Afrikaner nationalism. With regard to calvinism as a 'life-system' we may refer to the policy of Christian National Education; with regard to the idea of 'sphere-sovereignty' we may refer to the widely held conviction that the church has no right to interfere in political matters and that when it does it is transgressing its boundaries. In these and other respects Kuyper has been rightly interpreted, though he may well be wrong. But his ideas have also been interpreted in other ways, which have distorted his views.

We have already noted some of the ways in which calvinism at the Cape was modified during the nineteenth century. The crucial modification, however, took place in the early decades of the twentieth century. This modification was given expression in numerous tracts and books, the most important of which was the three-volume *Koers in die Krisis.*[17] Its underlying theme was that calvinism had to be adapted to meet the particular situation pertaining in South Africa, namely, the struggle of the Afrikaner against British imperialism, against humanism, liberalism, communism, and against being swamped by blacks. The sovereign-sphere of Afrikanerdom had to be protected. Kuyper's ideas provided a point of departure, but the end product was significantly different both from his view of calvinism and from calvinism generally understood. Two important modifications must be mentioned.

Firstly, Kuyperian calvinism in South Africa was wedded to the German romantic view of history. Kuyper's mentor Van Prinsterer had certainly flirted with this view of history, and the idea not only of national sovereignty but of each nation having a particular historical calling, destiny and cultural mandate strongly appealed to the Dutch people. It was also very appealing for the ideologists of the emerging Afrikaner nation at the turn of the century. Kuyper certainly spoke of God creating separate nations, each with its own identity, but he never regarded the *volk* as a 'sovereign-sphere'. In fact, he saw calvinism as a means whereby nationalism could be transcended. His key interpreter in South Africa, however, H. G. Stoker of Potchefstroom, did not move in that direction. 'The people (*volk*)', he wrote, 'is a separate sphere with its own structure and purpose, grounded in the ordinances of God's creation.'[18]

Secondly, Kuyperian calvinism in South Africa was wedded to the German organic view of the state, in spite of Kuyper's antipathy towards such a view. This marriage was not performed by theologians, but by the political philosophers and leaders of Afrikanerdom in the 1930s.[19] As a result, individual human rights were subsumed within and made subservient to the rights and needs of the nation; service to God and service to the nation became virtually the same thing. Nothing could be more alien to Calvin, or, for that matter, more removed from Kuyper's intention. But because of the idea of 'sphere-sovereignty' the church was virtually rendered silent. It was to stick to 'preaching the Gospel' and was not prophetically to examine the political situation in the light of that Gospel. Afrikaner calvinism was virtually captive, in spite of some exceptions, to Afrikaner nationalism.

DIE ROOMSE GEVAAR

As we have already noted, according to Abraham Kuyper calvinism as a 'life-system' is not only in conflict with other non-christian ideologies and religions, it is also in conflict with what he referred to as 'romanism'. And the idea that calvinism is in principle in conflict with Rome has been central to Afrikaner calvinism's self-understanding.

The Dutch calvinists who settled at the Cape were not only heirs of the protestant reformation, they were also the products of a Europe that had been ravaged by the Thirty Years War between catholics and protestants, and a Holland that had struggled bitterly against catholic Spain for independence. Their natural antagonism towards Rome was further reinforced by the coming of the French huguenots to the Cape in 1688. It is therefore understandable that catholicism and its representatives were regarded with suspicion, and that catholic services of worship were generally proscribed until towards the end of the eighteenth century. It must be remembered that catholics were in a similar situation in Britain at the time, that the German lutherans at the Cape were only permitted to worship in public from 1778, and that the French huguenots were virtually forced to join the Dutch Reformed church.

It was De Mist's *Kerkenordre* of 1804 which granted the protection of the law on equal terms to 'all religious associations which for the furtherance of virtue and good conduct respect a Supreme Being'.[20] This Enlightenment point of view included Roman catholics and reflected the Batavian Republic's more liberal and tolerant outlook. But with the second British occupation of the Cape the situation changed, albeit for a short time. In 1806 the catholics were expelled. Whether or not this was aimed at pleasing the Dutch Reformed church in much the same way as Britain sought to do in regarding that church as the established church in the colony is difficult to determine. By 1820, however, catholics were again free to worhip. As E. A. Walker puts it, 'In keeping with catholic emancipation in the United Kingdom, full civil privileges were granted to catholics with the exception of a few religious orders, and priests were even paid Government salaries like the clergy of so many other churches in the colony.'[21] This remained official state policy until the passing of the Voluntary Bill in 1875 by the Cape Parliament.

The Voluntary Bill laid the legal foundations for church-state relations in emerging South Africa. It made all churches, including the Dutch Reformed, voluntary associations. Catholic opinion was divided on whether or not to support the bill but eventually did so, and, according to W. E. Brown, it benefited from it. As a voluntary association in law, it was, he wrote, 'able to act more spontaneously and to proclaim its teaching more freely than when it was assisted and therefore influenced by its association with the secular power'.[22]

As we shall see, the attitude of the Cape authorities was not always shared by the Afrikaner republics in the north, nor did it necessarily tally with the policy of the Dutch Reformed church in regard to the Catholic church. If the Dutch Reformed church was fighting rationalism and liberalism on the one side, it was also opposing catholicism on the other. This was not primarily for social or political reasons, but for theological and missionary ones. The Dutch Reformed church was against the steady growth of catholic missions among the 'heathen', and it was particularly wary of the influence of catholic schools on young Afrikaners. Several synods towards the end of the nineteenth century warned parents about the danger of the latter, and the warning grew stronger during the Afrikaner struggle for power this century. It was also not unknown for school teachers to be dismissed from public schools because they were Roman catholics.[23]

That this antipathy was largely theological to begin with can be ascertained from the fact that the catholic hierarchy and catholic missionaries were far less critical of Afrikaner racial attitudes and policies than were most of the other protestant missionary societies at the time, and least involved in public and in overseas protest.[24]

Indeed, catholic leadership displayed considerable diplomacy, tact and caution on such matters; an understandable approach given the anti-catholic sentiments of the majority of the colonists. And the Dutch Reformed church's reaction to the growth of 'high church' tractarianism within the Anglican church in South Africa was one of considerable fear and apprehension.[25]

Antipathy towards catholics was particularly strong amongst the Voortrekkers. The *Grondwet* (1856) of the trekkers 'discouraged all churches which did not hold by the Heidelberg catechism, and excluded Roman catholics' even if, as Walker adds, 'their bark was worse than their bite'.[26] Similarly, the boer republics of the Transvaal and the Orange Free State were generally anti-catholic. The Orange Free State law of 1880 required all school teachers to be protestants and also excluded all catholics from the civil service.[27] Similar restrictions were placed upon catholics in the Transvaal. In both republics, however, a more pragmatic policy was adopted when political considerations required it. For example, President Pretorius of the Transvaal gave full civil liberties to Roman catholics in 1871 in an attempt to please his new Portuguese allies in Mozambique.[28]

The Constitution of the Union of South Africa in 1910 did not prejudice catholics or their church in law. The same is true of the Republican Constitution of 1961. But no constitution can prevent ingrained attitudes from flourishing, or affecting policy decisions in government or education. Indeed, it could be argued that during the present century Afrikaner calvinism has hardened in its attitudes towards the catholic church, at least until very recently. Catholicism has been, and still is, regarded by many as a danger to the soul of the nation. It is an alien church, a church with an alien world-view. Its internationalism is contrary to nationalism; its multi-racialism ('look at what happened in Mozambique and Latin America where inter-breeding was rampant') is contrary to apartheid. Indeed, as *Die Kerkbode* suggested in August 1939, for the Afrikaner, catholicism is a danger equal to that of communism.

In his paper *Protestant Aksie Vandag*, which he presented to the Cape Synod of the Dutch Reformed church in 1975, Dr Gustav Bam, then Assistant Secretary of the synod, showed how since 1873 the Cape Synod had taken a stand against its members sending their children to catholic schools.[29] To begin with the synod simply issued warnings. But in 1906 a new accent emerged. The Synod took steps to counter the influence by encouraging its ministers to preach against such education. By 1953 it was made clear that parents who did allow their children to attend such schools were acting against their baptismal vows, and were therefore subject to disciplinary action. In other words, during the decades of this century Dutch Reformed attitudes, as evidenced on this issue, have grown stronger in their antipathy towards catholicism and its influence. That this has involved more than simply the school issue is made clear by Dr Bam when he says, 'The key words which we find here do not only describe the attitude of the synod towards catholic schools, but also reflect the attitude towards the Roman church itself. The key words are: rejection; admonition against; work against; reprimand.' Even at the very synod addressed by Dr Bam, who called for a new approach to the catholic church, a motion was adopted without dissent in which parents were urgently called upon to have more children as a means of 'combating the growth of the Catholic church'.

The synodical decisions of the Dutch Reformed church only reflect the general attitudes of Afrikaner calvinism as a whole. These work themselves out in a variety of ways. For example, considerable pressure has, from time to time, been brought upon the government to restrict catholic immigration into South Africa. There has also been a concerted attempt to convert catholics, especially recent Portuguese immigrants, to the reformed faith on the basis that the Catholic church does not proclaim the true gospel of Jesus Christ and is not therefore a true church. Furthermore, even in this ecumenical age, the involvement of catholics in inter-church gatherings or projects has usually meant the non-participation of the Dutch Reformed church. There is also a strong antipathy towards mixed marriages between members of the Dutch Reformed church and catholics.[30] In short, the traditional attitude of Afrikaner calvinism has been, and to large measure remains, that the Catholic church is a danger to true christian faith, and many would also regard it as a threat to the well-being of the nation.

CALVINISM VS CATHOLICISM

We have maintained that Afrikaner calvinism's antipathy towards catholicism has not only remained constant but that it has also grown stronger this century as Afrikaner nationalism has struggled towards and achieved power. Is it possible, however, especially in the light of Vatican II and present political developments in South Africa, that this traditional attitude might be modifying itself?

Dr Gustav Bam's address to the Cape Synod in 1975 certainly reflected a new approach. Without compromising on his church's

reformed confession, and without in any way suggesting that 'Protestantse Aksie' should cease its operations, Dr Bam maintained
that a new situation had arisen which now called for a different
approach to the problem. *Inter alia*, he referred to some of the
important changes which had taken place in the Catholic church
since Vatican II, and to the new constellations of churches which
had begun to emerge as a result, which no longer follow the old
pattern of protestant on the one side and catholic on the other. In
this connection, Dr Bam referred to the fact that the Roman
Catholic church in South Africa was increasingly involved with
those churches belonging to the South African Council of Churches.
But Dr Bam went significantly further. The Catholic church, he
declared, has become indigenous to South Africa, it is no longer an
alien church; it is a church which is anxious to help shape the
future of South Africa; and the forces which threaten South Africa
and the Dutch Reformed church also threaten the Catholic church.
In this respect, he maintained, she is an ally. In the light of all this,
Dr Bam suggested that the time had come for the Dutch Reformed
church to reappraise its attitude towards the Catholic church. In
doing so, he raised eight sets of relatively radical questions, which,
if answered in the affirmative by his church would bring about a
revolution in its traditional position. That Dr Bam was not an isolated voice in this regard can be seen from the reactions of some
other leading Dutch Reformed theologians to his paper. Without
denying the basic differences between the two traditions, there
was a strong feeling that Rome should be regarded no longer as an
enemy but as a partner in dialogue.[31] Professor J. A. Heyns, Professor of Theology at the University of Pretoria, put it in this way.
'The attack on christianity is so violent and at the same time so
subtle that all christians should hold hands in their common struggle. The power of unbelief may not be strengthened. At the same
time error may not be underestimated. That is why dialogue with
Rome must continue.'[32]

It is doubtful whether the insights and concerns of the theologians are shared by the majority of the laity or the ministers of the
Dutch Reformed church, but there have been some changes in
social attitudes. For example, since 1974 Roman catholic priests
have been allowed to conduct prayers on the radio and television.
Monsignor Hughes, the catholic leader responsible for this aspect
of his church's life, indicated at the time that the then Director of
Programmes for the SABC, Mr Douglas Fuchs, had said that the
policy of 'South Africa is a protestant country', which might

affect catholic TV broadcasts, needed to be reconsidered. Mgr Hughes reported that specifically catholic themes would have to be avoided, as well as political issues. He then went on to say: 'But Mr Fuchs paid us a rather dubious compliment by saying that in the matter of racialism and politics in general, the Catholic church was more realistic than the South African Council of Churches and others.'[33]

What this latter comment suggests, and this is confirmed by other things as well, is that despite the traditional attitude of Afrikaner calvinism towards Roman catholicism, changes since Vatican II, but even more importantly the deepening social and political crisis in South Africa, are making some Afrikaner calvinists more pragmatic in their approach. This does not necessarily mean a compromise with regard to theological issues, but it does mean a reassessment of the Catholic church as a danger to the nation and the state. Of course, for some, especially in the light of the role of significant sections of the Catholic church in the liberation of Zimbabwe, that church will continue to be seen as *die Roomse gevaar* 'the Roman danger'. The fact of the matter is, however, that the Catholic church is itself divided on political issues. In Rhodesia most lay white catholics aligned themselves with majority white opinion, and most black catholics with liberation movements. Similar allegiances are becoming evident in South Africa. So at this stage in South Africa's history it is clearly more advantageous politically for the Nationalist government to encourage the support of the Catholic church as much as possible, rather than to antagonise it through overt support for anti-catholic sentiments. To do otherwise would be to encourage the more radical sections of the church and increase the possibility of its becoming a supporter of revolutionary change, as in Latin America. At the same time, it seems equally clear that the predominantly black Catholic church is unlikely to allow itself to be co-opted by the Nationalist government.[34]

To return to Alan Paton's comment quoted at the outset of this essay. Are catholicism and calvinism so irreconcilably different in their world-views that they must inevitably come into conflict given the South African situation? Is it really the calvinism of the Afrikaner which is the problem, so that if, let us say, the Afrikaners had in fact been Catholics all would have been significantly better?

It is interesting to note that the most outspoken ecclesiastical critics of Afrikaner calvinism have not been Roman catholics, but anglicans of an anglo-catholic persuasion. This may well be the case because there has been a much more intense interaction between the Dutch Reformed church and the Anglican church in South Africa with regard to political and ecclesiastical matters than between the former and the Roman church. Moreover, the Roman catholics have tended to be more diplomatic than prophetic, more cautious than critical in their relations with the state. It was Trevor Huddleston, an anglican, who wrote in *Naught for Your Comfort*:

The truth is that the calvinistic doctrines upon which the faith of the Afrikaner is nourished contain within themselves—like all heresies and deviations from catholic truth—exaggerations so distorting and powerful that it is very hard indeed to recognise the Christian faith they are supposed to enshrine. Here, in this fantastic notion of the immutability of race, is present in a different form the predestination idea: the concept of an elect people of God, characteristic above all of John Calvin.[35]

It would obviously be incorrect to deny that there are basic differences between calvinism and catholicism, but it is equally incorrect to suggest that their different ways of looking at man and the world imply irreconcilable attitudes towards such problems as race or social justice.[36] On the contrary, both confessions have a long tradition of concern for social justice, even though this may often have been forgotten by them, and both would regard such ideologies as apartheid as un-christian, though neither have been very successful in combating racism in church and society. What has been so largely at fault in this regard has not been calvinism, but the way in which Afrikaner nationalism has distorted the reformed faith so that it could lend credence to such dehumanising policies as apartheid. Which leads us to a final comment related to the questions we have posed, and one which opens up another important dimension for understanding the church in South Africa, be it catholic or protestant.

The history of European colonisation shows that it does not matter materially whether colonisers are calvinists or catholics. What is crucial is whether they enjoy power to acquire the land, cattle and labour of indigenous peoples.[37]

References

1. Alan Paton, *Apartheid and the Archbishop* (Cape Town, 1973), p. 47.

2. A series of essays, *The Catholic Church and Southern Africa* (Catholic Archdiocese of Cape Town, 1951), published to commemorate the establishment of the hierarchy in South Africa, attempts to see the Catholic church in terms of its social context, but it virtually ignores other christian traditions

including the dominant calvinist one.

3. Cf. John de Gruchy, *The Church Struggle in South Africa* (Cape Town, 1979); cf. also John T. McNeill, *The History and Character of Calvinism* (New York, 1957).

4. Ian Linden, *The Catholic Church and the Struggle for Zimbabwe* (London, 1980).

5. Quoted in Paton, *op. cit.*, p. 113.

6. W. E. Brown, *The Catholic Church in South Africa* (London, 1960) p. 5.

7. T. R. H. Davenport, *South Africa: a Modern History* (Johannesburg, 1977) ch. 3.

8. Irving Hexham, *The Irony of Apartheid: the Struggle for National Independence of Afrikaner Calvinism against British Imperialism* (New York, 1981).

9. J. du Plessis, *The Life of Andrew Murray of South Africa* (London, 1919).

10. Hexham, *op. cit.*

11. Abraham Kuyper, *Lectures on Calvinism* (Grand Rapids, 1931), ch. 1.

12. *Ibid.*, p. 17.

13. *Ibid.*, p. 81.

14. *Ibid.*, p. 104.

15. Cf. Helmut Thielicke, *Theological Ethics*, vol. 2 (Philadelphia, 1969), p. 598.

16. Cf. *Gaudium et Spes* in *Documents of Vatican II*, ed. W. M. Abott and J. Gallagher (London, 1965), para 76; cf. also Martin Versfeld's essay 'Relations of Church and State' in *The Catholic Church and Southern Africa*, especially p. 50.

17. Eds. H. G. Stoker, F. J. M. Potgieter and J. D. Vorster (Stellenbosch, 3 vols., 1935-1941).

18. Quoted in T. Dunbar Moodie, *The Rise of Afrikanerdom* (Berkeley, 1975).

19. Cf. Moodie, *op. cit.*; D. S. Bax, *A Different Gospel: a Critique of the Theology behind Apartheid* (Johannesburg, 1979).

20. T. R. H. Davenport in Monica Wilson and Leonard Thompson, eds., *A History of South Africa to 1870* (Cape Town, forthcoming), p. 275.

21. Eric Walker, *A History of South Africa* (London, 1964), p. 165.

22. Brown, *op. cit.*, p. 290.

23. *Ibid.*, p. 185.

24. *Ibid.*, p. 181.

25. Cf. P. R. J. Le Feuvre, *Cultural and Theological Factors Affecting Relationships between the Nederduitse Gereformeerde Kerk and the Anglican Church (of the Province of South Africa) in the Cape Colony, 1806-1910* (unpublished Ph.D. thesis, University of Cape Town, 1981).

26. Walker, *op. cit.*, p. 278.

27. Brown, *op. cit.*, p. 188.

28. *Ibid.*, p. 33.

29. Gustav Bam, 'Protestantse Aksie Vandag' (unpublished paper, 1975).

30. The Director of Ecumenical Affairs of the DRC, Dr P. Rossouw, spoke

out strongly against 'mixed marriages' in *Die Kerkbode*, October 1980.

31. Cf. *DRC Newsletter*, no. 180, December 1975.

32. *Ibid.*, p. 2.

33. *Ecunews* (South African Council of Churches) no. 32, 1974, September p. 5.

34. Cf. the pastoral letter written by Cardinal McCann, Archbishop of Cape Town, giving the reasons why the Catholic church would not celebrate the twentieth anniversary of the Republic of South Africa in 1981. This letter was read at mass on Sunday 24 May throughout the republic.

35. (London, 1957), p. 50.

36. Cf. André Bieler, *The Social Humanism of Calvin* (John Knox, Richmond, 1961); W. Fred Graham, *The Constructive Revolutionary: John Calvin and his Socio-Economic Impact* (John Knox, Richmond, 1971). The first theological critique of apartheid written in South Africa was by the DRC professor of theology at the University of Stellenbosch, B. B. Keet, *Suid-Afrika, Waarheen?* (Stellenbosch, 1956). See also the position adopted by both the World Alliance of Reformed Churches, and the more conservative Reformed Ecumenical Synod, on such issues during the past decade.

37. Heribert Adam and Hermann Giliomee, *The Rise and Crisis of Afrikaner Power* (Cape Town, 1979), p. 92.

6 EDUCATION: POLICY AND PRACTICE

Brigid Flanagan

The year 1976 was of crucial importance for all those engaged in South African education. Following an initial protest against the introduction of Afrikaans as a compulsory medium of education in Soweto schools, black pupils began to rebel against the entire educational system. There followed a wave of violence and retaliatory action from the police which left over 500 dead and caused widespread damage to schools, public offices and equipment.

Two lessons were learnt from 1976, the most violent year in South Africa's recent history. The first was that blacks rejected the system of 'Bantu Education', which they saw as a means for indoctrinating and equipping them to fit easily into apartheid society; the second that education is the most important means for both the maintaining and the reforming of society, and that whoever controls the educational system lays the foundation for the society of the future.

All those engaged in South African education were forced to review their policies. By 1978 the South African government had given notice of its intention to change the Bantu Education Act of 1953, and various institutions, including the Catholic church, began to review their educational systems.

At its February 1979 Plenary Session, the Southern African Catholic Bishops' Conference decided to make a thorough evaluation of the church's educational policy and practice. It intended to review the rationale for running catholic schools in South Africa, and to examine thoroughly its existing potential in personnel and financial resources to ensure their best possible use. For this purpose it authorised a major consultation on catholic schools aimed at formulating specific recommendations to be placed before the conference and the Major Superiors of Teaching Congregations responsible for schools. Significant changes are expected from these discussions.

BACKGROUND

It is impossible to understand how the church's educational policy
in this country developed without situating it in its historical context. The formal history of the Catholic church in South Africa
began in 1837 with the appointment of Bishop R. Griffith O.P. as
Vicar Apostolic of the newly created Vicariate of the Cape of Good
Hope. On his arrival he found a small white catholic population
composed of Dutch, German, French and Irish elements. He understood that his primary task was to attend to the needs of these
'members of the household of the faith', to build up a local catholic
community of the traditional type, and to break down the barriers
of religious intolerance so that the Catholic church could develop
peacefully. Interest in the conversion of the indigenous population seems to have been secondary, to be attended to only 'when
the wants of the children of the household of the faith had been
provided for'. (Brown: 194) Thus right from its beginning the
Catholic church shows a two-pronged approach: a settlers' church
for whites, and a missionary church for blacks.

This approach also characterised its various institutions. The first
catholic schools in South Africa were established for whites. They
aimed at raising the standard of white education and at breaking
down religious prejudice by the admission of protestant pupils.
'The first convent school in South Africa run by the Assumption
Sisters in Grahamstown was so popular that many protestants sent
their children to the nuns.' (Brown: 46) Various religious congregations were later invited by bishops to open schools for whites. By
the 1870s, the catholic system of education in private schools by
the religious orders had entered into the cultural formation of
South Africa.

With the coming of the Missionary Congregation of the Oblates
of Mary Immaculate in 1852 and, at a later date, the arrival of the
Cistercians (who developed into the Missionaries of Mariannhill),
the church in South Africa turned its attention to the evangelisation
of blacks. It gradually began to establish schools for the black,
'Coloured' and Indian population as part of its programme of evangelisation. Most black schools were concentrated in Natal and the
Transvaal. For a while, like all the other mission churches, the
Catholic church had to bear the main financial burden for these
schools, but eventually a system of state subsidisation grew up,
and a fairly happy and productive partnership developed. The system enabled the churches to train and employ great numbers of
lay teachers. For the black schools in South Africa this system

came to an abrupt end in the 1950s, when the state withdrew its financial support for church schools.

'BANTU EDUCATION'

In 1949 the newly elected National Party government appointed a commission of inquiry into education for blacks, and in 1951 it presented its findings, which ultimately formed the basis of the Bantu Education Act. The report asserted that existing educational facilities were not 'an integral part of a plan of socio-economic development' for blacks, and that an educational system be devised both more closely related to the needs of the country's economy, and also in conformity with the traditions and characteristics of the people for whom it was designed—with the social purpose of preserving and propagating black culture.

The main reasons for black educational change given by the Nationalists were then twofold: to develop the occupational skills demanded by the increasingly complex industrial sector, but in such a way that the 'rightful place' of the white worker was not threatened, and to provide ideological formation geared towards short and long term social control. This latter idea was formulated in 1940 by Dr W. Eiselen, Chief Inspector of Native Education in the Transvaal, who was later to become a major architect of the apartheid system. 'Native Education is essential in the urban areas, because in these areas, where tribal institutions have been completely revolutionised, some other disciplinary agent has to take the place of tribal control, and the most efficient agent we can think of is the school.'

The provision of 'Bantu Education' was not a concession won by blacks, but an imposition upon them. The policy shows a close ideological and practical connection with the concept of 'Christian National Education' as spelt out by the *Federasie van Kultuurvereeniginge* in a pamphlet of 1948. The preface declares that 'we want no mixing of languages, no mixing of cultures, no mixing of religions and no mixing of races.' It highlights the calvinist principles of election and predestination and applies them to the Afrikaner *volk*, to whom it accords the divinely ordained role of trustee for all the peoples of South Africa. Articles 14 and 15 spell out principles applicable to the 'Coloured' and 'Native' groups. These are: (1) a christian national outlook; (2) group separation; (3) each group is responsible for its own education; (4) mother-tongue education; (5) each group must provide its own teachers; (6) the Afrikaners are a senior or trustee group.

Not only does this concept of education oppose the liberal principle that only free enquiry can discover truth, but it presents apartheid, not as a possibly fallible human arrangement, the rightness of which can be proved or disproved, but as a God-given truth. In 1953 the Bantu Education Act extended these principles to educational policy.

'Bantu Education' aimed to generate and maintain a social structure based on apartheid. At the level of ideological transmission it was intended to ensure that blacks identified with the roles assigned to them by their white rulers, and, as a result, to legitimate apartheid. Its success would depend upon the degree to which the racial structure of South African society would change from one with a high degree of potential conflict because of low consensus, to one with a low conflict potential and a high consensus. 'Bantu Education' was to be the means of transmitting and finding acceptance for the apartheid ideology.

Social control was the immediate aim of 'Bantu Education', and its means was by promoting ethnic loyalties through mother-tongue education. This policy ran counter to the prevailing tendencies of urbanisation, by means of which ethnic identification was losing its significance and an urban black culture was beginning to emerge. More importantly for the life-chances of young blacks entering the labour market, this mother-tongue policy resulted in increasing the difficulties of obtaining higher education in which the language medium was English or Afrikaans. Mother-tongue education at the early stages of school was to serve as a filter for those proceeding to higher education, and it resulted in relatively few blacks entering the labour market to compete with whites for jobs. With the 1953 Act, control of black education passed from the provinces and the missionaries to a new Department of Bantu Education. Churches that proposed to retain control of their schools had to face a loss of subsidies.

By 1953 the Catholic church was deeply involved in black education. It ran 688 state-aided schools and 130 unaided schools, with an enrolment of 111 361 students. This represented approximately 15 per cent of the black schools of the time.

The coming of the Bantu Education Act provoked a crisis in the church. The bishops opposed it on purely religious grounds, not because it was the 'cornerstone of apartheid'. They regarded the school as an essential part of the church's evangelising effort, and certainly large numbers of converts were made from among the non-catholic pupils admitted to the mission schools. But they considered the school to be essential not only for gaining converts but for continuing the education of catholic children in a distinctly catholic atmosphere. 'As elsewhere in the world and as mandated by the pope, the catholic school was to survive beyond the missionary era and independently of the state system. The school was the kingpin of a catholic upbringing and the catholic school was the centre for consolidating the gains made in evangelising the African.' (Bixby: 22).

Many bishops simply could not conceive of a Catholic church without schools. The majority felt that, without schools, the church would lose its influence, vocations would diminish and many catholics would fall away from the church. Religious instruction given in state schools would be incapable of combating the consequences of secularised education. Besides, there was no guarantee that the church would have free access to state schools for the teaching of religion to catholic pupils.

The bishops therefore decided to keep the schools going at all costs, justifying their decision on religious and not political grounds. Records of the plenary session discussion on the black schools reveal that there were many differences of opinion and of attitude among the members of the Conference. Some recognised that the Bantu Education Act was part of the apartheid policy and that opposition to it was an opportunity to take a tangible stand against apartheid: any step the church took in opposition to the Act would be a positive act of defiance of apartheid. On the other hand, awareness that the Act was part of the policy of apartheid did not necessarily evoke strong sentiments in favour of overt defiance. Some urged that it was better to acquiesce to some extent in the scheme of 'Bantu Education' in order to protect the interests of the church. Others urged the bishops to worry not about the principle behind the Act, but about how to safeguard their right to teach children.

Though the bishops were determined to keep the schools, they knew that the Minister of Education could refuse to allow a private school system to exist; therefore they had to avoid antagonising the government. Co-operation with the other churches was made difficult because most denominations were not opposed to the state takeover as such, but to the proposed content of 'Bantu Education'. Some bishops even went so far as to express publicly their willingness to co-operate in all aspects of the Bantu Education Act, apart from giving up control of their schools, and were clearly attempting to dissociate the church from the widespread (particularly Anglican) opposition to 'Bantu Education'.

The decision to keep the schools and the consequent need to avoid incurring government displeasure led to a public strategy that appeared to compromise the church's stand against apartheid. However successful the bishops may have been in retaining their schools they paid a price both in moral credibility and in worsened relations with the government.

A whole host of other problems was raised by the decision to keep the schools. Raising the money necessary to keep the schools open from the church's own resources appeared to be an impossible task. The situation of the lay teachers of whom there were about 2 000 in 1954. also presented problems. Those who stayed on in the church schools after 1 April 1955 would cease to be considered government employees. They would be the responsibility of the church, and where would it get the money to pay them? The decision to reduce salaries by 25 per cent without any consultation was resented by the teachers. The church too readily expected them to make tremendous sacrifices for catholic education. It failed to realise that the teachers' opposition to 'Bantu Education' came primarily from the fact that they saw it as an instrument of apartheid policy, and that the teachers naturally resented the compromising attitude of the church in agreeing to accept the inferior system.

The subsequent story of the teachers in catholic schools is not a happy one. Over the next ten years their position deteriorated as they experienced a continuing decline in salary, working conditions, morale and prestige. Equally important was the embarrassing position of the hierarchy as they witnessed the steady deterioration which was bringing them dangerously close to letting the end of keeping catholic schools justify any means of keeping them.

The Bantu Education Act placed the bishops in a cruel dilemma. Whatever decision they took was bound to have undesirable consequences. To close the schools would incur government hostility and deprive many blacks of a catholic education. To hand the schools over to the state system would almost certainly mean the total loss of catholic influence in black education, and would deprive blacks of anything remotely resembling an alternative to 'Bantu Education'. They chose the course which they took to be the lesser of two evils.

In deciding to maintain its schools the church was forced to become intimately involved in the new system. The bishops were led into simultaneous policies of co-operation and opposition. The stand against apartheid which some bishops saw in the maintenance of the mission schools was difficult to reconcile with the promises of co-operation regarding 'Bantu Education' and the attempt to get government support for training colleges and farm schools. Assurances of co-operation and goodwill preceded protests, and protests when they did come were framed in the name of 'religious' education.

There was a decline in the academic quality of the schools, owing to the increase in the number of unqualified teachers. There was a drop in the morale, quality and moral fibre of the teachers, and some people wondered how such poorly paid teachers could be proper 'lay apostles' (Collins: 1963). The shortage of teachers from the religious orders meant that salaries had to be found for more lay teachers, driving up school fees and increasing financial pressure. This in turn led to a drop-off in catholic enrolment so that by 1965 only 48 per cent of all catholic children were in catholic schools.

These factors combined with the growing concern for social justice that developed after Vatican II eventually led the church to review its decision to keep all its schools. The growing social and political awareness raised serious doubts about the church's acquiescence in apartheid and the acceptance of segregation in church institutions. The wide discrepancy in the quality and quantity of the white and black school systems was difficult to justify. A more widely acknowledged problem was the injustice of the teacher's salaries. This became the burning question with regard to maintaining the schools. Would not the counter-witness given by the flagrant, unjust underpayment of teachers counteract the religious influence of the schools? Realisation of these problems grew slowly but steadily during the sixties.

In July 1968 a bishops' plenary session admitted that it was impossible to keep all the schools. By 1970 the situation had become untenable. The number of catholic schools dropped rapidly from that date as the diocese of Mariannhill and the prefecture of Volksrust decided to hand their schools over to the government wherever possible. Umtata, Kokstad and Umzimkulu likewise decided to release schools to the Transkeian authorities.

A report on catholic education in South Africa written in 1972 confirmed what was already evident. It highlighted the insolvency of the black schools and drew together all the arguments against continuing them. It sharply criticised the wide discrepancy between the resources devoted to white and black catholic education and placed the problem in the context of post-Vatican Council orientations. In 1973 the bishops acknowledged this report in a statement that marked the end of a unified commitment to the catholic schools. After announcing that many dioceses were unable to continue financing the schools the conference paid a parting tribute to the ideal of the catholic school and regretfully noted its passing. The statement concluded on a hopeful note as it anticipated the development of new forms of apostolate.

DISTRIBUTION OF RESOURCES

In the foregoing section, reference was made to the unequal distribution of the church's resources. The inequality, as we have seen, dates back to the very beginning of the church's involvement in schools. In 1960 only 300 of the 2 400 sisters and almost none of the teaching brothers in South Africa were employed in black schools (Collins: 1960). In 1965 the *per capita* cost of white education was nearly twenty times more than that of black education. In 1970 the segregated school system provided Johannesburg with twenty white secondary schools but only one black. (Collins: 1970). The 1973 South African Catholic Education Study stated: 'The schools in the present distribution of 70 per cent (of the resources) for 30 per cent (of the population) and 30 per cent for 70 per cent do not reflect the presence of the church in society according to its present commitment to the development of peoples. The overwhelming evidence of this pragmatic priority needs to be reviewed in the light of post-Vatican II directions of leadership from among membership. This redirection is necessary to provide a credible service to a post-Vatican II Church.'

Unequal distribution still remains a fact, as can be seen from the 1979 school statistics. There were then 81 private black catholic primary schools and 27 secondary schools. In the state's 1975–76 Public Revenue account R645,6 million was spent on white education, and R66,3 million on black education. This came to an average of R644 *per annum* for each white pupil and R41,80 for each black child. The Catholic church's proportionate division of resources is not significantly different from this.

CURRENT CHURCH POLICIES AND SCHOOL INTEGRATION

In 1957 the Southern African Catholic Bishops' Conference included the following passage in its statement on apartheid. 'The practice of segregation, though not officially recognised in our churches, characterises nevertheless many of our church societies, our schools, seminaries, convents, hospitals and the social life of our people. In the light of Christ's teaching this cannot be tolerated forever. The time has come to pursue more vigorously the change of heart and practice that the law of Christ demands. We are hypocrites if we condemn apartheid in South African society and condone it in our own institutions.'

Nothing came of this. It was never followed up. Soon after the statement was issued the bishops were caught up in the Second Vatican Council, and South Africa was caught up in Sharpeville and in becoming a Republic outside the British Commonwealth.

In 1973 the issue of 'open schools' became a practical and real one within the church. In the meantime other religious and educational bodies were already deeply involved in the question. A study of the legal implications was made on behalf of the Association of Headmasters and Headmistresses of Private Schools and in April 1973 the anglican Archbishop of Cape Town applied for permission to accept suitably qualified 'Coloured' children as scholars 'in a number of private schools closely associated with the Church of the Province'. The application was turned down. When the Department of Schools of the restructured Commission for Christian Education and Worship met in August 1975, its first task was to investigate the possibilities of opening catholic schools to children of all races. The Association of Women and the Education Council of the Associations of Religious were also studying the question. These bodies had a particular interest in the issue as the government had specifically approached the church to request that a number of black diplomats' children be accommodated in the white private schools run by religious. Three schools found themselves faced with the very embarrassing situation of having to exclude South African blacks while admitting foreign blacks.

As a result of recommendations for a move towards opening white private schools to pupils of all races, the bishops' plenary session of February 1976 passed the following resolution. 'Realising that the church must give witness to the gospel in its institutions, the Conference favours a policy of integration in catholic schools, encourages individual schools to promote the implementation of the policy according to circumstances and directs the Department of Schools to continue to study the question with a view to enabling the Conference to confirm and concretise the policy.' With the passing of this resolution the die had been cast and though there was, and still is, a long and painful road ahead, there could now be no going back. The day of the exclusively white catholic school was over.

The original intention was that the year 1976 should be a period of information and preparation for all concerned, priests, religious, teachers, parents, pupils, and parish, 'in the context of a broader programme of education in Social Justice and Reconciliation'. At least two white schools admitted black pupils in 1976.

In the move towards open schools there were two major obstacles to be surmounted; on the one hand, the fear and reluctance of some religious to take any step that might in any way antagonise the government or jeopardise the good standing of their schools in the eyes of education authorities or white parents; on the other hand, the government's insistence on the policy of segregated schools. It was unrealistic to expect that all involved should come to the same degree of awareness of the issues involved at the same time. The change involved a long and painful process and there was much tension before all came to a whole-hearted acceptance of the policy. Thanks to the excellent communication and very close collaboration between the bishops and the Education Council of the Associations of Religious, the church was able to take a united stand on this issue.

It is not possible to deal here with legal problems encountered or with the seemingly endless negotiations between representatives of the schools on the one hand and of the government (either at provincial or ministerial level) on the other. These negotiations have been going on since February 1977 and still continue. All major difficulties seem to have been overcome in the Cape and in Natal, and black pupils enrolled in private schools in these provinces have the necessary authorisation. Progress is much slower in the Transvaal but the parties are still talking. Meanwhile, a considerable number of black pupils have already received two or three years of education in open schools.

In going ahead quietly and doggedly with this policy the church has tried to avoid confrontation with the government. It has also tried to keep the issue out of the 'political arena'. The motivation inspiring the church's policy was put very clearly by Brother Jude Petersen, Provincial of the Marist Brothers in 1979. 'The opening of catholic schools to pupils irrespective of race has been the response to an ever-increasing awareness of the implications of the gospel message in our South African society. The schools have sought throughout to keep the issue from becoming a political football. . . . At times the schools have been accused of seeking some form of confrontation with the state. This has certainly not been the case. The real confrontation that has taken place has been between those running the schools and the message of the Gospel.'

The development of the open school policy has affected the schools in many ways, and is leading to a re-thinking of much that has been taken for granted in the past. A new educational policy and programme is needed that will include black cultural values as well as white, in such a way that black pupils will not merely be assimilated into the existing system but will rather remain authentic blacks enriched by western culture, just as whites must be enriched by African culture.

Unfortunately, an awareness of what is necessary does not automatically supply the solutions. However, slowly and searchingly the schools have been seeking ways and means of meeting the challenge. At the beginning of 1977, a resource team was attached to the Department of Schools to work in collaboration with schools to facilitate the process of integration. One of its most valuable contributions was the organisation of a number of seminars on African studies. The most important result of these was to make people aware of their ignorance in this field. They caught glimpses of new insights into history which up to then they had seen only from a white viewpoint; they came to realise that there was a whole area of literature, African prose and poetry, which they had never heard of. They saw that existing school curricula needed to be broadened and enriched so as to include the contributions of other cultural groups. They realised the impoverishment of that with which they had so long been satisifed.

The concept of multiracial education is new, not only for South Africa but for the educational world generally. While a beginning is being made to come to grips with its implications and challenges, we have a lot to learn. That the South African Catholic Bishops' Conference has agreed to finance a Correspondence Course in African Studies being run by SACHED (South African College of Higher Education) is an indication that it realises the need to rectify and enrich existing school curricula. This course, which began in 1980, is intended for all who wish to improve their knowledge of African history, literature, economics and art, but is aimed primarily at teachers in the hope that the new insights into history and the new avenues into literature will bring a new vision and vitality into their classrooms.

SUCCESSES AND FAILURES

The (white) settlers' church established and maintained schools which undoubtedly achieved high standards in the fields of academic, vocational, religious and moral education. But that these schools unquestioningly accepted the segregated pattern of South African life for such a long period, that they turned out generations of young men and women who took the status quo for granted, who were unaware of the injustice of the society they lived in, and who knowlingly or unknowlingly co-operated in perpetuating it, indicates that the schools largely failed to impart a truly christian social awareness and conscience to their pupils.

As regards the (black) missionary church, it has no mean record in the field of education before 1953. Mariannhill, Mariazell, Inkamana, St Louis Bertrand, St Boniface, the Pax Institution, and St Bruno's (to mention only a few) all enjoyed an excellent reputation, and turned out some first class scholars and leaders. Just to take a few names at random: Dr B. W. Vilakazi (translator of Zulu literature and lecturer at the Witwatersrand University), Steve Biko (the Black Consciousness leader), and Percy Qoboza (former editor of the 'banned' newspapers *World* and *Post*).

It was undoubtedly a triumph that the church was able to create, operate, and in the case of secondary schools even expand, a private school system. By all logistical standards this was a tremendous achievement and a testimonial to the determination of the church to have its own schools. More impressive in some ways was the political achievement (though the church emphatically disclaimed any political motivation). Through an effective combination of public relations and private negotiations the bishops withstood the will of the government, clearly articulated by Verwoerd, to assume exclusive control of all black education. The retention of the black schools was not an unmitigated success. The bishops responded to the Bantu Education Act, not as an essential piece of apartheid legislation designed to perpetuate the subordinate status of blacks, but as a threat to its own apostolic and institutional interests. Apart from retaining control of its schools the Conference had to accept and implement most aspects of 'Bantu Education', so that in many respects the schools were state schools. In syllabus, medium of instruction, inspection and examinations they were tightly controlled by the Department of Bantu Education; even the religious syllabus required government approval. All this publicly compromised the church's opposition to apartheid. In its efforts to keep the schools at any cost, it was forced to pay its teachers less than a living wage and maintain a school system that was even more separate and unequal than that operated by the government. In short, it led the bishops to practise their own form of discrimination. In doing this their predicament was not unique. 'Many well-meaning institutions and individuals in South Africa have been forced to compromise their liberal convictions in order to satisfy other conflicting interests. The story of the catholic schools also illustrates how easily such a compromise can take place; it is only the harsh light of retrospect that makes clear the implications of the decision that were only dimly perceived in 1954.' (Bixby: 118)

The church's move towards open schools has a high symbolic value: it is a concrete gesture that denotes respect for the human person and the brotherhood of all in Christ. It also indicates that church personnel have at last become aware of this particular demand of the gospel and are determined to put it before all other social considerations. In practice also the open school seems to be working out successfully. The experience has shown that the problems anticipated in terms of human relationships have been those of the adults rather than the children. The pupils are learning to mix and relate to one another. Parents and staffs are learning to replace ignorance, fear and prejudice with understanding, friendliness and mutual respect.

There are many, however, who think that this gesture will have little nor no impact, that it will not change South African society. They argue that it will create an élitist minority, who will be ostracised by and alienated from other blacks, and that the gesture has come far too late to affect those who have long since decided that 'the black man must go it alone'.

WHAT OF THE FUTURE?

One does not need to be a prophet to foresee that within the next few years there will be a drastic reduction in the number of catholic schools. With the diminishing and ageing personnel at their disposal, neither the bishops nor the religious congregations will be able to staff and finance all the remaining catholic schools. We hope, however, that the few schools retained will be of high quality, and that they will be sufficiently adventuresome to try out new educational methods, and to meet needs in society which the state school is unable or unwilling to meet. We hope that the open schools will result in a system which will value, respect and utilise the cultural diversity of our society and achieve a solid education for all. The catholic school of the future must be a christian community, involving pupils, staff and parents in its plans and activities. Co-educational schools will develop by combining neighbouring schools for boys and girls. Children from several primary schools will be channelled into a few strategically placed, easily accessible, well-equipped, well-staffed secondary schools, whose teachers will be drawn from the most highly qualified personnel of several religious congregations. Pooling and sharing resources will be a characteristic of catholic schools of the future.

Finally, while the church will always maintain an interest in catholic schools and in the education of children and adolescents, this will no longer be considered a priority in the work of evangelisation. Much more attention will be given to adult religious education by means of such movements as Marriage Encounter, Family and Community Catechetics and Neighbourhood Gospel Groups. Efforts will be made to promote education as a lifelong process, and to involve the whole family and the whole christian community in a corporate effort to educate one another in the faith, and to grow 'into the perfect man, fully mature with the fullness of Christ Himself'.

References

Brown, W. E. *The Catholic Church in South Africa* (London, 1960).

Bixby, A. *The Roman Catholic Church and Apartheid in Education* (unpublished B.A.(Hons) dissertation, University of Cape Town, 1977).

Collins, C. B. In *Southern Cross*, 4 December 1960 and 6 February 1963; in *Rand Daily Mail*, 24 January 1970.

7 BLACK RELIGIOUS SEPARATISM

James Kiernan

The Catholic church in South Africa bears the unique imprint of its host society. South Africa is a country of many contradictions, not the least of which is that it is 'underdeveloped' yet highly 'developed' economically and technologically. A technologically 'advanced' and affluent white settler population lives side by side with a 'backward' and poor indigenous black population, and there is a marked disparity of life-styles between them. The possibility of the gradual and peaceful merging of these populations has been ruled out by forms of segregation and a ban on intermarriage imposed by the state. The two population blocks inhabit radically different social spheres, and a development, such as religious separatism, which may effect a transformation in the one sphere, can go largely unnoticed in the other. The Catholic church is squarely planted in each of these sectors and, as a result, tends to be ambivalent (flexible, if you wish) in its outlook. Indeed it is not unrealistic to discern two Catholic churches, rather than one, at work in South Africa.

There is an established network of parishes serving whites, mainly in the large urban centres, and there is a missionary church working with and upon a vast black population. It is a division which goes right to the top where it has on occasion riven the Bishops' Conference and profoundly weakened its statements, which, if they are to be seen to be unanimous, must rest on compromise. Some bishops are more missionary in outlook than others, not in the narrow sense of wishing to win more and more black adherents to the faith, but in the fuller sense of working to uplift and improve the lot of the poor, the oppressed and the weak. Some are more firmly anchored to the conservative interests of whites. Yet others veer hopelessly between the two sides. Generally, too, the staff of white parishes and those who man the mission outposts form distinct groups of personnel with largely divergent interests. Moreover, this internal division is not merely structural but it is part of the experience of living for all members of the church, despite the efforts of well-intentioned individuals to span the gap, thus rendering it less than absolute. The separation is not absolute for another reason. The missionary church is not financially independent but is tied to the purse-strings of the 'established' church. Given the structure of South African society, this 'second-hand' character of the missionary church could scarcely be otherwise. (Ramusi 1975) The church straddles the inequality of society and is torn by it. It should be noted, without comment at this stage, that the urban black is located somewhere in the margin of this division and fits somewhat uneasily into the scheme of this twofold concern.

There is another way in which the ministry of the church is governed and limited by the ideology of the state, namely in the area of tribal separatism. Tribal separatism is the tactical corollary of white supremacy, and, however much parts of the church may struggle against it, it is inescapably caught up in the coils of this sacred shibboleth. It is necessary, at this point, to distinguish two types of separatism, not unrelated to one another and both related in some measure to church and state. These may be described as political or tribal separatism and religious separatism. Political separatism is the ideology which nourishes the South African state and gives it life and purpose, an ideology which conceives South Africa to be a patchwork of tribal or national units, each ostensibly self-determining but each subject to the informal but decisive pressures and controls of the South African state. This is the ultimate concession of Afrikaner nationalism and the line beyond which there is no further retreat: that it will accord to others a measure of that self-expression which it jealously cherishes for itself. Everything else is negotiable and arrangements can be increasingly flexible but this ideology of separatism is the basic principle to which the South African state is firmly and rigidly affixed. Problems can be solved and crises overcome as long as the solutions to them remain within the framework of political separatism. There can be no doubt that this framework, variously labelled apartheid, pluralism, multinationalism and even federalism, is not without its attractions for many blacks, who are desperate to grasp whatever crumbs of self-respect may fall their way, and that it is particularly appealing to those who are recognised as tribal or national leaders and are anxious to acquire the limited power which is granted within the framework. Within recent years, such a confluence of interests has led to the establishment of a number of quasi-states and we can expect further implementations of the design in the near future.

Consequently political separatism is no longer a blueprint without substance, a speculative issue to be debated academically, but a political reality which cannot be dislodged by argument. Like other missionary agencies, the Catholic church must adapt to the new arrangement.

A great deal can be learned from missionary experience elsewhere in newly independent Africa, although the emerging 'federal' formation of South Africa will pose a unique challenge to the church. It will be difficult for it to shed entirely the taint of an alliance with élitism in black eyes, but the internal strain between settler church and mission church might be somewhat ameliorated by constituting separate ecclesiastical regions in the new 'homelands' and by drawing staff as far as possible from the local population—a task beset with its own difficulties. On the other hand, such an arrangement could scarcely avoid legitimating the inequality inherent in the political dispensation of the South African state. Thus, a familiar dilemma arises in a different guise, assuming new dimensions.

Once again, it should be noted that the pursuit of political separatism accentuates the anomalous situation of urban blacks. Living within or near white metropolitan areas, they are permanently removed from the 'homelands' to which they 'belong', and they do not 'belong' to the area in which they have settled. Their political rights are exercisable only from a distance. The import of political separatism for the urban black is that, no matter how deeply he may have set his roots in town, he is regarded there as a foreigner and as a permanent migrant. He is there in some respects; in other respects he is elsewhere. He is rendered doubly alienated, from where he is and from where he 'belongs'. In effect, he inhabits a political limbo. For the moment, this affects only some urban blacks, but, as political separatism is increasingly applied, it is a fate which will be shared by the majority.

In the meantime, and with much less fanfare, religious separatism has been steadily gaining momentum. Almost surreptitiously, a religious revolution has taken place in South Africa over the past ninety years, the dimensions of which are appreciated fully only by a comparative few, despite Sundkler's early seminal work (1948) and more recent publications on the subject (Barrett 1968; West 1975; Dubb 1976; Sundkler 1976). Shembe's and Lekganyane's churches are among the few spectacularly successful examples of this phenomenon, but there may be four thousand such sects today in South Africa alone. Their number defies accurate enumeration but the latest census figures (1970) reveal that about 25 per cent of the black population now belongs to one or other of such religious groups. Collectively, they command greater support than any single missionary church and their strength must surely constitute a challenge to the missionary churches as a whole.

The earliest attempt to set up a black church free from white supervision was that of Tile among the Tembu in 1884. Although it was shortlived, its major significance lay in its tribal composition. It was a Tembu church and its head was the Tembu chief. Tribal secessions from mission churches occurred among the Tswana and the Pedi (Sundkler 1961:39) before the turn of the century. But in 1892 a secession of a different kind occurred in Johannesburg with the formation of the 'Ethiopian' church, which was to set the style for a host of subsequent defections. These churches emerged in an urban setting and, far from returning to a tribal ethos, their membership cut across tribal divisions. They sought African, not tribal, autonomy and it now seems clear that this was a response to the experience of racial segregation and discrimination, not merely in South African society at large, but more particularly within the confines of the mission churches where the teaching that all men were equal in the eyes of God was found to be curiously qualified in practice and that whites appeared to be more equal than blacks. This disparity was sharpened by the special grievance of educated black ministers, who were denied positions of eminence consonant with their achievements within the mission churches. It was this blocking of black leadership which eventually provoked that movement towards religious separatism which, following Sundkler (1961:38), can be conveniently labelled 'Ethiopian'.

Since Ethiopianism stressed black identity and aspirations in opposition to white, it has been viewed with a measure of suspicion and alarm by the South African state, ironically unaware of the extent to which its own policies had contributed to the emergence of the Ethiopian churches. These churches were reputed to have provided a religious veneer for nationalist and revolutionary tendencies and to be an instrument for the shaping of an African political consciousness, best expressed in the slogan 'Africa for the Africans'. These suspicions were not entirely groundless. Ethiopian preachers vocally promoted enthusiasm for the Zulu Rebellion of 1906 and were listed among its leaders (Sundkler 1961:69). Later on, a number of Ethiopian church leaders were prominently associated with the aims and programme of the African National Congress. Successive government commissions, however, have grudgingly exonerated the separatist movement as a whole from seditious intent and political entanglement. Correspondingly, it seems likely that the Ethiopian churches have gradually withdrawn altogether from the political arena and have adopted a more accommodating attitude towards political separatism. Historically, there has been a considerable overlap of religious and political separatism, the two being inextricably intertwined for most of the time. The state has adopted a cautiously tolerant attitude towards religious separatism and has laid down stringent criteria for the recognition and registration of separatist churches. But only a handful of such churches now possesses this stamp of legitimacy. The National Party government regularly witholds this recognition, which is now all the more coveted by church leaders (if only because it entitles them to some travel concessions on the state railway system), and continues to regard the separatist movement with watchful concern.

If the Ethiopian movement has extracted a veiled hostility from the state, it has produced a reaction of guilt from the mission churches. It became clear that, whatever had prompted secessions on such an alarming scale, it was not a purely religious condition. After all, the dissident Ethopian sects did not repudiate or seek to discredit christianity as such. In general, each sect remained faithful to the teaching, mode of worship and organisational pattern of its church of origin. The fault lay in the state of human relations within the mission churches, in the inequality between black and white members, and thus the blame was laid squarely on the conduct of the missionaries themselves. As the mission churches came to terms with this unpalatable fact, self-reproach generated the hope that the fault could be repaired and some lost ground recovered. Efforts were made to come to a more sympathetic understanding of separatism; indeed it was just such a consideration which precipitated Sundkler's excellent study. The churches have organised consultations with the separatist leaders, have provided educational assistance for aspiring leaders, have set up an association of separatist leaders, endowed with its own fund, and commissioned West's recent study of churches in Soweto.

The Catholic church remained quite aloof from this flurry of activity and took no part in it. The reason for this apparent apathy is quite simple. The Catholic church in South Africa, alone of all the mission churches, has never experienced a separatist rift (and even throughout Africa as a whole has remained exceptionally free from such an experience). Such remarkable exemption from rampant sectarianism has not only rendered the Catholic church remote from the problem of reconciliation with separatism, which besets other mission churches, but it has raised the question of the source of its immunity. Numerous answers have been offered, among them the claim that the elaborate rituals of catholicism have neutralised the ritualistic appeal of a purely black church. This is not without some validity, although in recent years the Catholic church has greatly simplified its liturgy. However, it rather misses the point, since the Ethiopian separatists did not break away to gain ritual satisfaction but, primarily, to protest against white domination in social relations. The simplest answer and the one which best fits the facts is that given by Hastings (1976:25). Separatism is simply an extension of denominationalism. It followed a precedent firmly established in the recent history of certain protestant churches imported from northern Europe. Where such a precedent did not exist, as in the Catholic church, there was no model on which to base separatist expression. It would follow that, even if inequality based on colour inheres in the organisation of the Catholic church, grievances arising from it would not—could not—be expressed in schismatic form. The separatist tendency was either faithful to or was contained by received tradition, either that of denominational diversity or that of a unified universal church. For this reason alone, the Catholic church remains unshaken and unaffected by the Ethiopian secessions.

An Ethiopian church is separatist in the strict sense of the term, in that it becomes independent by separating itself as a unit from a parent body. However, there are black independent churches which have not travelled the path of separatism but have sprung from the inspiration of a visionary or a charismatic figure. These have been called 'Zionist', a term which lacks the precision of 'Ethiopian'. It is rather a broad label which accommodates quite diverse religious strains, from the inimitable black theology of Shembe, through various degrees of syncretism, to a fairly straightforward adaptation of christianity to modern black requirements. Some consciously call themselves 'Zionist'; others may style themselves 'Apostolic', 'Pentecostal', 'Gospel' or 'Holy'; still others may bear more exotic titles, for example the 'African Castoroil Dead Church'. Many derive from the ephemeral influence of American black churches, yet may be able to trace connections back to an original foundation in the 1920s; others have sprung up and mushroomed from a purely African impetus and may just as suddenly disappear without trace. Some, like Shembe's Nazarite church, may count their adherents in thousands; at the other extreme are churches which consist of little more than a single family hoping one day to attract a large following. Some restrict women to secondary subordinate roles; others allow women equal opportunities for advancement and may acknowledge a female leader or bishop. These distinctions do not exhaust the bewildering variety to be found in churches of the Zionist type and, yet, they do exhibit a number of common features.

1 The most apt descriptive term to cover the whole gamut of churches of the Zionist variety would be that of 'Spirit churches', because the source of their appeal lies in the harnessing and deployment of the power of the Holy Spirit, mediated by a rich religious technology which is steeped in complex symbolic meanings and consists of clothing, staves, flags, water, ashes and salt (Kiernan 1978 and 1979). Although much of this meaning and usage is derived from an African heritage, frequently it is explicitly justified by recourse to Old and New Testament precedent. Scriptural support is most obviously available for the two principal manifestations of the operation of Spirit in the course of worship, that is, *prophecy* and *glossalalia* ('speaking in tongues'). Prophecy is a specialised ministry with which certain individuals are endowed and which is fostered by morally impeccable conduct and the practice of asceticism, particularly in fasting and other forms of abstinence. Through the mediation of visions and voices, the prophet gains insight into the nature and source of the troubles afflicting individuals and congregations and he receives some indication as to the best way of treating them. It can be seen, therefore, that prophecy is an indispensable element of Zionist 'healing'. The phenomenon of 'tongues' is an ancillary and unspecialised contribution to the healing process. When the Spirit bubbles over into speaking or praying in tongues, even the ordinary congregant can offer garbled clues as to diagnosis and treatment of an illness, which a prophet can elucidate and build upon. Should no prophet choose to decipher such messages, the content of 'tongues' can still convey an expression of concern for, and solidarity with, the sick. Spirit and healing, prophecy and 'tongues', together form the primary distinguishing feature of the Zionist type of religious experience.

2 The second common feature is the scale of the worshipping and healing congregation or band. In my experience, the strength of a congregation rarely exceeds forty adults and is usually much less, while attendance at regular services always falls below the known strength. On occasion, congregations come together at larger

gatherings. Nevertheless, the effective religious unit is very small in scale and this increases the likelihood of its being a real community resting on thorough, even intimate, personal mutual knowledge. One's actions and omissions, successes and failures, strivings and troubles are well known to others and any change in individual circumstances can be quickly absorbed by the congregation and appropriate action taken. The congregation is, therefore, small enough to be a community which dispenses both discipline and compassion.

3 The third noticeable feature is the multiplicity of offices which are held within such a small congregation and which, because they are seldom arranged in a clear hierarchy, appear to render it structurally unbalanced. Not all such offices confer authority on the incumbent; many are merely an entitlement to carry out some simple task, however infrequently. Some offices, for instance 'prayer for the sick', are so widely held that they are virtually synonymous with being a member in good standing. Authority ultimately rests with the congregation as a whole, with all the possibilities of abuse that attend this, but it is taken to be voiced by a clearly designated leader, usually the minister. The dignity of office, however, is not withheld from those who persevere for a while and each one is accorded his or her share of the limelight and an area of responsibility in the management of events. The heightened feeling of participation which this arouses strengthens the communal base of the congregation.

4 The Zionist movement grows through a steady recruitment of adults from the surrounding population, of women much more than men. These gains compensate for the alienation of its own children, particularly male children. Zionism appeals especially to the physically sick and the socially handicapped, to whom it offers relief and support and the possibility of self-improvement. It holds out to the very poor and oppressed a rigorous programme for economic survival and to women, especially, the backing and solidarity which many of them require to maintain viable families in adverse circumstances (Kiernan 1977a). Because these are churches of the very poor, education is seldom in evidence, although it is highly valued. Few of the leaders are educated even to a moderate degree, most struggle to read the bible to their congregations and many are completely illiterate. The ministry is, therefore, untrained in the accepted sense. Experience and proven ability to win converts emerge as the practical qualifications for becoming a minister.

5 The Zionist churches neither pursue nor lend support to any political cause. They tend to see politics and other engagements not of a strictly religious nature as futile time-wasting activity. Their concern is not with institutional and educational administration but with 'the resolution of private rather than public problems' (Hastings 1976:26), although it should be added that a private problem could well have a public context. Not only are Zionist sects apolitical, they are also non-tribal in outlook. In practice, membership may be predominantly drawn from one 'nation', but the boundaries drawn are not territorial or ethnic or cultural and the composition of congregations faithfully reflects the composition of the surrounding population. These churches are purely a socio-religious manifestation of the modern black South African milieu and, to the extent that they display exclusiveness, it tends to be of a strictly religious nature.

6 A line is drawn between those who practise sorcery and those who do not. Zionists abhor sorcery and the substances it employs to translate personal feelings of envy, jealousy and enmity into physical harm. By definition, all non-Zionists are regarded as either actual or potential sorcerers. The reality of sorcery is not denied; neither is any attempt made to stamp it out. It is acknowledged to be a pervasive evil and Zionists are engrossed in resisting its intrusion into their lives and in neutralising its baneful effects. Indeed, it is part of their appeal that they claim to possess special expertise in this area. The same claim is made by traditional diviners and herbalists, with whom Zionists are, therefore, in competition; yet Zionists disapprove of diviners as strenuously as they condemn sorcerers. There are several reasons for this. It has always been the case that diviners are suspected of being sorcerers themselves, since they employ a power akin to sorcery in order to combat it, a power that can equally well be used for good or evil. Zionists are concerned to tap an entirely different and novel source of power and always to the benefit of others. Herbalists and many diviners make use of the same range of substances employed in sorcery, while Zionists rely on prayer alone, for example in order to impart a blessing to water. Furthermore, diviners receive inspiration and insight into illness from their ancestral spirits. Zionists vary in the degree to which they concede power to ancestors, but, in general, there is a tendency to accord them a diminished capacity for intervening in the affairs of the living. This may amount to a protective role, confined to the relaying in dreams of warnings about impending dangers, but ancestors are not credited with any contribution

to the healing process. Cases have been reported of their being assimilated into the structure of the angelic intermediaries between God and man (Sundkler 1961:261; West 1975:181), and this would seem to be a logical phase in their eventual elimination. It can be concluded from the foregoing that Zionism constitutes a significant departure from traditional religious forms.

7 Fundamentally, Zionism is an urban phenomenon. Zionist groups are plentiful enough in country districts, but the movement's strongest base and the scene of its most spectacular growth in recent years has been the major industrial complexes around Johannesburg and Durban. It is not without relevance that these areas of greatest population density, where strangers are thrown into association with one another and perforce must live in close proximity, are precisely the places where the fear of sorcery is rife and widespread. Undeniably, the spread of Zionism owes much to the rise of cities and the experience of migrant labourers flocking to industrial centres. The movement has its roots in Johannesburg at the beginning of the century (Sundkler 1961:48, 80), although evidence recently uncovered (Sundkler 1976:43) shows that it had a secondary independent origin in the little town of Wakkerstroom, strategically situated midway between Johannesburg and Durban. Today, churches of the Zionist variety have their strongest following in the vast city of Soweto. Even Shembe's church, atypical in some respects, is situated on an urban periphery. West has argued (1975:196) that, in Soweto, churches of this type owe much of their success to the fact that they provide forms of association which enable people to adapt to urban conditions, and there is no reason to suppose that such an argument lacks general validity, since there can be few rural areas in a country of advanced technology which are untouched by urban influences. The urban dimension has shaped the Zionist churches in a number of ways. The place of worship is normally a room in a modest township house and this in itself limits the number of participants and determines the optimum size of a congregation. More strikingly, Zionism has in recent years taken to the trains and I have argued elsewhere (Kiernan 1977b) that the holding of services on commuter carriages is a clear demonstration of how religion can be employed to come to terms with a peculiarly urban hazard. In fact, it can be siad that Zionism represents an attempt to erect a bastion against all that is repulsive in township life.

8 A further definitive characteristic of the Zionist movement is its inherent tendency towards fragmentation, and this constant

reproduction largely accounts for the multiplicity of churches of this type. Fragmentation occurs almost with the force of a general law to which there are few, if any, exceptions. Until recently, Shembe's church had defied this rule, but today it is riven by rival factions contesting succession to the leadership and the conflict may yet prove to be insoluble without the parties going their separate ways. The contentious issue of succession upon the death of a leader may often be a precipitating factor, but it cannot be regarded as the root cause of the tendency to fragment. The cause would appear to be twofold. First of all, the incidence of fragmentation seems to be a function of scale. The more successful a church is in increasing its membership, the more likely it is to experience a secession. An increase of scale to the point at which the structure becomes unwieldy and unmanageable and at which the periphery becomes isolated from the centre will almost certainly generate a duplication of the most effective scale of operation. Fragmentation is thus an outcome of growth. But it can also occur in the absence of significant growth and this is related to competition for positions of supreme leadership (Sundkler 1961: 296–7). Granted the situation created and supported by the South African state, in which it is virtually impossible for a gifted black to attain a preeminent position in politics, commerce or industry, it is often in the religious arena that such men realise their potential. Granted, further, that this realisation is to some extent blocked in the mission churches, it becomes clear that only in the black independent churches is there unfettered scope for blacks with ambition and ability to exercise leadership at a high level of organisation. Often enough, a talented and forceful man can rise to the position of vice-president or deputy leader within his church, but he cannot supplant the founder or his successor during his lifetime and, moreover, the leader's son may be waiting in the wings to succeed his father. The temptation is almost irresistible for the deputy to strike out on his own, taking his followers with him. Thus as the proliferation of office creates opportunities for leadership at the congregational level, the segmentation of churches circumvents the bottleneck of leadership at a higher level.

9 Finally, there has been much agonising over whether or not the black independent churches can be described as christian, and Sundkler may have given a misleading impression when he claimed (1961:297) that Zionism was a bridge back to paganism. One should be equally wary of asserting that Zionists are christian without exception or qualification. What can be said with some certainty

is that there are more christian churches among them than is credited by those who have only a passing acquaintance with their practices. Their services, which may initially appear esoteric, bear the impact of their christian witness. In many essentials they display a fidelity to christian belief and worship. The form of baptism by triune immersion is a valid one, as I can attest from close and repeated observation, and the eucharistic celebration, though infrequently held, keeps closely to the institutional narrative, the reading of which (John 13) accompanies the action. For christian Zionists, the indispensable core of regular services is the bible. Preaching is firmly anchored in its familiar texts, and it is drawn upon as a constant reference point and as a source of inspiration and precedent for daily living. Concern with healing is not only based on biblical precedent but it is firmly believed that it can be accomplished only by prayer. The power of communal prayer is transmitted to healing instruments such as water by means of a blessing, and prayers for the well-being of congregations and individuals are unambiguously addressed to the 'Father'. However, the central religious principle to which christian Zionists adhere is the saving power of Christ, applied through the agency of the Spirit, but here the emphasis diverges somewhat from that of mainline christianity. While the Resurrection is not rejected, it is not the pivotal belief and, in practice, it tends to be submerged in a preoccupation with Calvary. The climax of the christian calendar for each church is its collective celebration of Good Friday with its leader.

More than anything else, Christ is the suffering Saviour whose death releases the means of overcoming affliction and hardship. This accentuation of the Christ 'who died for us' is quite in keeping with a number of other aspects of Zionism. The poor and the disadvantaged who make up the membership of Zionist churches easily identify with the sufferings of Christ and derive comfort from his example. Moreover, the emphasis on suffering and death, and the corresponding neglect of the Resurrection as the prelude to an eternal afterlife, fits in with Zionist concern for the everyday problems besetting individuals in this temporal world. Somehow, the Crucifixion has a space-time dimension which the Resurrection lacks. Furthermore, the death of Christ has particular resonance for African cultures in which the management of the transition from the world of the living to the realm of the dead has been a dominant concern. There may, therefore, be some truth in the suggestion that Christ has usurped the traditional role of ancestors and that an equivalent role, much extended in scope, is now attributed to him. In a sense, then, Christ emerges as *the* ancestor par excellence. There are more obvious ways in which Zionist christianity retains its African heritage, but Hastings (1976:55) is undoubtedly correct when he asserts that what is carried over are the concerns and techniques and material of traditional religious culture. In essence, these churches are christian; they have at their core a christian spirituality. According to Hastings (1976:54), they are to be viewed as 'an eruption of traditional African religion integrally transmogrified by faith in Christ'. Perhaps the emphasis is misplaced. Of a great proportion of them it would be more correct to say that they constitute an expression of christian religion adapted to the requirements of modern blacks, who are whirled along in the flux of rapid social and cultural change.

* * *

In reconstructing Zionism as an ideal type, I have isolated its main features and, if I have provided a somewhat lengthy and elaborate account of these, it is because it is important that the Catholic church take cognisance of this religious development. Whereas the Ethiopian churches appear to be moribund or even in decline, the Zionist churches are still expanding, and the main thrust of religious innovation and experimentation belongs to them. They are increasing both in overall membership and in the number of churches, and a tendency has also been noted for the Ethiopian churches to adopt a Zionist style of worship (Sundkler 1961:144, 182). This swing towards Zionism must pose a challenge of sorts to all mission churches, Catholic or otherwise. Does the success of the Zionist sects point to needs not met and opportunities not available in the mission churches? While the ephemeral appeal of extremist groups on the fringes of the movement can be discounted, there is at the centre a solid christian core tailored to the needs of urban blacks, especially the urban poor. Christian Zionism may well fill a gap not filled by the Catholic church.

There is evidence to support this suggestion and it is to be found in the steady drift of converts from the mission churches to the Zionist groups. In a survey of 237 Zionists, which I conducted while doing field research in KwaMashu township near Durban, 26% had come from paganism whereas 44% had been attracted away from the mission churches. In the case of the remaining 30% who were Zionist born, the conversion rate in their parental generation was 56,5% from paganism and only 27,5% from mission churches. These figures indicate a definite trend over the years for Zionism to recruit increasingly from the mission churches and to make less impact among non-christians. Of the 44% in the survey who had been won from the mission churches, only 5,2% had been Catholics, on the face of it a relatively meagre leakage. However, any inclination towards self-congratulation on this score would be groundless. Catholic losses compare unfavourably with those of the Anglican (3%) and the Calvinist-Presbyterian churches (3,5%) and are superseded only by the Lutherans (5,6%), the American Board (7%), the Methodists (8%) and other Protestant sects (11,5%). Moreover, real Catholic losses may exceed the figure cited, as I was known to be a representative of the Catholic church and information of this kind may have been concealed in a number of cases. Furthermore, there seems to be no good reason to suppose that this drain will not continue and will even assume more serious proportions in the future. Consequently, the Catholic church can no longer adopt a holier-than-thou attitude towards the problem, nor can it, in the face of the evidence, affect to be immune from encroachment by the independent church movement. Zionism lays down a serious challenge which the church cannot ignore.

How to meet this challenge is a question to which there is no easy answer and, certainly, I would not presume to suggest ways and means of doing so (cf. Shorter 1975:145ff.). However, if the broad strategy is to learn from Zionist experience and, where possible, to assimilate its most desirable features, then attention must be directed to a consideration of three basic issues.

Foremost is the question of organisational scale and leadership. Providentially, circumstances are forcing the Catholic church to adopt a mode of organisation akin to that of Zionism, in that it must be small scale and built around local leaders. Having relied until now on the importation of trained personnel without being able to supply indigenous ministers in sufficient numbers to meet its needs, the church must now adapt to a relatively priestless situation. Areas of pastoral responsibility are becoming so vast and the exercise of pastoral care so remote and intermittent that the creation of small-scale communities of worship under autonomous and untrained local leaders seems to be unavoidable. The Zionist congregation or band might well serve as the model for the construction of such communities. Indeed, in some places, the Legion of Mary, though selective in membership, already exhibits some features of this model (cf. Shorter 1973:210).

Secondly, note must be taken of the predominantly urban appeal of Zionism. The townships are the centres of religious innovation and within them may be discerned the trends of future religious development among blacks. One suspects that the church is insufficiently aware of this and that, in any case, the strength of its urban presence is inadequate to use such knowledge to advantage. Granted that its personnel and resources are already stretched to the limit, it will have to take the decision radically to re-order its priorities: and the first priority must be to concentrate its efforts on the urban masses and to address itself particularly to the problems of the urban poor. Some laudable steps have been taken, such as the staffing of some township presbyteries with black priests, but the impression has been gained that this was the outcome of dire necessity in Soweto rather than of enlightened foresight. It is on its performance in the townships that the future of the church in South Africa rests.

Finally, it is almost a truism that people are attracted to Zionism for its healing services. It is not simply a matter of visiting the sick, which the church encourages and in some places organises. Besides, the church does have its own ritual for the sick, although it is not enacted on the same congregational scale as in Zionism. But it must be recognised from the outset that, in nearly all cases, Zionist healing is an emphatic deliverance from sorcery and, therefore, entails some recognition of sorcery as a fact of life. For Hastings (1976:74), this presents an insurmountable obstacle (although he refers to witchcraft rather than sorcery, the distinction is not relevant here): 'Witchcraft accusations may grow in intensity at a time of social dislocation; if they are somehow countenanced by the proponents of christian truth, they may take on a wild new certainty of a very simplistic kind, while the concept of witchcraft is so evil that, once its existence is admitted, there can seem a terrible logic in a ruthless campaign for its eradication. Is it not here, above all, that a christian view of sickness and death does clash quite decisively with the philosophy of African tradition?' Quite so, but I submit that Zionists have discovered a way out of this impasse by offering protection from sorcery while suppressing the accusation of others as sorcerers. In a different idiom, Zionists confine themselves to hospital work without turning detective. The danger of a witch hunt does not arise. And yet their view of healing is thoroughly christian; God alone heals and he is prevailed upon to do so through the power of prayer. Deploying the good to overcome evil is basic to the notion of salvation, and every convert to Zionism is redeemed from the realm of sorcery.

At the very least, the Catholic church should throw its considerable weight into the programmes of aid and co-operation undertaken by other missionary bodies in their approach to the black independent churches. Such a step would be ecumenical in the widest sense. Beyond that lies the possibility of discovering and nurturing something of the essence of African christianity. South Africa, with all its shortcomings, presents a unique opportunity for accomplishing this, for nowhere else in Africa has a purely indigenous christianity flourished to the same degree. The church, however, will absorb some of the vitality of this African incarnation only to the extent that it can heal its own internal division and thus sharpen its perception of itself as a missionary church with its own vision—a vision of the future which is meaningful to the African population. 'The only answer . . . to the Ethiopian-Zionist movement is the revival of the churches in Africa in such a way as to give satisfaction to all the *legitimate* demands of African christians for freedom, self-expression and self-government.' (Neill 1965:501) The missionary quest must not be smothered. It must be rediscovered and refined to its quintessential striving to liberate and to reconcile all men.

References

Barrett, D. B. *Schism and Renewal in Africa* (Nairobi, 1968).

Dubb, A. A. *Community of the Saved* (Johannesburg, 1976).

Hastings, A. *African Christianity* (London, 1976).

Kiernan, J. P. 'Poor and Puritan: an Attempt to View Zionism as a Collective Response to Urban Poverty', in *African Studies* (1977a) 36(1).

— 'Public Transport and Private Risk: Zionism and the Black Commuter in South Africa', in *Journal of Anthropological Research* (1977b) 33(2).

—'Saltwater and Ashes: Instruments of Curing among some Zulu Zionists', in *Journal of Religion in Africa* (1978) 9(3).

—'The Weapons of Zion: Powers and their Media among Zulu Zionists', in *Journal of Religion in Africa*, (1979) 10(1).

Neill, S. 'A History of Christian Missions', vol. 6 of *The Pelican History of the Church* (London, 1965).

Ramusi, C. 'Church and Homeland' in T. Sundermeier (ed.), *Church and Nationalism in South Africa* (Johannesburg, 1975).

Shorter, A. *African Culture and the Christian Church* (London, 1973).

—*African Christian Theology—Adaptation or Incarnation?* (London, 1975).

Sundkler, B.G.M. *Bantu Prophets in South Africa*, (2nd ed. London, 1961).

—*Zulu Zion and some Swazi Zionists* (London, 1976).

West, M. *Bishops and Prophets in a Black City* (Cape Town, 1975).

8 BLACK CATHOLICS

Mandlenkhosi Zwane

Why does the southern African Catholic church fail to keep its militant members within its fold? How do black catholics feel about the social and political situation in southern Africa?

There is no simple answer to these related questions. To begin with, the level of a person's political awareness determines the way he reacts to a social situation and, at present, there is no uniformity in the way black catholics see southern African society. I believe that this is changing: shared experiences are forcing black catholics to a common view of their society. At present there are many different views and perceptions; in the future blacks will unite in the perception of their society.

THE SOUTHERN AFRICAN SITUATION

To answer these questions I shall give a personal view of the area of the world in which I was born and brought up. Since a personal account can be simplistic I shall start by giving an interpretation of the situation in southern Africa. In the first place there is the complexity arising from the presence of many very diverse groups with their various political, social and economic interests.

The polarisation between black and white, fomented by institutional violence and economic protectionism, is all too well known, and has led to the paradoxical situation of white Africans who, while appealing to their many generations of ownership of land, are still very conscious of their European origins and refuse to identify themselves with black African people. Instead they have created powerful enclaves supported by the nations of the western world. While oppressing indigenous peoples they have claimed to be christian. This has made the proclamation of the gospel very difficult.

Southern Africa is the meeting place of two giant ideologies— capitalism and marxism-leninism. In siSwati we say, 'When two bull elephants fight, it is the grass that is destroyed!' There are also other tensions which are either glossed over or exploited. Whites divide into Afrikaner and English; so-called non-whites are fragmented into 'Coloureds', Indians, and blacks. Setting up puppet 'homeland' principalities allows for the endorsing out of urban workers who become immigrant foreigners. Tribe is played off against tribe, middle class comfort and worker security against the aspirations of the young. 'Homeland autonomy' is set against the solidarity of the black consciousness movement; and the new student movements are distinguished from the exiled and long banned African National Congress and the Pan-Africanist Congress.

The area is also characterised by differing political realities. Some areas are still in a period of pre-revolution where force of arms ensures relative calm with only sporadic outbursts of violence; in others, civil war and the struggle for personal power claim their toll of lives; in yet other areas there is a post-revolutionary phase where a new socialist regime is endeavouring to establish itself.

Finally, besides these internal factors there is an external force bearing upon the area. The strategic position of the Cape sea route makes both East and West concerned to have it on their side. Added to this is the attraction of controlling or having access to the region's rich mineral resources, which makes the industrialised world's motives for its interest morally questionable.

NATIONAL SYSTEMS IN SOUTHERN AFRICA

There are diverse national systems in the area. Botswana, Lesotho, and Swaziland hardly seem to have defined their socio-political position or their economic orientation. They are drifting along, sometimes adopting the opinions of the expatriate-managed western corporations, at other times accepting the more radical opinions of African nationalists proposing conflicting solutions to their countries' problems.

Angola and Mozambique have publicly made their blend of socialism quite clear in their choice of marxism-leninism; Zimbabwe has yet to define its system in practice but is firmly committed to the road of socialism. Namibia is the scene of a retreating colonialism which keeps on delaying the inevitable of allowing the Namibian people to develop freely with the other free peoples of the world.

Moving northward, Zambia gives the impression that it is caught up in a web of international intrigue over southern Africa. It appears to look towards the Soviet Union for support while, at the same time, aligning itself with the western world. Much as it has tried to design and act on an African philosophy it is under the constraint of economic realities and as such its position is nebulous. Malawi persistently ignores Africa's opinion and continues to maintain trade and diplomatic links with South Africa.

Finally, South Africa itself is a fiction. It is a country seen by the west as it wants to see it: a defender of western interests, a defender of christian civilisation and a staunch bulwark against communism. The fictitious nature of such a view is manifest to us who are in touch with the socio-political realities of the area. We know the true state of affairs and we think it is frightening! We believe that the present liberal pronouncements of the National party are making the image of South Africa even more fictitious since basically South Africa has not changed. As a South African politican has predicted, whites will tend to choose the politics of confrontation rather than negotiation; rather than compromise or surrender they will tend to fight to the last man. In 1978 a meeting of catholic bishops had this to say: 'The southern part of the African continent is in turmoil. Dissensions spring from within countries and are exploited from without. Some are poised on the brink of war, others are locked in conflict and the rest wait to be engulfed by the consequences.'

BLACK RESPONSE

How do black catholics respond to the South African situation? In place of the simplistic divisions I want to suggest that the position is complex. Blacks react to South African realities in a variety of ways. I have divided them into five groups.

1 *The traditional* Probably most black catholics fall into this group. They are those who are good cultic christians: they attend church regularly and they obediently carry out their religious duties. People from a variety of occupations fall into this category: they may be domestics, shop assistants, industrial drivers, policemen, security men, or petrol pump attendants. These are the people who say 'Yes Father', 'Yes Sister', 'Yes Madam', and 'Yes Master'. When talking to a priest or employer they deferentially use the third person, 'I wonder what Father thinks?' These are the people the government and a large section of the white population call the law-abiding element of the black population, which has to be protected from agitators and communists. This section of the black community is likely to adopt the same attitude toward the situation as those who have influence over them, be they government propagandists, the clergy, employers, the madam or the master. This is the unquestioning section.

2 *The co-opted* These are the blacks, from all walks of life, who

have bought the idea of 'separate development' and who have
been co-opted into the system: some because they find themselves
in a given geographical area or because they belong to a particular
group, others by choice, sometimes a very difficult choice. Their
present feeling about the situation is difficult to assess. We can,
however, say that they are the most cheated in the country.
Sooner or later we will probably know their feeling—which I
suspect will be that of anger.

3 *The liberals* These are found among the growing educated
middle class, in good jobs. They aspire after, and fight for, equality with whites. Their attitude is similar to that of the white
opposition political parties. They imagine that if the National party
disappeared tomorrow, South Africa would be a non-racial state
where people would be judged on merit for jobs, education,
residential areas, and political power. These people have been
extremely impressed by the Catholic church's policy of de-raciali-
sing its schools ('open schools'). The industrialists see them as a
cushion for the whites against the black masses because if South
Africa were an open society this group would have a stake in the
white man's good life.

4 *The angry rejectors* These are the products of institutional
evangelisation and the system of apartheid. They are black christians coming mostly from high schools, seminaries, colleges and
universities. They are young graduates and undergraduates who
have totally rejected the God revealed in what they term 'white
man's christianity'. For them the church in South Africa has been
and continues to be part of the oppressive system. Christianity was
used as a means to colonise, suppress, and alienate the blacks.
They are angry people. They have stopped thinking in terms of
peaceful settlements. They think they have learnt that the white
man does not understand the language of peace. They see every
white man's institution as an instrument of oppression—his industry, his education, and his christianity. They are prepared to align
themselves with anyone if that brings about a total liberation of
the black man in South Africa. In this section of the black community apartheid has produced its natural and logical result—violent reaction.

5 *The concerned rejectors* This is a sizeable number of deeply
committed christians in the black community who reject that brand
of christianity which fails to address itself to the black community's
socio-political struggle. They reject christianity as projected by
whites and their church institutions. Going to church and observing

the cultic practices can no longer impress them as long as the church is found wanting in the exercise of justice. They have a deep human concern: they value and look for peace. However, they too are militant and angry. They cannot be won over by pious and sanctimonious platitudes. My fear and concern is that if these people cannot make their peace with the church they may join the angry rejectors.

Any general statement about the black community's feeling about the present socio-political situation in South Africa is inaccurate because there are no unities of thinking, understanding, and reaction towards the situation.

It will be a great mistake if this diversity gives comfort to whites. The apartheid system leaves no room for rational reaction. It is not a system practised in good faith. It is full of too much hypocrisy. The day is rapidly approaching when the lies will surface and be seen by all sections of the black community.

THE CONCERN OF THE CHURCH

The last two groups characterised above reflect the movement in the whole sub-continent towards militancy against the white status quo. More and more young people are joining these groups. As political awareness among them expands so these groups increase in size. And the number of the young in southern Africa is growing rapidly: for example, in 1977 the Ministry of Education in Swaziland estimated that about sixty per cent of the population was under nineteen years old. I believe that the church should focus much more of its energies on this group.

The church has a duty to conscientise the 'traditional' catholics: to develop in them a responsibility to the community in which they live. Christian life is a community life, and living a christian life means to care about, and take responsibility for the community. This applies to priests and parishioners equally. You will find men who provide much assistance in running the church, but go and look at the way they treat their wives! The priest is often not too much concerned because the man appears to show signs of piety. Both priest and parishioner should become aware that their first duty lies towards the people and the community and not to a building.

Bishops, priests, brothers and sisters are prepared to suffer and die if the South African government closes their churches. But would they be dying for social justice? In the nineteenth century, if the church had not merely spoken about justice but actually

practised it, Marx could not have dismissed it. The fact remains
that catholics are often more dedicated to the ritualistic practices
of their religion than to the quest for justice.

In the scriptures there are two ways in which man is expected
to serve and worship Yahweh—through prayer and through service
to the community. The prophets of the Old Testament had frequently to bring this to mind. 'God says, now your prayers and
sacrifices are stinking because you have forgotten the poor of
Yahweh. You have forgotten the widows, the orphans, and the
strangers.' This emphasises that one cannot be true to God if one
is not true to one's neighbour. As a christian one should be aware
of the dual nature of this responsibility, and aware too that the
mass, the sacrament of unity, should both signify and reflect the
unity of the community.

It seems to me therefore that if the exercise of justice were an
integral part of our spirituality, our rulers would find christianity
a little difficult to handle. And the church would not have such a
problem with the angry or the concerned rejectors.

CHRISTIANS AND VIOLENCE

May those catholics who react angrily to social injustice use violence to combat this injustice? Can the demands of christianity be
reconciled with violence? The dilemma for South African christians is that it is the apartheid social structures which are conditioning people to react violently. Apartheid will eventually conscientise all South African blacks to a violent rejection of the
entire system, and of those who benefit from it. So unless apartheid is dismantled, this violence is inevitable. And South African
christians can express their opposition to violence by working to
change those social structures which induce people to violence.

THE 'OPEN SCHOOLS'

How does one assess the 'open schools' policy of the church? Surely,
one might say, this must be seen as one of the vital things that must
be done if there is to be any hope of peaceful change. It is important for white children to learn, by mixing and meeting with blacks,
that they share the same hopes, fears, and ambitions. In principle,
it is a bold move. But it can be dangerous too.

The open school experience can be extremely dangerous if a
black child comes from a family with a liberal consciousness. Such
a child may have the idea that 'I must prove that, although I am
black, I am intelligent.' If he does not succeed that child will believe

that the white man is, after all, more intelligent. It seems to me that the church wants the white children to know that the blacks are as intelligent as they are. I do not however think that the schools can 'prove' this, as the experience of the United States has shown.

What should be emphasised is that blacks have a right to be in the schools rather than an obligation to prove that they are intelligent. Blacks should not be in these schools because a privileged concession has been made to them, but because it is their right. It follows from this that the schools should lay emphasis on the development of the person and not merely on achieving adequate examination results.

CHURCH LEADERSHIP

How effective is the church leadership today? It is discouraging to see how little the bishops' statements have achieved over the last twenty years. The bishops have failed to help priests impress what they say on their parishioners. The bishops also have very little awareness of what is going on in the black community. They do not even know what their black priests are thinking. Perhaps the reason for this is that the bishop is more an administrator than a pastor. He is like a minister in a government ministry. He depends on the civil servants. If the civil servants want to 'let him down', they can do so. It seems to me that this is comparable to the situation of a bishop and his priests in southern Africa.

Another question concerning church leadership is that of the small number of black people entering the church ministry. The percentage of black people in the total South African catholic population has grown phenomenally in the last sixty years—today black catholics make up over eighty per cent of the church, but they make up a small fraction of its priests and nuns. Why is this so? There is no easy answer to this. During the last century, a number of black priests were ordained in South Africa. This was an unsuccessful experiment. Was it because they were sent to Rome for their training? Or that they were not accepted when they returned to South Africa? I do not know, but these were the last people to be admitted to the ministry until 1925. From that year people like Bishop Dlamini entered the ministry.

Another sore point in this connection is that most of the religious orders did not want to accept, or found it difficult to integrate, local vocations. It is notable that the one religious order which did try from the start to get vocations, namely the Oblates (O.M.I.'s), produced results and is still producing results. Now too we have black Dominicans and, in Swaziland, black Servites.

When it was eventually realised that the church needed black vocations these were not forthcoming. Was it because of the early experiences of blacks in this regard? Or because blacks did not wholly identify with the church? The South African missionary orders were not an attracting force. With many vocations from Germany, Ireland, and elsewhere, and with adequate foreign money, there was little pressure on the local black people to provide support for the church in the form of trained personnel. By constantly obtaining assistance from abroad, the missionaries did not create a sense of self-reliance among black catholics. As a result blacks were unable to develop a sense of full responsibility for the church, and tended not to feel wholly part of it.

It is also extremely difficult today for a black seminarian. He is aware that there is change all around him, and he seems irrelevant to what is happening. This creates an inner tension. While his peers are involved in the political and social affairs of the black community he 'sits back' and is fed and clothed. This makes it difficult for many blacks to complete their training for the priesthood.

STRATEGY FOR CHANGE

Let me return to my original question. Do we allow for militants within the church? Do bishops and religious superiors recognise 'militant priests' as true witnesses to the Christian message?

Pope Paul VI once said, 'The hour is late but the human concern is urgent.' In southern Africa it is indeed late, and the issue is urgent. But given the kind of church we have in this area I feel pessimistic. The machinery and the structure of the church are simply not geared to minister to the people I have described as the 'rejectors'. None of them is yet to be found in lay, parish, or diocesan organisations. The ordinary priests and parishioners tend to label them communists, anarchists, or agitators.

The example of Mozambique is instructive in this regard. There the churches are now fuller than they used to be, and their commitment to the social life and justice of the people is strong. It was Frelimo who walked in and said, 'Dear sisters, these buildings are too big for you. Get out.' They went to the bishops and said, 'Listen, get rid of these buildings. In any case they do not belong to you. They were built by the Portuguese and therefore they are not for you as religous. Give us the cars. You have taken them from the people.' I have heard that during the period of the interim government one religious order asked their Mother General to come out from Portugal as things were getting tougher. The Mother General said, 'Thank God; it had to be done by Frelimo.' She had been asked to come and comfort the sisters but she replied, 'This is what our life should be.'

I want to challenge the South African church by asking whether she is prepared to lose many of her material benefits for the sake of the liberation of all the people in the country. Or does she have to wait for a government to come and say, 'Get rid of these things.' 'Institutions' can be dangerous: they can immobilise people. A painful example from South Africa is the case of the hospitals. When these were taken over by the government the sisters went to the bishops and asked helplessly what they should do next. They feared that their useful life had come to an end, because they believed they had no alternative. Everyone knows that to vacate a room you have occupied for twenty years is not an easy thing. One has attachments. What could help us now is to forget the past and to walk into the unknown with the hope that God is leading us: to throw away those things that hinder the spiritual life and limit effective action in the community. We must be prepared to move ahead by asking, 'Lord, what will you do for us?', and by trusting that something will be done.

THE ROLE OF THE CHURCH

I should like to offer a few suggestions as to the church's role in South Africa today. Our starting point must be that large numbers of blacks have accepted the gospel despite the colonial and clerical church, and sunday christianity.

1 The task of the church is to reassert the principle of justice as an essential dimension in the proclamation of the gospel. The late President Kenyatta told the Association of Episcopal Conferences of East Africa in Nairobi in 1976:

One of the services you give to others is to help them keep going in the right direction. We have many distractions and can wander off the path. We need constantly to be put back on it again. We may not even know that we are going astray, that we are taking the wrong direction. That is why we need the church in our midst to tell us when we are making a mistake. The church is the conscience of society. . . . Do not be afraid to speak. If we go wrong and you keep quiet, one day you may have to answer for our mistakes.

2 It is imperative for the church to work out a sound, forceful and popular biblical theology of the development of the whole

human person with special emphasis on social justice. This theology must be developed in the context of evangelisation. 'For the church, evangelisation means bringing the good news into all the strata of humanity and through its influence transforming humanity from within and making it new.' (Declaration of Commitment, Southern African Catholic Bishops' Conference, 1977.) Seeing Christ hungry and making food available for all; seeing him thirsty and providing a clean supply of water for all; seeing him sick and treating the disease with curative and preventative health care; seeing him without shelter and working to provide decent housing for all; seeing him imprisoned and striving to make such institutions unnecessary. This task is relative to the need of seeing the gospel in the context of South African society and working for its incarnation on African soil. A true African christianity has not yet found roots here. The Africans have not yet sung God 'a new song'. The only authentic context for evangelisation is the local cultures, and the contemporary historical circumstances and consciousness of those to whom the gospel is addressed.

3 The church must come out very strongly in defence of 'man'— men, women and children. It must work towards a world where man is the prime consideration in plans for the future: man as the centre of social, political and economic life. 'For us what is at stake . . . is man, the African man, irrespective of the colour of his skin, his ethnic origin, his social condition, or his cultural or religious environment. What is at stake is his aspirations and hopes, his struggle and sufferings, his success and his failure.' This statement of the African bishops in Nairobi must ring in every christian heart in southern Africa and it must be accompanied by a systematic education of all christians in the scriptural vision of the human community. Our situation is calling upon the church to say clearly what it understands by 'man'. Pope John Paul II's first encyclical letter calls this understanding 'that deep amazement at man's worth and dignity' and equates such understanding with the gospel, the Good News, and so with christianity itself.

4 The church has a role in society as a medium of truth. One of the most exciting developments in the last decade has been the way christians in a number of different countries have played a practical role in providing information about human rights. In countries with strict governmental control of the mass media, the churches have at times been the only alternative source of news and data for the outside world. Such a role has been played by the church in, for example, Brazil, the Philippines and, nearer home,

Zimbabwe. Pope John Paul II has said that 'truth is the power of peace'. It is our task to harness such power. In South Africa we hear of arbitrary arrest, detention without trial, torture, and unequal access to health and educational resources. Once we have established the truth of these facts there is the need to push courageously ahead and investigate the real cause of evil and injustice in order to look for appropriate remedies. The church has to analyse the causes of injustice in South Africa if it is seriously to sponsor action to redress them. A mere catalogue of injustices and inhumanity makes people feel hopeless. Because there are not visible causes, there are no visible remedies. A horrible fatalism may creep in. This is not the truth! To analyse and to understand, to seek causes and the roots of evil are essential tasks for the churches. The truth, which has real power to change minds and societies, and to bring peace, is the reward of struggling with the complexity of the modern world.

The church must occupy an uncomfortable position in the modern nation-state. She must retain the right to make judgements about political, social and economic matters in the light of her belief about man. She may find temporary identity of interests with certain political movements and structures. But at no time must the church use its knowledge of violations of human rights as an instrument to achieve limited party-political goals, or to influence narrow ideological struggles between competing nations and communities. In the final analysis, faithful to its goals—'truth the power of peace' and man as the centre of social and economic life —it must carefully define the distance between the churchman and the statesman.

9 BLACK AND WHITE PRIESTS

Ken Jubber

As is true of most societies, South Africa is a class society. What is somewhat unique about South Africa is that for historical reasons class groupings and racial/ethnic groupings coincide to a large extent and are made to coincide. Power and wealth are effectively reserved for white South Africans. This power and wealth is maintained primarily through using it to keep black South Africans poor and powerless. Because of the coincidence of race and class and the conspicuousness of race, the class struggle in South Africa has come to be viewed as a struggle between blacks and whites. The fact that class and race boundaries do not coincide exactly is beside the point politically. The coincidence is sufficient to encourage and warrant an 'us-them' judgement on primarily racial grounds. Effective political action requires this simplification and polarisation.

Because the dividing line in the liberation struggle in South Africa is drawn largely in terms of race, it follows that all organisations which are made up of members of different race groups are exposed to severe conflict expressed in racial terms. The clearest forms of such conflict are obviously that between 'black' workers and 'white' management, and that between 'black' freedom fighters and 'white' security forces. These classic forms of conflict provide the model for conflict in less clear contexts. This paper looks at one such problematic context: the Roman Catholic church in South Africa. It shows that despite its opposition to racial prejudice and domination, the church itself stands accused of these practices. The paper argues that the liberation struggle in South Africa forms an integral part of the struggle for power within the church itself and the struggle over the role of the church in South Africa. It is no accident that conflict within the church is conflict between blacks and whites representing the oppressed and the oppressors respectively.

While conflict expressed in racial terms exists in various contexts within the church in South Africa, this paper focuses on that within the priesthood and the body of seminarians. The 'representation' issue within the South African Council of Priests and the troubled history of St Peter's Seminary are described and discussed as case studies of race/class conflict within the church.

THE CHURCH IN SOUTH AFRICA

Doctrinally the church is opposed to racial segregation and discrimination. From time to time the Southern African Catholic Bishops' Conference has issued statements outlining church policy on matters pertaining to race and race relations. The policy of the church in these matters clearly contradicts the policies of the present government of South Africa. In 1957 the catholic bishops stated the following.

The practice of segregation, though officially not recognised in our churches, characterises nevertheless many of our church societies, our schools, seminaries, convents, hospitals and the social life of our people. In the light of Christ's teaching this cannot be tolerated forever. The time has come to pursue more vigorously the change of heart and practice that the law of Christ demands. We are hypocrites if we condemn Apartheid in South Africa and condone it in our own institutions. (Brown 1960:360–351)

In 1966 the Bishops' Conference issued a further important statement:

In racially pluralistic countries like South Africa, racial prejudice takes on a crucial prominence. It is for this reason that this plenary session finds it necessary to reiterate the vigorous condemnation of the Vatican Council: 'Discrimination is to be eradicated as contrary to God's intent.' (Catholic Directory 1971:21)

The above statement is still regarded as reflecting the views of the Bishops' Conference as it is reproduced in the 1981 Catholic Directory. The published pastoral letters of the Bishops' Conference from 1952 to 1966 provide further information regarding the church's stand on racial issues. These letters claim that the church does not attach any importance to skin colour. While it is common to speak of different races, the church is concerned with the plight of the whole human race. In September 1980, at a meeting held at St Peter's, Hammanskraal, attended by some two hundred representatives including bishops, clergy, members of religious orders and lay-persons, it was decided that the church needed to identify itself more strongly with the poor, the oppressed and the suffering. At the meeting the church committed itself to the liberation of all South Africans (Argus 1980:3).

In the church, despite the forces and ideology of apartheid, blacks and whites may (and in some cases do) worship together. No deliberate attempt has been made to build separate places of worship for each racial group. The church is not opposed to racially mixed marriages and regards it as the christian duty of every catholic to unite people rather than divide them, to dissolve differences rather than perpetuate them. According to the Bishops' Conference, the present government deprives South African blacks of many of their fundamental human rights. On behalf of the church they have strongly criticised the policy of separate development and many of the restrictive laws enacted by the government which operate to maintain white privilege and domination.

The above statements operate in the realm of ideals; it is natural under the circumstances prevailing in South Africa to expect reality to diverge somewhat from these ideals. Though the church is open to all races for full and equal participation, it is not unaffected by the wider socio-political milieu. While people of all races may worship together, this is seldom in evidence since white and black are generally residentially segregated. In terms of existing legislation the government is empowered to order that no black shall attend any church in any urban area outside a black residential area if this is considered desirable. The Group Areas Act and its amendments result in most instances in the *de facto* segregation of worship. Sexual intimacy and marriage between blacks and whites is illegal. This and the segregation of schools, places of entertainment, places of residence, public transport, parks and beaches make any normal relationships between people of the various statutorily delimited population groups difficult and, in many cases, impossible. The fact that the white group is the only fully enfranchised group, and enjoys many educational, economic and social privileges denied the other groups, implies that whites constitute the dominant class in South Africa and blacks the dominated class. Whether individual whites support the status quo or not, they are as a group structurally and symbolically placed in the position of oppressor. Such differences in class position result generally in different perceptions of interest. Thus, even in situations in which black and white South Africans can act 'normally', the fact that they represent and are part of opposed political/economic constituencies means that severe conflict is almost unavoidable if such interaction is anything more than trivial.

The peculiarities of the South African situation have made their impression on the church in many other ways. In 1972, Higgins pointed out that there had never been a call for racially integrated church schools in catholic circles in South Africa. This remained true until March 1976 when the Bishops' Conference adopted a resolution to integrate all the schools under their control (see Flanagan in this book). While the number of black catholics in South Africa far outnumbered white catholics in 1980, the number of white priests far exceeded the number of black (see Table below). Roughly one priest in ten was black. As regards the hierarchy, one out of every four was black. Though the proportion of blacks in the hierarchy has increased significantly since 1974 (when the proportion was one in ten), the proportion of black priests to white priests has remained roughly the same (see Jubber 1976:29 for the figures). As is suggested below, this state of affairs may be attributed to the failure of the church in recent years to attract blacks to the priesthood and to the problems surrounding the training of black priests. The hierarchy, as is evident from various statements and actions, is keen to attract more blacks into the priesthood and promote those suitable to positions within the hierarchy.

	Laity	%	Priesthood	%	Hierarchy	%
Black	1 632 887	84	95	7	9	26
White	311 026	16	997	91	20	74
Total	1 943 913	100	1092	100	27	100

The racial[1] composition of the Catholic church in South Africa[2] in 1980[3]

The numerical disproportions in the priesthood and hierarchy led a group of twelve black catholics, including three priests, to walk into a national conference of bishops in Pretoria in 1971 with protest placards. One placard asked, 'Must we tolerate white bosses in the church as well?' Another stated, 'Christ is black—bishops act for white interests.' The demonstrators then distributed copies of

1 The church no longer keeps records or supplies information in terms of race. This Table has been constructed from the partial information available from various sources.

2 Excludes Namibia.

3 Based on figures and facts taken from the 1981 Catholic Directory of Southern Africa and information supplied by the Southern African Council of Priests and the South African Bureau of Census and Statistics.

a memorandum denouncing certain catholic religious leaders for their discriminatory attitudes and demanded the appointment of a black cardinal. The leader of the demonstration pointed out the discrepancies between the numbers of blacks and whites in the laity and in the hierarchy (Sprocas 1972:43). Sentiments similar to these recurred in the survey now to be discussed.

RACE CONFLICT WITHIN THE SOUTHERN AFRICAN COUNCIL OF PRIESTS

The Southern African Council of Priests (SACP) was founded in 1970, and since its first meeting has been confronted with the problem of tension between black and white delegates. In the middle of 1972 I was asked by the SACP executive to conduct a survey on its behalf, with the aim of investigating and, if possible, resolving this tension.

Priests

Postal questionnaires were sent to the 114 black priests working in South Africa, Namibia, Botswana, and Swaziland. The final number of completed questionnaires returned was 54. As the completed questionnaires were received they were dated. The responses to certain key questions were later analysed according to the date of receipt in order to detect whether there was any marked alteration in the response pattern with time. No obvious trend was detected. This could indicate that the replies received were fairly representative. However, this cannot be known with certainty.

The findings of the survey revealed that a clear majority of black priests felt that the SACP did not adequately represent them, while it did adequately represent white priests. The reason given for this was that white priests dominated the Council. Some respondents suggested that there were elements of discrimination evident in the selection of delegates to the Council and also during deliberations of the Council.

The frequency with which white domination of the Council was cited as the major factor affecting the representative nature of this body was considered an important finding. It suggested, firstly, that a large number of black priests saw their interests as so different from those of white priests that white priests were unable to represent them satisfactorily, and, secondly, that significant numbers of black priests felt that the white delegates to the SACP generally acted in their own white interests.

It became evident in the analysis of the returned questionnaires that an overwhelming majority of the priests expressed themselves in the racial terminology peculiar to South Africa. It was apparent that they were conscious of racial cleavages not only within the society, which is to be expected, but also within the church and the SACP, which might be considered surprising. One respondent wrote the following:

The present council of priests appears to me to be just a mere coming together in meetings to find out how one group thinks and feels (i.e. blacks wanting to know how white priests think and whites doing the same) . . . and thereafter going out to team up one group against the other.

A variety of suggestions was offered by the respondents as to ways of improving the Council. More than a third of these dealt with re-constituting the Council. Most of those making this suggestion felt that the representation of black priests on the Council should receive attention. A large majority of the respondents were of the opinion that the racial composition of the Council should be altered. While a quarter of the priests wanted separate councils for black and white priests, more than two-thirds indicated that the Council should remain integrated. The priests who held the opinion that the Council should remain integrated cited religious arguments most often as their reason for holding this view. 'The Church is one, therefore the clergy must be one,' was a recurrent statement. Another reason related directly to relationships between the races: separation breeds racism while integration fosters racial harmony. A few priests offered practical reasons: 'Priests are mutually dependent,' and 'Priests share common problems.' Those who desired racially separate councils wrote most often of white domination of the integrated council as the major reason for their stand. As one priest phrased it, 'If the body is to function properly, open discussion must be present; if this is inhibited by integration, the solution is segregation.' Some priests felt that segregation was a necessary prior step to integration. This sentiment is reminiscent of the premise enunciated by Carmichael and Hamilton (1969:244), 'Before a group can enter the open society, it must first close ranks.' Or, more recently, as re-stated by George Wauchope, publicity secretary of the Azanian People's Organisation, 'No matter how much a white may oppose apartheid, he remains, in South Africa, in a privileged position. He is unable to *live* the struggle with us.' (Argus 1981:10).

Bishops

In response to questions dealing with the hierarchy, slightly more than half the respondents stated that the number of bishops should be in proportion to the number of white and black catholics in Southern Africa. At that time (1973) there were 23 bishops, one of whom was black. Since approximately eighty per cent of South Africa's catholics are black, the proportion of black bishops to white was judged to be highly unsatisfactory. The remainder of the respondents indicated that bishops should be chosen without reference to race at all.

The arguments for a proportionally constituted body of bishops were most frequently couched in terms of the black numerical majority in the church. This justification was followed in frequency by the view that a greater number of black bishops would lead to better understanding between black laity, priests, and bishops, while it would also improve the services provided by the church. A few respondents expressed the view that black bishops would provide the black laity with the political leadership expected of a bishop and not forthcoming from the white bishops.

Those respondents opposed to considering the racial composition of the church as a criterion for the appointment of bishops supported this opinion most often with the statement that racial considerations had no place in the church. Instead, they felt that such factors as ability, suitability, spirituality, as well as formal qualifications should be the only criteria for the selection of a bishop. Among these respondents were some who suggested that the non-racialism of the church should serve as an example to South Africa. One priest stated that there were signs of favouritism in the selection of bishops and he, together with five other priests, felt that more black bishops could justifiably be appointed on non-racial grounds. One priest went so far as to propose that when a capable black priest was ready for the position of bishop, he should be given it, even if this meant displacing a white bishop.

Some priests were particularly critical of the white bishops. One wrote, 'Some white bishops show no interest in the black community.' Another, 'As a result of the political set-up in South Africa white priests and bishops fail to reach the black people except perhaps in the sacraments, which is superficial.' A more radical reply was, 'The church is black, it is unjust and to its detriment that it is headed by white bishops.' One priest suggested that, if there were more black bishops, 'the outlook of the church would change quickly. We would understand that the church is for the people

and not only the people for the church. The church would cease
to be a colonising power.'

The church
Asked what one change they would introduce into the church in
southern Africa if they could do so, more than a third of the respondents stated that they would change the church structure to
permit blacks a greater influence in its running. The next most
often mentioned change was a change in race relations within the
church. One priest wrote, 'Remove the present bishops (perhaps
retaining Bishop Hurley) and get gospel-centred bishops interested
in living and preaching it even in the face of strong opposition
from their flock. Pastoral bishops must direct the flock and be
seen to be doing so.' It is obvious that this recommended change
was also a criticism of the bishops of the church. Another priest
wrote, 'The church must stop bowing its head to some of the unjust laws of this country.' A further suggested change was to 'make
most of the bishops black and reduce the number of white bishops.
Make the majority of parish priests black with most white priests
as assistants.'

Almost all the respondents felt that the black clergy played less
than an equal part in the running of the church, and they offered a
variety of reasons why this was so. The most frequently stated reason was that whites held responsible positions in the ministry. Surprisingly, nearly a quarter of the black priests gave as a reason for
this unequal influence the lack of money on the part of the blacks.
This was conveyed by one priest in the words, 'Because the man
with the money has a better part to play since the church has become too money-oriented, so, brother, like it or not money speaks
but not the gospel of Christ.'

A few priests wrote of the 'job reservation' in the church which
favoured whites and the feeling that whites regarded blacks as inferior. One priest felt that whites were better equipped to run the
church while two respondents stated that blacks were inclined to
take a defeatist position and be reluctant to take command. With
evident bitterness one wrote, 'The church is a white man's club. A
black priest is not trusted, his short-comings are exaggerated. He
seems to be an unwanted interlude into the white man's domain.
There is no charity between white priest and black priest, in the
way they run each other down.'

The priests described a large number of difficulties they experienced in working among blacks. A frequently mentioned difficulty

related to the fact that since many priests are assistants to a white
priest they lacked the status and trust they felt was necessary for
being an effective priest. A few priests wrote of having too little
power but were not specific. Other difficulties mentioned were:
insufficient money; too few priests for a given area; blacks found
some doctrines difficult to accept; doctrinal contradictions; the
distrust of a white man's religion; lack of transport; the faithless-
ness among the blacks. On the difficulty of securing the status of
a priest in the eyes of the congregation, one priest wrote, 'The
main difficulty is that my people are wrongly informed by the
white missionaries that I am incompetent, and my people tend to
believe them because I have nothing to offer them, whereas the
whites have surplus things to give them.'

The majority of the black priests considered that the church
was losing influence among black people. Fifty-seven per cent
were of this conviction. Thirty-seven per cent felt the church was
not losing influence.

The following quotation, from the reply of one respondent,
touches on some of the reasons offered by the priests for the loss
of influence of the church on the black community.

The church is losing influence amongst the educated especially. This poses a
serious threat to those of my flock who are uneducated. It is futile to preach
about the priesthood let alone the brotherhood and other religious congregations. The very illiterate people can *see* the way I am treated, thus becoming
reluctant to see their children in the same plight as I am in. On the other hand
the church has never had any 'influence' amongst the people I am serving—
except in terms of a 'charitable institute'. The church was and is (unfortunately) regarded more or less as a 'means to an end' and not much more. It is
exceptionally difficult to let the people realise what the church really is and
of course who Christ really is. It seems futile to speak of the church without
speaking about Christ. I think we simply have to proclaim the Gospel boldly,
to identify ourselves with the poor: the poor in this context means the oppressed, those deprived of their rights, etc. Secondly, let those in charge of us
treat us as persons and not as 'mechanical components' (for lack of a better
word). We are ordained priests just as much as our white priests; let us have the
same opportunities; let me have enough latitude in the serving of my people.

Those respondents who felt the church was losing influence
among blacks attributed this to white domination and paternalism.
The estrangement of the intelligentsia was the second most frequently cited reason. Other reasons were: the church is too critical
of black religious and tribal customs; the church is pro-government;
some theological ideas are difficult for blacks to accept.

The priests listed a large number of catholic beliefs and practices which were difficult for blacks to accept, for example the church's marriage requirements, and its rulings on divorce and polygamy. The condemnation of ancestor worship, the discouragement of the practices of circumcision, elopement, sacrifice, and other tribal customs were further hindrances. Some catholic theology caused problems. Specific mention was made of the doctrines of the Trinity, original sin, the infallibility of the pope, the virgin birth, the story of Genesis, and the body/soul distinction.

State and church

When asked what they thought the major role of the church was in South Africa, the most frequently encountered response was, 'to evangelise white and black.' This was followed by statements to the effect that the church must unite all races and stamp out injustice and unchristian acts. Seven priests stated in strong terms that the church's role was to help liberate blacks from white domination. Respondents made a number of suggestions as to the role the church should play in South African politics. Most of these centred on the part she could play in reducing racial discrimination. Two priests felt that she should have nothing to do with politics. In contrast, seven priests suggested that the church should agitate vigorously for political change.

Eighty per cent of the respondents held the opinion that their church had ideals which clashed with those of the present government. They described the main differences in terms of the government's racial policy and the denial of basic human rights. A significant number of priests drew attention to the 'theoretical' differences but the 'practical' convergence between government and church. One priest stated, 'The church has to sweep its own house before criticising the government. The church and the government have different languages but they work hand in hand.'

There was considerable agreement among the priests as to the proper course of action of a church member when confronted with a clash between church doctrine and the laws of a country. Most of the priests stated that the church members must abide by the laws of God. A few went further, saying that practices contrary to God's will should be actively opposed. This sentiment was pithily phrased by one priest. 'God first; Caesar second, even if this means imprisonment or death.' Another considered the correct course of action to be 'to proclaim the truth as it stands in the

Gospels. To fight any form of injustice without fear of punishment. Christ said, The truth shall set you free. It is the duty of the church to free mankind from slavery and any form of oppression.

When asked their opinion about the political structure they would most like to see in South Africa, sixty-three per cent of the priests stated that they favoured a fully integrated and unified country. A federal plan was chosen by twenty per cent and only four per cent selected the segregation plan of the present government.

Follow-up enquiries

The survey suffers from the obvious defect that it captures the views of the black catholic priesthood at one moment in time. Not only is the membership of this priesthood undergoing gradual and constant change as new members are added and others leave, but the views of the individual priests are subject to change over time. It had been my intention to conduct a proper follow-up survey of black priests in 1980 but owing to the fact that the church would not or could not supply me with a list of the names and addresses of all its black priests, and the late publication of the 1981 Directory, this survey was not possible. Instead, the SACP executive was contacted and a number of questions put to its members in November 1980.

According to the executive, a group of black priests split from the SACP in 1973 over the issue of representation and the running of St Peter's Seminary. This group called itself the Black Priests' Solidarity Group. Before this group broke away, there had been a call for eighty per cent black representation on the SACP. The 1973 formula which required that at least thirty per cent of the delegates be black was unacceptable to this group. In 1974, in order to better meet the demands for greater black representation on the SACP (black delegates comprised a third of the SACP in 1974), the Council established a department of Black Pastoral and Priestly Affairs. This consisted of three members elected by the black delegates of the SACP and a further three black members elected by the entire SACP. This department had access to the Bishops' Conference through the executive of the SACP or direct access if this was desired. In 1977 this department ceased to function although it was never formally disbanded. The need for it had passed. It had been, according to the executive, a necessary transitional body which helped to defuse the representation issue. This issue was also defused by the formation of the Black Priests' Solidarity Group, which effectively withdrew the more 'radical' black priests from the SACP. According to the SACP executive, the representation issue seems now to be satisfactorily resolved (at least as far as priests other than members of the BPSG are concerned). The constitution of the SACP still requires that at least thirty per cent of its delegates be black, and procedures have been agreed upon which ensure that this percentage will be achieved.

ST PETER'S SEMINARY*

The tension between black and white priests on the SACP provides an illustration of the ways in which the structural tensions of South African society penetrate even 'non-racial' organisations opposed to racial injustice and oppression. A further illustration is provided by the history of St Peter's Seminary, Hammanskraal.

In 1947, following the initiative of the Apostolic Delegate, the church decided to establish two racially segregated seminaries in South Africa. Thus St John Vianney, Pretoria, was established for white seminarians and St Peter's, Mariannhill, was established for black seminarians. In 1963 this latter was transferred to new buildings at Hammanskraal, fifty kilometres north of Pretoria. It is interesting to note that at the time of the decision, no one challenged the establishment of the two seminaries. It seems that the practice of racial segregation was accepted as 'normal', even within the church (SACBC 1979:2).

Between 1947 and 1972 official support for the notion of racially segregated seminaries gradually waned. This was due both to the church's growing opposition to racial segregation and domination and to the academic, administrative and economic difficulties encountered in running two seminaries. In February 1972 the Bishops' Conference appointed a Committee of Inquiry to investigate the whole question of priestly training in South Africa. After its investigations, this Committee drafted a report which was considered by the Conference in February 1973. Two resolutions were adopted relating to this report. The first was that the two seminaries should be united and staffed by members of one Academic Institute. The second was that the seminarians, seminary staffs

---

* What follows draws heavily on a report (SACBC 1979:1) and various press releases from the Bishops' Conference, on information supplied by the executive of the SACP, Sister Brigid Flanagan, and on priests and others who know something of the history of St Peter's.

and all priests in South Africa should be polled about the establishment of an integrated seminary. The response to the poll was poor; nevertheless, it was decided to have a professional sociologist, Professor Franz Maritz, analyse the results.

He interpreted the responses received as indicating that the people polled were not clearly in favour of the integration of the seminaries. He recommended that a joint Academic Institute for priestly training be set up, with the seminaries remaining separate and racially segregated for the immediate future.

At a joint meeting of the Administrative Board and the Seminary Commission, following on discussions with the rectors of St John Vianney and St Peter's, the various documents and recommendations regarding the organisation of priestly training and the seminaries were considered. It was decided that, given the state of the two seminaries and the views of those polled, it was not possible to proceed immediately with either the formation of the joint Institute or the integration of the seminaries. At the plenary session of the Bishops' Conference, held in July 1974, these decisions were upheld.

Since the idea of a joint Academic Institute made organisational sense, and 'racial integration' or 'non-racialism' was becoming increasingly valued as an end in itself by the hierarchy, 1975 saw further efforts to achieve these two objectives. In that year, the bishops resolved that a black rector should be appointed at St Peter's, that in 1976 students of St John Vianney and St Peter's should share some classes, and that the two communities should live together in one community for part of 1976 and for all of 1977, in preparation for the realisation of the proposed Institute.

By early May 1976 it appeared that everything was set up for the amalgamation of the seminaries as the first step towards the Catholic Academic Institute. On 6 May Bishop Naidoo, on behalf of the Bishops' Conference, had informed the staffs and students of both seminaries of the procedures to be followed in establishing the Institute. This information was apparently enthusiastically received, especially by the staff and students of St Peter's. The bishops were therefore unprepared for the bombshell which exploded at the end of May 1976 and which shattered all their plans for amalgamation and integration.

On 28 May 1976, their (black) rector being away at the time, the students at St Peter's staged a boycott, ostensibly over food. The staff then present, all white priests, took a serious view of this. They had been unhappy from the beginning of the year about the admission of certain students and now felt more strongly than ever that these students should not be allowed to continue at the seminary. Unsuccessful attempts were made by them to contact the rector. When he did return, on learning of the events that had taken place in his absence he gave his sympathies to the students, and he refused to support the expulsions called for by the white staff members. The polarisation between the white staff and the black rector and students was exacerbated by the involvement of black priests belonging to the St Peter's Old Boys association and the group of radical priests known as the Black Priests' Solidarity Group. Both groups sided with the rector and the students.

On 15 June, six bishops met the rector and staff in an attempt at reconciliation. It failed. By way of illustrating where his sympathies lay, the rector asked the bishops to replace the white lecturers with suitable black lecturers. To this end, he presented the bishops with a list of candidates.

The Soweto uprising occurred on 16 June. Many of the issues behind this event also lay behind that at St Peter's. Though the expression was different, both protests were symptomatic of conditions common to black South Africans, experienced in particular institutional settings: in Soweto, initially, the system of black education, at St Peter's the system of priestly training.

A number of lecturers resigned from the staff of St Peter's. It was decided to close the seminary. Plans to integrate the two seminaries and to establish an Academic Institute were suspended.

The decision to close St Peter's was attacked in a letter to the bishops from the Black Priests' Solidarity Group. In this letter the Group also informed the bishops that they were calling a meeting at Regina Mundi church, Soweto, on 8 August to discuss the problems of the church in South Africa as well as the problems at St Peter's. The discussions at Regina Mundi led to a meeting between a delegation from Regina Mundi and a number of bishops at Hammanskraal on 23 August. The delegation presented the bishops with the 'Black People's Memorandum', which insisted (1) that St Peter's seminary re-open in August, (2) that the present rector remain as rector, (3) that black priests be released at once to staff the seminary, (4) that only the rector be entitled to dismiss students.

The outcome of this meeting was a defeat for the delegation. The bishops decided that St Peter's was to remain closed until February 1977. They also decided to postpone the integration of the two seminaries.

During the later half of 1976, steps were taken to re-open St Peter's in 1977. The Constitution and Statutes of the seminary were amended to accommodate some of the demands for change and a number of new black staff members were appointed. In November 1976 the staff consisted of nine members. All four full-time members were black, while the part-time members consisted of one black and four white lecturers. As planned, St Peter's opened again on 6 February 1977 with a full complement of staff and 20 students. The rector, vice-rector and bursar/administrator were now all black.

The re-constituted and re-staffed St Peter's did not, however, come up to expectations. By November 1977 it became clear that things were 'not going well' and the bishops called for a comprehensive investigation. As a result of this, the bishops decided to close the seminary from 31 December 1977. They also established a special committee to investigate the matter of the future training of priests in South Africa. The rector resigned his post on 15 December 1977.

Though this closure of St Peter's marked the culmination of various developments, the Administration Board of the Bishops' Conference gave only one reason for the closure: it was anticipated that student enrolment in the near future was likely to be too low to justify keeping the seminary open. The anticipated poor enrolment requires some comment. For one thing, it suggests that a number of students enrolled in 1977 had decided not to return or had been debarred from returning. It also suggests that few, if any, new applications for enrolment had been received for 1978. What could account for this state of disaffection? The anticipated low enrolment, viewed against the events of the time elsewhere in South Africa, may be regarded as signalling a boycott undertaken as a rejection of the existing educational system and a call for a new system.

Though the church has been successful in gaining black converts in South Africa, it has not been successful in attracting blacks to the priesthood. According to a personal communication from Archbishop Hurley, little was done before World War II to promote black vocations to the priesthood. In 1947 a vigorous effort at recruiting black candidates was launched on the initiative of the Apostolic Delegate of the time, Archbishop Martin Lucas. By the early sixties this effort had paid off so well that it was envisaged that the intake each year would be in the region of twenty-five to thirty. For this reason the new St Peter's was built at Hammanskraal with accommodation for two hundred students. Sharpeville, increasing domination and exploitation, the intensification of apartheid, the liberation and nationalist struggles and successes in Africa, the influence of Black Consciousness ideas, Soweto 1976, the schools boycott, white domination in the church, and the nature of black priestly training are all factors which account for the fact that St Peter's never became the success it was intended to be and that the recruitment of black candidates for the priesthood remains one of the most urgent and intractable problems facing the church today. The calls by black priests for greater black involvement in the planning and execution of priestly training and the role which Regina Mundi and certain black priests have assumed in socio-political affairs in South Africa are clear indicators of the path which some black catholics wish the church to take.

The special committee established after the closure of St Peter's to study priestly training met throughout 1978 and 1979. In September 1979 the committee submitted a report to an Extraordinary Plenary Session of the Bishop's Conference. In February 1980 the bishops decided to divide priestly training into three stages: orientation, ordination, and post-ordination. They also decided that from 1981 St Peter's would provide the orientation stage for *all* new students for the diocesan priesthood, black or white. The ordination and post-ordination stages would take place at St John Vianney.

Thus amalgamation and integration were achieved at last. At the end of 1981 the new arrangement seemed to be working. Of St Peter's opening class of twenty-nine students, twenty-one completed the orientation stage of their priestly training. During 1981 St John Vianney, which had enrolled black student priests for the previous three years, provided training for its own post-orientation students as well as for the ex-St Peter's students whose studies had been interrupted. During 1981 black students made up more than half the student body at both St Peter's and St John Vianney.

CONCLUSION

The report of the views of black priests, the conflict within the Southern African Council of Priests, and the history of St Peter's Seminary has been presented to illustrate the way in which the church, though it is opposed to racial labelling as well as to racial discrimination and oppression, is nevertheless itself confronted with serious internal conflict along racial lines. This conflict stems obviously from the defining class-race structure of South African

society. Because black priests come from and minister to the oppressed it is not surprising that they have come into conflict with
an institution where white priests and bishops are seen as having
vested interests in the status quo in South Africa. The church is
clearly in a state of crisis. It is a crisis that cannot be avoided because it reflects the major crisis in South Africa itself. If the church
is not split into warring factions, as it seems on the verge of doing,
it will have to commit itself to a colossal work of reconciliation: a
reconciliation which, it seems, can only be achieved if the church
openly participates in the struggle to rid South Africa of the in-
humanities which so sharply divide both church and society.

References

Argus, The, 'RC leaders committed to liberating all in SA', 2 September, 1980, p. 30.

— 'Hard whites vs hard blacks', 7 March, 1981 p. 10.

Brown, W. E. *The Catholic Church in South Africa* (London, 1960).

Carmichael, S. and C. V. Hamilton 'Black power: its needs and sub-stance' in J. McEnvoy and A. Miller (eds.), *Black Power and Student Rebellion* (Belmont, California, 1969).

Catholic Directory of Southern Africa (Cape Town, 1970–81).

Higgins, E. 'The religious functionary in multi-racial South Africa: Some Calvinist and Catholic profiles' in *Social Compass*, (1972) xix: 29–47.

Jubber K. C. 'The Roman Catholic Church and Apartheid' in *Journal of Theology for Southern Africa*, (1976) 15: 25–38.

Southern African Catholic Bishops' Conference. *Pastoral Letters* (Pretoria, SACBC Press Commission, 1966).

— *Background to the closing of St Peter's Seminary, Hammanskraal, in December 1977* (Pretoria, SACBC Commission for Seminaries, 1979)

— Various press releases. (Pretoria, SACBC General Secretariat, 1974–81).

Sprocas. *Apartheid and the Church* (Johannesburg, Christian Institute of Southern Africa, 1972).

10   THE FUTURE

Bernard Connor

In South Africa as we look to the future there is a general expectation that a storm is brewing and the going will be rough, but little agreement over what it will bring and even less on how it should be met. Owing to the distortions of propaganda and conflicting perceptions of what is taking place at present, it is extremely difficult to know and assess accurately what is happening, let alone estimate what it all portends. As Heribert Adam points out, 'literally hundreds of qualified writers come to dozens of contradictory conclusions' (1979: 16) about the future of South Africa.

The Catholic church, likewise, has come to realise that its future is much less definite than was conceived twenty years ago. There is far less certainty now about the shape or institutional form required of the church. Gradually the realisation is dawning, though the pace varies from one diocese to another, that the church's exact stance in society, its pastoral priorities and way of relating to the state must vary from one situation to another. From regarding itself as 'an immovable city' the church is coming to understand itself more as 'a pilgrim people', called upon to move ahead all the time adapting, improvising and trying to respond appropriately, as circumstances demand.

The purpose of this paper is to examine some of the present trends and movements at work in both the church and South Africa, so as to suggest how the church can prepare for the future. This, to my mind, is not simply a matter of reacting, usually in a defensive posture, to events as they come upon us. Nor is it even a matter of working out how the church can accommodate itself to social changes as though its basic tasks would always be the same irrespective of historical circumstances. It is much more a question of working out how the church can be true to its mission in making a real, even if modest and limited, contribution to society. In particular, how can it provide a new view of the future based upon the memory which it cherishes of Jesus Christ? Following

Metz (1980: 89), though with some adaptation to the South African situation, we say: 'The church must understand and justify itself as the public witness to and bearer of the tradition of "a dangerous memory of freedom" in South African society.' In adopting the above statement my wish is to indicate the standpoint adopted in this paper, which is one based upon a particular theological understanding of faith. Anyone with a different theological standpoint would both give a different interpretation of what is taking place in South Africa and envisage the church taking up a different role in society.

THE SELF-UNDERSTANDING OF THE LOCAL CHURCH

Before any assessment can be made about the role the church should play in society, some grasp is required of how it is reshaping itself. The Catholic church has, over the fifteen years since Vatican II, broken out of its rigid framework of rules and practices. This has resulted in new expectations, some confusion, and a shift in meanings for many of its members. The outcome is that the church in South Africa, as elsewhere, finds itself in the midst of a transition period, where there is no certainty about what will be important for the future.

My hope here is to convey on a qualitative level, rather than on a quantitative one, some sense of where things are going. There is little point in making projections about, say, the number of black and white clergy in the year 2 000, because their role, importance and degree of influence is likely to be considerably altered by then. Admittedly this itself will be due to diminished numbers, but also to changed conceptions of community and ministry. Similarly, accurate figures about the numbers of catholics are of less importance than a knowledge of how they are incorporated into the church and how they view their responsibilities there. A mass of individuals, hardly knowing one another and minimally supportive of each other, are much more likely to be victims of propaganda than a number of smaller units who see themselves as mutually accountable to and for one another before God. The social role and significance of the church will depend more on the meaning and quality of its life and organisation than on having a large number of adherents. In fact, somewhat paradoxically, too high a membership would diminish the church's social impact and make it less of a force for significant change, especially if members were inadequately trained to understand and affect their society.

Diversity within the church

A first point to notice about the Catholic church in southern Africa is its heterogeneity. It draws members from all population groups, and even more importantly from both affluent urban areas and the impoverished countryside, together with a large number of migrant labourers. The liturgy is conducted in all the local African languages, English, and Afrikaans; and there are also quasi-parishes of Portuguese, Italians, Germans, Poles, Dutch, Hungarians and Yugoslavs. There are well-established catholic Indian, Mauritian and Lebanese communities, whose vitality is shown in the number of priests they have produced. The character and outlook of the church in different areas has also been shaped by missionaries from different religious congregations and of varying nationalities. This great diversity creates its own difficulties in administration, and there is a great need for improved communications between the different sectors of the church. But it does force the church to be 'catholic', and does not allow it to be identified with any narrow form of nationalism.

The consequence of this diversity is that liturgical practices, pastoral priorities, methods of organising and delegating responsibility vary from parish to parish, and from diocese to diocese. The inclusion of Swaziland and Botswana, as well as the 'homelands' of Transkei, Bophuthatswana and Venda in the Southern African Catholic Bishops' Conference means too that the church has to deal with and try to co-operate with an increasing number of local authorities. A policy, say, regarding schools or youth ministry that will work happily in one area could be a failure in another.

The consequence of this is that the church has no common centre with which people can effectively identify. There is no single place, tradition, particular outlook, theology, or religious devotion that can be singled out as the hallmark of the Catholic church in southern Africa. Great diversity can be healthy in that there is always life and initiative in some corner of the church, and it is not stifled by a monolithic uniformity. Yet such diversity can also lead to fuzziness and make it impossible for the church to act as one cohesive unit. Because of its diversity and its relatively small size (about ten per cent of the population), the church cannot be expected to play a role similar to the present church in Poland *vis-à-vis* the communist regime, or to nineteenth-century Ireland *vis-à-vis* the British government. How far it might adopt the same stance as the church in Zimbabwe did towards the Smith government remains an open question.

Decisive events for the church

In trying to discern how the church will shape its future, some attention needs to be paid to a number of events in its recent history. In the past twenty years certain events have taken place whose significance is not yet clear. They are likely to continue shaping the church for some time in the future, either because its members draw inspiration and guidance from them or because they are forced to react against them. Brief mention will first be made of some whose origin is outside South Africa, but whose full repercussions are still to be felt here, before going on to some more local events.

Easily the most important event was the Second Vatican Council (1961–5), which clearly stated that the building up and enhancement of the social order was a service christians should undertake. Quite apart from the many other issues dealt with at the council, it gave the church a renewed understanding of how God is at work transforming the secular sphere through man's activity. This has brought a sense of confidence that far-reaching social change is both possible and desirable, and that the church is not inevitably committed to supporting the political status quo. As the church has abandoned its siege mentality, so it comes to be asked why cannot white South African society do the same. It is interesting to note that almost the same metaphors are used about the 'garrison state' in South Africa as the church was using about itself twenty years ago. Some groups in the church have resisted this change, insisting on what Michael Novak (1964) calls 'non-historical orthodoxy', because they wish its life and thought to be suspended, as it were, outside history and society. Almost invariably such groups, for example the Catholic Defence League, wish to retain the established socio-political order.

Partly as a consequence of the Council the international organisation of the church has changed, and now allows considerably greater scope to the third world. This was seen particularly in the 1974 Synod of Bishops in Rome, where it was recognised that former mission territories could now take on their own evangelisation. The local South African church has been and still continues to be precariously balanced between the first and third worlds, with white 'parishes' belonging to the former and black 'missions' belonging to the latter. (In 1977 the South African bishops asked that these invidious distinctions be dropped: a call for a whole change in outlook.) In future the local South African church is likely to receive, at every level, more of its direction and impetus from what Walbert Buhlmann (1976) calls 'the third church'. This

'pull of christianity . . . towards the third world' has been recognised and welcomed in some lay circles (Farnan, 1980). Another
way in which the third world influence will grow in the church is
through the bishops' conference being linked with the other episcopal conferences of Africa, viz. IMBISA for southern Africa and
SECAM for the whole of Africa. Whether these lines of communication will have an impact beyond the episcopal level is still questionable, but at any rate the local church leadership need not feel
itself mentally confined to the South African laager.

Another event in the church that is likely to have an increasing
influence on the relations between church and state is the rise in
Latin America of 'liberation theology'. This approach, with its
concentration on 'doing the truth' rather than speculation about
the implications of christian belief, provides a method for reflecting in faith on one's social situation with a view to eventually
changing it. A door has been opened here for South African theologians, though few, so far, have yet ventured across its threshold
(see Gremillion 1976).

Within the South African church four events are worthy of mention. In 1977 the bishops' conference committed themselves to
work for social change and added their 'corporate voice as leaders
of the Catholic church in this country to the cry for a radical revision of the system'. Their formal declaration containing twenty-
one commitments still requires implementation at most levels of
the church; little machinery was established at the time to carry
them through. However in 1980 the Interdiocesan Pastoral Consultation, itself a result of one of the commitments, was held. Its
recommendations showed a clear realisation that the church's pastoral problems, for example those connected with marriage, catechesis, parish structures and youth, all have a social dimension. It
was also realised that adequate structures and channels of communication were needed before the church as a whole could move
further. One result which could be of importance on a socio-political
level is the establishment of a full Commission for Justice and Peace,
with some authority to act on a national and international level.

A third important event was the decision in 1977 to open all
catholic private schools to children of all races. The number of
children involved is small, and so this venture is not substantially
going to change the educational scene. Nevertheless this action,
undertaken at considerable risk, has spoken louder than many
words in showing where the church's concern lies. The ultimate result is still difficult to foresee as, in a number of centres, the black

children in the open schools are caught in the dilemma of whether or not they should also stay out of school in solidarity with those boycotting 'Bantu Education'. It is becoming increasingly evident that the church now has the role of striving for a unitary system of education in all its schools, which will stress service and co-operation rather than 'western' competition and individualism.

Fourthly, considerable numbers of catholics, mainly blacks, have been banned, imprisoned without trial, repeatedly questioned and beaten up. All this, together with the lack of concern shown by the authorities, has brought home to the church that it is regarded in some circles as an enemy of the state. As far as the future is concerned the church is having to brace itself for further persecution.

TRENDS IN THE CHURCH

Despite the diversity in the church it is still possible to single out some overall trends, although the various dioceses, national organisations and parishes are carrying them out at different speeds. There is a shift of emphasis from being a white to a black church, from being clergy-centered to laity-centred, and from being passive observers to active participants.

From a clergy-centred to a laity-centred church

Although the church in South Africa was founded by the labours of priests, religious brothers and sisters, their number is now steadily declining. Coupled with that is the realisation, even impetus, given at the Vatican Council that everyone has an active role to play. This has been more easily accepted in black parishes than in white ones, as they have never had many clergy catering for them; more people have always been involved and were able to take the initiative. Some obvious signs of increased lay participation are training schemes for lay ministers and parish councils. Parallel to this is the recent growth of 'family and community catechesis'. In these approaches there is the realisation that it is not sufficient to train only a few people for leadership roles, but that the christian community as a whole has to be prepared to accept and work along with their lay leaders and priests. Furthermore, considerable attention has been given, for instance in the winter schools for clergy and religious, to the promotion of 'base communities'. At present there seems to be more theory about how these communities could work than activity at the local or base level.

The shape, outlook and degree of socio-political engagement that a laity-centered church would have is unclear. Initially at least it is likely to be conservative, with the laity trying to keep christianity within the bounds laid down by social norms and the laws of the state, and trying to pass on the faith from one generation to the next in much the same form as it was received. However as more lay people, particularly the young, are being forced by circumstances to think for themselves about the relation of christianity to the social realities of South Africa, a more socially engaged church might gradually emerge. But this will require an increased grasp of the church's social teaching, so that people see their sociopolitical involvements and responsibilities within the full scope of christianity. At present many people, especially but not only whites, regard social questions as something apart from religious questions. Many blacks on the other hand look to the church for guidance and support in their social struggle.

From a white led to a black majority church

Parallel with and partly owing to the growth of lay participation the church in South Africa is discovering itself as a predominantly black body. Until recently the black 'mission' was regarded as an appendage to the white 'parish', even though the former usually had more members. Only in the last few years has there been more thinking about the place and contribution of black church members in their own right.

A continually pressing question is whether the church might split between black and white. In the past the St Peter's Seminary Old Boys' Association and then the Black Priests' Solidarity Group have threatened to break off from the Council of Priests. The call by the black caucus in the South African Council of Churches to set up a 'Confessing Church', on the lines of the Barmen declaration in Nazi Germany, unless there is a definite move by the church to break with social injustice, finds some echoes in the Catholic church But how much support this would have, or even what is envisaged, is far from clear. Nor again is it clear how much support and sympathy the more outspoken black clergy enjoy among their parishioners. The difficult question arises as to whether the church is being used for political purposes or even an individual's own political advancement or whether it is giving genuine backing to the black struggle for liberation. If the church co-operates with or supports any one black cause this creates difficulties for itself not only among whites, but among other blacks, owing to the many divisions within the black population.

Sacramentalism vs evangelisation

Linked with the decline in the number of priests, and hence the lack of people to administer the sacraments, more scope is being given to a church of the Word. This trend is not pronounced at present, but there are more and more people taking part in prayer groups, neighbourhood gospel groups, or following a course of biblical or theological studies. More laity are also conducting catechetical instruction because of the declining numbers of religious brothers and sisters. An overall result of this is to give much greater scope for conversion and evangelisation within catholic life, and not to rely so exclusively on the 'sacramental machine'.

The question arises, however, about the form that evangelisation might take. There could be a trend towards a fundamentalist evangelical pietism cut off from social concerns, where mutual support, even across racial lines, would only be on a personal basis with little or no concern either about social structures or people beyond a prayer circle. Such 'private' religion would tend to be supportive of the established power structure, and would tend to regard any social action as beyond its scope or even as a threat to its spirit-filled tranquillity. It is notable that the charismatic movement in the Catholic church has usually avoided any social commitment or witness to the gospel which demands the support of the oppressed in society.

Amongst white clergy and religious, considerable interest is shown in the 'renewal movement', which however is almost exclusively confined to 'psycho-spirituality'. There is concern about personal discernment, the charism of particular orders and religious institutes, about personal growth and wholeness. Although there are undoubted merits in this movement it has come to absorb so much energy, money and time that it saps people's interest in social matters. In some quarters it has become a form of escapism from socio-political responsibility, and plays into the government's hands by providing a private religion that keeps people quiet and avoids asking awkward social questions.

On the other hand a renewed stress on evangelisation could lead to a 'servant' church, with a concern for all people and their embeddedness in the social and economic structures that shape their lives. In this case the drama of salvation is seen as being enacted in the secular world, and not as something confined to a purely religious and personal realm of life. Pope Paul VI stated: 'The church has the duty to proclaim the liberation of millions of human beings, many of whom are her children—the duty of assisting the birth of this liberation, of giving witness to it, of ensuring that it is complete. This is not foreign to evangelisation.' (*Evangelii Nuntiandi*, 30) To judge from the overriding concerns of parish and diocesan pastoral councils this realisation has not spread far through the church as a whole. There is a fear that the church will be emptied of religious concern and limited to being a vehicle for socio-political change. On the other hand, if it has nothing effective in this matter to offer on a local level, the church will alienate both its members and those outside it who are engaged in the struggle for justice.

It needs to be stated, although it would take too long to explain here, that there is no irreparable division between prayer and politics, between the 'charismaticals' and the 'politicals' in christianity. There are certainly different tasks and vocations within the church, but the same demands of sacrificial love are required in a life of prayer that leads to mystical union with God as are required in a life of service to others so they can realise their God-given dignity. Both mysticism and political involvement can be spurious but one test of their authenticity is the ability of the one to recognise the genuine value of the other.

On examining, then, the internal life of the church, no single clear social commitment or direction which embraces all its members is visible. There is considerable awareness of the struggle for justice in some quarters and a sense of responsibility for this on an episcopal level, but by and large amongst white clergy and laity there is a lack of both organisation and conviction to go beyond a personal and domestic interpretation of christiantiy. Now we can proceed to examine some of social influences and problems that the church has to contend with in the coming years.

THE NATIONAL SECURITY STATE

A double challenge the church is increasingly having to face already is the rise of South Africa as a national security state, on the lines of Brazil, Chile or South Korea. Here an attempt is made to bring all facets of national life, including the legislature and executive, the business community, the police, the information community, the scientific and industrial communities into a national security system. Louw (1978: 29) advocates this and goes on to point out, 'The supreme test for the effectiveness of a national security policy lies in the way in which its constitutent functioning parts and processes can be related so that they complement, strengthen and support one another and attain, in a total pattern, the strength of unity.' One reason this policy poses a threat to christianity is that everything is subordinated to the security of the state, a concern which comes to override all consideration of justice for the population as a whole, particularly the disadvantaged. In the name of 'national security' all manner of injustice can be tolerated or even advocated, and anyone who dares question this is branded as a 'subversive' or 'traitor'. Under the pretext of supressing subversion, due process of law is suspended in the form of banning, imprisonment without trial, and arbitrary arrest. Religion is tolerated, even encouraged, but only so long as it is a private religion that legitimates the civil and military authorities. This brings out the second challenge the church is increasingly having to face: the idolatry of the national security state. The state comes to have a mystical or divine quality, so that its tenets, policies and even its officials are seen as unquestionable. In a national security state it is easy for a government, which may only represent very limited interest groups, to fall 'prey to a vertigo of power, to a desire for divinisation' (Ricoeur 1974: 216). This gives the church the task of making it clear to the state, in both its words and deeds, yet without denying the state's real but limited authority, that it is a fallible instrument and itself subservient to a higher law.

We can therefore expect increasing tension between church and state as the government continues with its 'total strategy'. A main task of the church in the social field will be to keep alive a concept of justice for all and consistently denounce the notion that 'extreme' forms of action may be justified in the name of 'security'. The notion of 'security' is interesting in that it directly contrasts with the basic christian attitudes of faith and hope; neither of these latter provide an existential certainty about what will happen in the future, whereas the security outlook tries to control the future, and not merely to make prudential plans to cope with it in the best way possible. The continued promotion of the national security state is going to involve the church in an intensified struggle both for people's allegiance and against religion being used as an instrument of state security.

THE CHURCH AND THE BLACK POPULATION

Besides the polarisation between black and white in South Africa, there are also considerable political differences amongst the blacks themselves, which the church has to be aware of in planning its pastoral work. Apart from the more obvious differences between different groups, between supporters of 'homeland' rulers and

urban leaders, and between the proponents of black consciousness and non-racialism, there are—following du Toit (1980: 3)—
three different types of black response to the government's strategy of maintaining itself in power, while granting some indirect
rule to black people.

The first type of response is 'self-interested collaboration'. This
fits in with the government's policy of co-opting a black middle
class who would form a buffer against the vast black proletariat of
migrant workers and people in the 'homelands'. The success of the
government's programme here, which brings a certain measure of
economic advancement for some, depends upon splitting black solidarity and encouraging people to have an attitude of possessive
individualism towards life and one another. This policy is also
implemented by a number of firms seeking to draw blacks, even
ones who have had trouble with the authorities, into their companies. This may be a mixture of genuine concern and a way of
neutralising and isolating outspoken people from the rest of the
population. If one has enjoyed some privilege and luxury, it is
difficult to lay it aside or possibly lose it in a political struggle.
The church has to discern when such people are thinking only of
their own benefits and neglecting, even exploiting, the poorer and
more powerless sections of the population.

'Collaborative opposition' is the second type of response, where
people are using the structures, frequently ones provided by the
government itself, as a means of combating the evils of the present
system. This has been dubbed the 'Buthelezi strategy'. Leaders in
this position have to be enough of an opposition to keep their con-
stituency satisfied, and collaborative enough not to be ousted
from power by the central government. Hence it is a tight-rope.
Because of its lesser degree of self-interest, people adopting this
position may be in a better position to promote social justice for
the whole of the community, the poor included, and so could well
be helped by the church. In any event a fair degree of co-operation
and support could be given to this group. But the church also has
to assess, and maybe at times warn, where this position of collaborative opposition simply does not work and people are being duped
and taken advantage of.

The third response is 'non-collaboration', seen in election and
school boycotts, and strikes. But with the present powerful system
of state control, it is difficult to achieve anything that has more
than nuisance value. In this situation the church has very limited
scope for pastoral work. Here its task may be to understand what

drives people to this degree of negativity, and keep alive—though usually only in small dedicated groups—the human good which is worth striving for. Where frustration and resentment are paramount, and during times of violence, there will be little public acceptance and recognition of the church's work. People will be either too scared or too bewildered to welcome the visible presence of christianity, and then the church will increasingly have to recognise that its role is one of being a supportive presence, even if it gets no thanks at the time.

THE CLASH OF IDEOLOGIES

Mainly because of its mineral wealth and strategic importance, combined with its being a turbulent meeting point for different races, South Africa is becoming an arena where several different ideologies are competing with each other. Superimposed on the old ethnic and racial loyalties and animosities, there are three views of man contesting the shape of his future. In the words of Edward Schillebeeckx:

I think that the urgent question which will prove decisive for the future of our world and of christianity over the next thirty years is whether the most powerful impulse in world history will prove to be 'marxism' or 'the christian gospel' or the technocracy of humanistic 'critical rationalism'. For these are the forces which are in question here and now as historical impulses towards an improvement of our secular society. For all the perceptible affinities and points of contact, the concern for humanity and the 'vision' (dream, promise or planning) which these three movements bring are *by nature* very different. (1980: 653)

Marxism has been adopted as a programme by the African National Congress, and appeals to many frustrated and antagonised blacks who cannot see how anything could be worse than the present system. The present government, which has shifted its power base from parliament to planning boards, is making South Africa into a well controlled technocracy; anyone who cannot fit into that scheme is relegated to the 'homeland' periphery.

This is the scene in which a very heterogeneous Catholic church has to work for the next few decades. It has to beware of tying christianity to any single ideology or political programme. Circumspection will be required in welcoming any political or social movement; at the same time it has to immerse itself in the struggles and perplexities of the region's divided peoples. To accomplish anything at all will require both the simplicity of the dove and the cunning of the serpent.

References

Adam, H. and Giliomee, H. *The Rise and Crisis of Afrikaner Power* (Cape Town, 1979).

Buhlmann, W. *The Coming of the Third Church* (Slough, 1976).

Du Toit, A. 'Different Models of Strategy and Procedure for Change in South Africa' in F. van Zyl Slabbert and J. Opland (eds.), *South Africa: Dilemmas of Evolutionary Change* (Grahamstown, Institute of Social and Economic Research, 1980).

Farnan, G. H. Editorial in *Trefoil* (1980), 47 no. 184.

Gremillion, J. *The Gospel of Peace and Justice* (Maryknoll, New York, 1976).

Louw, M. H. H. 'The Nature of National Security in the Modern Age' in M. H. H. Louw (ed.), *National Security* (Pretoria, Institute of Strategic Studies, 1978).

Metz, J. B. *Faith in History and Society* (London, 1980).

Novak, M. *The Open Church* (London, 1964).

Pope Paul VI. *Evangelii Nuntiandi*, Evangelisation in the Modern World (1975).

Ricoeur, P. *Political and Social Essays* (Athens, Ohio, 1974).

SACBC. *The Bishops Speak* vol. 2 (Pretoria, SACBC, 1980).

Schillebeeckx, E. *Christ: the Christian Experience in the Modern World* (London, 1980).

11 WHY THE CHURCH IN SOUTH AFRICA MATTERS

Adrian Hastings

'Why South Africa?' is a question frequently put to those outside the country who show a very special concern with its problems. Are they really so different, or so much worse, than those of a host of other countries in this confused world? Has South African society, and the church within it, some very special relevance for christians in other parts of the world? This chapter is the attempt of one British christian to say why we should answer 'Yes' unhesitatingly to those questions. To do so one must put the South African situation into a far wider context.

Oppression, systematic discrimination against 'second-class' citizens, torture, the murderous elimination of dissidents are common features of many countries in the world today. One has only to think of Kampuchea, Ethiopia, Equatorial Guinea and Uganda, to name four of the bloodier tyrannies of the 1970s. It is but the start of a long list. The world is in an increasingly oppressed condition; horribly divided and in conflict. But the characters of oppressions and conflicts differ. While opposition to inhumanity is finally undivided, it can only be effective if it is based on as clear an understanding as possible of each type of inhumanity—its historical causes and current mechanism, the ideology used to justify it, the external forces which profit from it and maintain it in existence. Some are blinder, more arbitrary, more wholly irrational, maybe briefer; others are more systematic, more thought out, more subtly defended, more lasting. The oppression of Amin falls into one category, that of Soviet intervention in Afghanistan into a second, that of the South African state system into a third. While one's immediate horror may well be more for the holocausts perpetrated by an Amin or an Nguema, they have a madness which probably ensures that they will not last too long or be effectively significant for the future structures of our world. The more thought out and rationalised, the more legalised, the more moralised a system of oppression is, the more money there is in it for someone, the more it requires among the free the most exacting sustained analysis and inflexible opposition. This is true alike of Marxist tyrannies and of anti-Marxist varieties of the South African or Argentinian type.

It is well to begin by outlining the particular characteristics of South Africa which both make of it a quite special case and slot it, in various ways, into a global context. We shall list six. The first, and the core of the whole thing, is of course not just the racial division of its population but the systematic structuring of society, economically, politically and educationally, in terms of race. And this not as a matter of habit or of individual prejudice but of the dominant theory of society and of a mass of meticulously detailed law, much of it recently enacted, all of it sharply enforced. No other country in the world has so clear a racial divide within its citizenry, but the clarity of that divide is itself not a matter of race but of law. Many other countries face racial conflict, breed racial prejudice, and in various ways practise racial discrimination. But elsewhere this is a matter of public regret. Nowhere is it a matter of legal principle. This sets racial conflict in South Africa clearly apart from racial conflict elsewhere, and makes of it indeed a specifically different phenomenon—transforming it from disorder into a symbol.

Secondly, South Africa is an integral part of the African continent. It is no island of its own. No major geographical feature separates it from the rest of Africa. Nor, on the side of the large (black) majority of the population, is there a racial separation. Nor is there any decisive historical one. The white conquest of most of today's Republic of South Africa in the nineteenth century was simply part of the wider scramble for Africa. The Zulus and the Xhosa, like the Ashanti and Benin, were conquered by British arms. The subsequent transference of power over black natives to white settlers was achieved by act of parliament in Westminster. Neither the past nor the present of South Africa can be seen apart from the history of imperialism and anti-imperialism in the wider continent. The oppressed majority in South Africa is but one wing of the great black population of Africa as a whole. Poor as most African countries are at present, volatile as their political systems may be, their numbers and potential importance for global history are vastly greater than those of white South Africa. The turbulent tide of black independence, development and self-expression was not stopped at the Zambezi. Nor will it be at the Limpopo. A decade here or there and that tide will have flowed irresistibly on.

Thirdly, South Africa still (just) remains a country within the western democratic tradition. Its constitution, its parliament, its party system, its universal franchise (for whites), its courts, its universities and newspapers: all these things make historical sense, and only make sense, within the tradition of western Europe. It is impossible for Europeans not to think of South Africa very differently from, say, Iran or Vietnam. This cultural and political affinity does, of course, reflect a racial affinity. The ancestors of the white rulers of the country today came from Holland, from France, from Britain or from Germany. And it is because they did so and then continued for long to be governed from Holland or from Britain that the institutions of western Europe were implanted so firmly and so recognisably at least within the white segment of South African society.

Fourthly, South Africa remains a crucial member of the western economic system. British, American and West European investment in the country is enormous and growing. The same companies operate across western countries. There is a constant interchange of personnel as well as of finance. This, of course, both vastly increases the responsibility of western countries for what goes on in South Africa and inhibits effective action to right what is wrong, lest in one way or another their own economies should suffer. At present British investors profit as much as South African from cheap black labour, long black hours, and no black vote for the parliament which makes the laws that govern them.

Fifthly, South Africa in church-going terms is an extremely christian country, both on the white side and on the black. Christians do not control the world today and their responsibility for what happens in many countries, large and small, may be next to nothing. If the government of Russia or Albania misbehaves, christians may and do condemn what is done (and it may indeed be done to their direct disadvantage) but it is not being done within their own family. Christians share responsibility for Constantine in a way they do not for Nero. What is done in South Africa is done emphatically by christians, many of them members of the same churches or families of churches that exist elsewhere; moreover it is seriously defended in christian theological and moral terms, by 'leading' members of white South African society. Hence the reputation of christianity, its very word to the world, is at stake here in a way that cannot be the case in Albania or Afghanistan.

Sixthly, and finally, South Africa is increasingly taking on the characteristics of the 'national security state'. This is a fairly recent development and it is worth being clear about it because in some ways it is altering the focus of attention. South Africa's traditional contradiction has been the attempt to reconcile a liberal western political system for whites with the exclusion from that system of eighty per cent of the population, so as to ensure that the twenty per cent should always control the eighty per cent. Verwoerd's philosophy of apartheid was the most laboured attempt to overcome this contradiction through the discovery of the 'bantustan'. If profoundly unconvincing as an apologia for what was actually going on, it temporarily filled the gap between theory and practice and enabled well-wishers to argue for the wait-and-see policy: what would come of the bantustans? The more unsatisfactory they have looked in practice, and the more wholly incapable they are of saying anything to Soweto and the basic urban problems of South Africa, the more apartheid is seen finally to have run out of steam. At the same time the collapse of white rule in Mozambique, Angola and Zimbabwe has almost completely removed South Africa's protective covering, and the internal contradiction between democracy and racial domination has itself become a security risk both theoretically and practically. The consequent shift is away from what measure of civilian democracy has survived the piecemeal repressive legislation of thirty years of Nationalist government to a system more and more characterised by dependence upon the military coupled with the tight control of civilian patterns of expression: the 'police state', in fact, of Paraguay or the Argentine. As liberal safeguards are progressively removed it becomes—almost but not quite paradoxically —easier also to remove a few of the irritations of 'petty apartheid' which were really required to feed the ego of the poorer members of a white 'liberal democratic' society. As ordinary whites increasingly lose what political power they formerly possessed and the control of power is withdrawn to an inner laager, an oligarchy of the security, political and big business bosses, it becomes practicable, and internationally desirable, to soften the hard dividing lines between white and non-white: to remove the 'whites only' notice from the park bench. Superficially, that is to say, the development of the national security state can go with a diminution in overt racialism (just as Salazar's Portugal did not need to be overtly racialist to hold its black population ruthlessly under control).

All this is straight-forward enough. Democracy has, after all, an authentic meaning. If it is abused for too long by those simply repeating its rhetoric, then it dies. If it cannot be shared with blacks then it cannot for long be shared between whites either. White domination and privilege (the true, underlying commitment of most of the ruling minority) can better be maintained by a basic shift of model and it is that shift which would now appear to be taking place. Nevertheless, at least for the time being, chunks of the liberal tradition are still there, not in themselves to be despised, and still partially usable: just as anything that remains from Chile's old liberal tradition is still to be used for what it is worth to fight Pinochet's tyranny, or what there is of legal objectivity in Russia to fight Soviet tyranny. The weapons may be weak, and weaker than they were, but one uses what is at hand. Let us remind ourselves too that the progressive taking over of 'liberal democracy' by 'national security' is not a phenomenon peculiar to a very few states. It was happening fast in America under Nixon. It is probably happening to some extent in almost every western state subject at present to major political pressures.

These factors, coming together in South Africa and nowhere else in anything like so acute a form, oblige the rest of the world, and christians in particular, to wrestle with the South African case and its meaning for them in a way that they hardly have to with some more immediately blatant examples of miserable oppression. There is a world-wide spiritual and moral struggle facing mankind in these final decades of the twentieth century. Within this moral struggle South Africa and its image bear what is quite possibly a decisive role. Our world is growing more sharply divided than ever before between rich and poor, haves and have-nots, the 'North' and the 'South'. Very roughly speaking, the rich consist of the white world plus elsewhere a privileged coloured elite; the poor consist of the non-white world plus the lowest strata of older white societies. Furthermore, and still more roughly, the white/ rich world is very largely co-terminous with countries which at least in regard to their past and their cultural traditions are regarded as christian, while the non-white/poor world is, by a large majority, non-christian. Japan is one obvious exception to such a simple characterisation. Another is presented by the deprived masses of Latin America and black Africa: have-nots, but in large part christian. To the significance of that we shall return. Yet the overall image remains, one paradoxically in contradiction with what—in gospel terms—the christian image surely should be: a fellowship, not of the rich and the powerful, but of the poor of God.

Is the poor, southern, non-white world also to become antichristian because the white, capitalist world is claimed as christian?

Such a scenario is certainly not wholly devoid of plausibility, and developments could make it more and more probable as the years pass: let liberation theology be 'excommunicated' in Latin America; let the black millions of central Africa be alienated from the churches by a prolonged white-black conflict centred upon a South Africa firmly backed by the United States and western Europe; let the basic christian communities of the southern continents be deprived of the eucharist, and starved of life; let a diminishing priesthood retreat into the realm of the sacral, reasserting its segregation from the laity, and its concern with more important spiritual matters than torture and starvation; let an other-worldly and authoritarian form of christianity be proclaimed again as the only one fully acceptable to Rome; and we are almost there. It is not impossible.

Now the whole nature of the South African situation, as it has been engineered by its white overlords, is such as to provide a paradigm for this scenario: a microcosm almost capable of forcing the macrocosm into its image. For the spokesman of the South African official mind, the world is indeed thus so divided today. On the one side, the white, christian, capitalist west, of which South Africa is to be recognised as a bastion and integral part; on the other, communism. And that is not, of course, only a South African view. It is one held by numerous sincere conservative 'western' christians. Moreover, still more interestingly, it is the Russian view. The Kremlin and Pretoria do not disagree in their pragmatic analysis of the contemporary situation. For both, christianity goes (or must be made to go) with capitalism, in its present multi-national form above all, and with the world hegemony of the white Euro-American states. Whether christianity is in this context 'true' or whether it is 'false' almost ceases to matter. Its function becomes the same and is one inherently set against the inescapable immediate aspirations of the large majority of mankind.

If theirs were an adequate analysis, things would be grave indeed for christianity. In fact, thank God, it is deep down, despite its plausibility, a fearful travesty of reality. Russia is not a genuine friend of the third world oppressed—in Afghanistan, Equatorial Guinea (where it backed Nguema's regime, a particularly horrible little dictatorship) or anywhere else. South Africa is not a standard bearer of freedom, democracy or christianity. It is the poor, the black, the oppressed who form the great majority of christians in South Africa as in so many other parts of Africa, Latin America and Asia. Nevertheless in the eyes of many in the international academic world, in the international leftist movement and in the world of international capitalism it does not appear such a travesty, any more than it does in the eyes of the rump of white middle-class 'western' christians. It is too convenient to their spiritual comfort, their particular type of intellectual myopia, their accustomed rhetoric, their economic advantage. However profoundly mistaken, there has long been something of a consensus, an integral element within the mental substructure of twentieth century orthodoxy, shared by both 'left' and 'right', to see the whole pattern of modern world history, intellectual conviction and group commitment in what is really a very simple binary model of 'left' and 'right'. With 'left' goes 'communism', 'marxism', the rights of oppressed people (particularly non-white people), the rejection of religion, the 'revolution'; with 'right' goes 'capitalism', 'the west', white supremacy, religion, christianity. This latter group will promote the political model of liberal democracy in white societies but in less-than-white societies it will promote instead the national security state. 'White' and 'less-than-white' are not here precisely racial categories: Portugal and Spain have lately been permitted to move from one to the other; Chile, however, was taken in the 1970s in the opposite direction. What is so profoundly shocking (shocking to agnostics, very often, as well as to 'conservative' christians) about, say, 'the theology of liberation' or the grants of the World Council of Churches to liberation movements, is that they undermine the intellectual categories assumed by the 'orthodox' of both left and right, including the politicisation of christianity in the service of the 'right'. That is why, equally, right-wing agnosticism (a very widespread phenomenon) has, so often, politically to be hidden: 'attending church occasionally' is an almost necessary characteristic of the successful right-wing politician lest he flout the categories.

Beneath layer upon layer of intellectual junk passed down in the accepted traditions of western middle-class christianity, agnostic academe and marxist myth, what is in truth valid at the core of this analysis of the world predicament is little more than the existence of two rival power-blocs, operating from different bases and with different types of strength. The heart of one is American big business and its wider network, the multi-nationals. The heart of the other is the Soviet communist party, heir to traditional Russian nationalism at least as much as to the institutionalisation of early twentieth century European revolutionary movements. Each controls, in different ways, massive military and economic machinery. Each justifies itself in ideological terms which are in fact entirely subservient to military and economic operations and objectives. One may have reasons to dislike or fear one less than the other, but the differences between them have certainly in principle next to nothing to do with religion, with human freedom or with justice for the oppressed. Genuine struggle for religion, for freedom or for justice in the world must include El Salvador as well as Afghanistan, Czechoslovakia as well as South Africa, and it must in a real way be a struggle against both power blocs.

The significance of South Africa lies, for both sides, in the opportunity provided by the catching up of a local struggle into the global one, the reality of both being at the same time obscured by its smoke-screen translation into religious and ideological terms derived from this false consciousness common to left and right, and of its nature profoundly misleading as to the true spiritual lines dividing today's world. The local struggle is that of a rich, white minority to maintain its political power and consequent economic privilege over a poor black majority. This is not just a class conflict: rich/poor. If it were, it could and would be defused in all sorts of ways, but which in fact are largely ruled out by the profound psychological preoccupation with race and the effective redrawing of class division on race lines. The identification of class and race immeasurably hardens the lines of division and increases the fears and bitterness upon either side. The racial re-ordering of class does not, though, mean that this is not a class conflict. It is. And the particular characters of the South African economy (the world's greatest gold producer, etc.) and geography (the Cape routes, etc.) slot South Africa into the world order in an important way, and the dominating South African class into the dominating class within the western economic and political system. South Africa's dominated class is, as a consequence, at least potentially, an ally of the West's enemy: the Soviet Union.

Black people were far worse treated in Nguema's Equatorial Guinea than in Vorster's South Africa, and Russia and Cuba did their best to ensure the survival of Nguema's unspeakably awful regime, just as they—and they alone—enable Mengistu's appalling tyranny in Ethiopia to survive. Nevertheless, as the conditions of Equatorial Guinea were not widely known throughout the world, and as Nguema was himself a black man, representing no philosophy worth even two minutes consideration, but simply a maniac addicted to torturing his fellow human beings, Soviet support for Nguema had little wider significance, beyond confirming the wholly opportunistic character of Soviety policy decisions. Western support for South Africa is different. Too big and rich to be ignored, its oppression, precisely principled on racial grounds, is necessarily an affront, not only to its twenty million black citizens, but to the three hundred million black people outside its frontiers. The effective west/South Africa alliance coupled with the increasingly effective Soviet/African National Congress alliance then appears as proof positive of the thesis that there really is a global confrontation linking Soviet and black interests upon the one hand, and western and white racialist interests upon the other.

But the identification does not end there. Soviet propaganda is continually anti-religious, white South Africa has continually justified its stance in christian terms and its leaders are manifestly church-going christians harping—like Russia—upon the christianity/communism chasm. South Africa has thus become the most practically effective piece in the validation of the binary thesis for world interpretation:

Russia	*West*
communism	*capitalism*
atheism	*christianity*
black liberation	*white domination*

The more this model can be seen pragmatically to work, the more it will work: it can be self-fulfilling, with each side conforming to expectation. And, of course, as already suggested, it is simply taken for granted by a sort of twentieth century orthodoxy and its upholders that they do so conform. Most lamentably of all, time and again white church leaders blatantly demonstrate by their words and actions that they too absolutely presuppose this model, whereas if they have one function in the world today, it should be to confound the model. Yet the model *is* confounded—by the people. In objective fact, as already stressed, it does not provide a true interpretation of the world at present in regard either to power politics or, and this matters much more to us, to religion. The realities of church life in the latter years of this century are simply not so, but far otherwise. The churches have, in the last few decades, and above all in Africa, witnessed what is already appearing as one of the decisive achievements of all church history—a major breakthrough into the non-white, non-dominating, non-capitalist world. Just as the white establishment seems in the deafness of its affluence to be more remote than ever from the gospel message, the non-white world in its wide-awake poverty seems to have taken to itself the figure of Christ as never before.

Christianity's present vitality is quite simply to be found among the poor of Latin America, central and southern Africa, parts of Asia. Most bishops in South Africa are as white as can be, Catholic or Anglican. They share the wearisome sense of responsibility for clerical propriety common to most bishops the world over. But all the lot of them have not conceivably half the spiritual or historical significance for the church of the 1980s that Desmond Tutu has. He is no mere aspiration, no day-dream. He is a fact. He is christianity in South Africa, while his colleagues are but over-dressed, timid administrators, of little more significance in terms of the spiritual combat of a globe in agony than the countless butchers, bakers and candlestick-makers who marry in their churches, vote for the National or opposition parties and do not positively torture their fellow men but are not tortured either.

Desmond Tutu does not just represent a South African reality, but a far wider one: the reality of the christian consciousness, of the thirst for justice within millions of hearts, christian, black and poor. The geographical vitality of popular christianity has shifted very rapidly in the second half of this century, even if there are plenty of hierarchs who have hardly noticed it. Christianity is no longer the religion of the western European dominator, any more than it is the religion of the Soviet dominator. It is, increasingly, the religion of the non-European dominated. It would seem that in the South African ethos the vastness and significance of the ecclesial change between, say, the early 1950s and the late 1970s has not really been appreciated. The canonical institutions look not so very different from the way they looked thirty years ago; their control continues for the most part to belong to the white élite, but the reality of christian life is now simply different and if the catholic institution cannot conform to that changed reality (cannot, in the case of South Africa, recognise that its principal homeland is its eighty per cent black, not its twenty per cent white membership) then the tide will simply sweep on in other courses, leaving that institution—as it has done many a time before—high and dry.

Still, conceivably, Moscow and Pretoria may together get their way. All this new life may still be crushed between the upper and the nether mill stones, between the generals and the multi-nationals and the bishops on the one hand, the generals and the commissars and the purveyors of atheism on the other. If that should happen, then the greatest achievement of the twentieth century church—its breakthrough, after centuries of encapsulation, to the non-white world—would be lost. But Desmond Tutu and his like stand up as the sign in the present of hope for the future. And they stand up precisely in South Africa, as South Africans: in the place where all they stand for (the integration of blackness with christianity and freedom, and of what is good in the tradition of the west with what is good in the tradition of Africa) has been most explicitly and systematically denied.

It is surely not surprising that the church in a racialist society should so largely and long have succumbed to racialism. It tallies with too much christian history. The weakness of so much official ecclesiastical protest against apartheid has been the manifest racial discrimination practised by the church herself. There is very often in catholic life, in all sorts of fields and countries, a divorce between official statement and ecclesiastic reality which must puzzle the observer, whether he be an outsider or insider, but seldom more so than here. Yet if in one way such a gap must be puzzling, in another the absence of such a gap might be held to be even more surprising, for the church is—in part of its nature—a corrupt body, partaking of the corruptions of the society it is part of. Were it not so, it would in some extraordinary way have to be divorced from the mankind of which it must be the inner light. The precondition to offering light is, in a strange way, that one is first part of the darkness, part of the problem. It would be miraculous if in a very racialist society the church were not to some considerable and damaging extent racialist too. And church life is not miraculous. Everywhere it partakes of the sicknesses of society. How could it not do here? Of course it has done, and it does. But the corruption of a church can become such that it only receives, it ceases to give: it becomes but an ecclesiasticised image of the mess around it. What one looks for in a living church is not the absence or exclusion of sin, but surges of life, of repentance, of hope, of prophetic vision, a sense of spiritual struggle with the 'weapons' of Cross and Resurrection used. One looks too for at least some partial and provisionally effective overcoming of the major evils of the contemporary world within a fellowship which offers by its sheer existence a sign of the power of God's grace, manifest already, ultimately invincible. Does the church in South Africa do that to its own society and to the wider world—a world which shares the responsibilities, problems and ultimate fate of South Africa?

The witness that one expects of the church in South Africa has, it seems to me, to be of at least three different, if interlocked, kinds. First and foremost it must be, and be seen to be, what it most deeply claims to be: a fellowship of men and women, classless and raceless, a manifest *koinonia*, a church in which the body and blood of Christ are shared by black and white, in which white christians receive the Lord's body and blood from black hands, as black do from white, a body of people in which this experience of divine condescension achieving human unity is realised in that at least some of its members when outside ecclesiastical walls are quite obviously and decisively influenced in the pattern of their personal and social behaviour by the eucharist.

Secondly, it must be a church which is so clearly and publicly identified with its poorer and therefore black members that no observer can doubt which sort of person this institution most cherishes.

Thirdly, a church is inevitably itself a power institution, and the Catholic church is more so than most. The character of its hierarchy matters. It is necessary to the church's public witness that the black majority does not have some mere token presence within the hierarchy of ministry and power, but an effective participation within it, so that the church precisely as an institution, as a responsible decision-making body, to some genuine extent confronts rather than mirrors a racially discriminatory world. The catholic hierarchy is in public eyes very much the 'sacrament' of the church to the wider society and so the colour of its skin, the pass book it is humiliated to carry, the marks of the police truncheon on its middleaged shoulders, the comfortable suburbs in which it is not allowed to sleep, may be much more meaningful than the verbal message it utters. The bishops have, time and again, protested forcefully against formal injustice. But it would not appear to an outsider to have woven that protest into anything at all of a confrontatory life style. It could, on the contrary, be argued that its life style still remains in all sorts of ways racialist while its statements alone are anti-racialist. The wider catholic world today has for its criteria the day to day life of Archbishop Helder Camara, and the life and death of Archbishop Oscar Romero. Their behaviour has been so much more important than their words. No South African catholic bishop yet has been imprisoned, deported or placed under house arrest. One bishop in prison is worth a score outside. He will be remembered, they will not. And what is the church but a chain of remembrances forged around an initial sacrificial death?—'Do this in remembrance of me.'

There is a necessary and explicit peak of christian witness which is certain to be minority witness: a sort of personal and prophetic playing out amid contemporary agony of gospel truth, an approximation to the high hill of Calvary, to which very few are called. But in every living church some are, and the survival—certainly the healthful survival—of the many depends upon the witness of those few. South Africa has indeed provided witness of this sort: Trevor Huddleston and Albert Lutuli, Beyers Naudé and Desmond Tutu, and other less known or unknown figures, martyrs among them. A handful in all maybe, but perhaps, for the needs of evangelical warfare and the soul of the world, sufficient to give the lie to the Moscow/Pretoria model of man's current predicament. The church's power is a symbolic, 'spiritual' power and that power is carried along the line by the few who are ready to suffer 'even to death'.

There seem in scripture to be two patterns for the destiny of the little flock within the body of dull mediocrity and hard disobedience which so often constitutes the city of men and even, alas, the people of God. One is that the little flock, small though it be, is just sufficient as salt and light to save the whole, to rescue its neighbourhood from the judgement of destruction: if there be but ten. The other pattern is that the remnant is indeed saved but through the flood, by exodus. It goes out. The mass is lost. The society goes under. The mills of God have ground it so very small. The city of God can and must find some new temporary environment. It will go on but the empire, the kingdom, the republic will not. We cannot ourselves choose or predict the pattern of our own destiny. We cannot know in South Africa which it is to be. We do know that witnesses are there because through the bonding of word and action, accepted suffering and unflinching perseverance, the sense of lived identity with the gospel of divine and human reconciliation, we have recognised the authenticity of their prophecy. In the life of the Afrikaner Naudé, of the Xhosa Tutu, we have seen clearly enough the breaking down of every middle wall of partition, the hallmark of Christ's presence. A small host of witnesses have demonstrated the fallacy of identification between whiteness, christianity, capitalism, the oppression of the poor. They have spoken to their own society of its discarded people, and they have spoken to the world too. To be able to speak thus from the ground of personal and ecclesial experience in the eye of the storm is to make clear the truth of the gospel and the relevance of even our poor, broken, corrupted church to the loosing of bonds and the reconciliation of men.

APPENDIX: THE BISHOPS' STATEMENTS

1962: STATEMENT ON RACE RELATIONS
In 1952 the South African Catholic bishops made their first official statement on race relations. For four years the National Party had ruled South Africa and had started structuring the country in the light of the apartheid policy. Rather surprisingly, the bishops do not mention the word apartheid, possibly because they thought the National Party would be voted out of office and that the policy was a passing political aberration. The statement is mildly reformist in tone: the bishops condemn racial discrimination; they argue that whites should be responsible trustees of blacks; and they propose that whites should gradually incorporate blacks into their society.

The Archbishops and Bishops of the Catholic Church in South Africa have judged it opportune to draw attention to the racial problem in our country and to the Christian principles that must govern attempts to solve it.

As a result of historical circumstances, the Europeans,* who constitute about one-fifth of the population, hold most of the land, wealth, and, for all practical purposes, the entire political power. The non-Europeans (Africans, Asians and Coloured people) have practically no share in the government of the country, and are debarred by law and customs from enjoying equal opportunity with Europeans in the field of gainful employ, and consequently in other spheres of social life.

This political, economic and legal 'Colour Bar' has its psychological counterpart. Whatever be its origin, it induces many Europeans to look upon non-Europeans as persons of inferior race who can

*In the context of the time 'Europeans' meant 'whites'. Later terminology distinguished between 'white' and 'non-white'. In the early 1970s the term 'black', referring primarily to indigenous Bantu-language-speaking people, but often also to all those who suffer racial discrimination, replaced the word 'non-white'.

never be entitled to full citizenship and complete equality. A stigma of social debasement is attached to the condition of non-Europeans. The natural consequence is the growth among non-Europeans of resentment, animosity and distrust.

Were the attitude of Europeans the sole reason for South Africa's racial problem, it would be simple enough to condemn it as unjust and unchristian, and, by a determined process of education, endeavour to modify it. However, the problem is far more complex than that. Its complexity arises out of the fact that the great majority of non-Europeans, particularly the Africans, have not yet reached a stage of development that would justify their integration into a homogeneous society with the European. A sudden and violent attempt to force them into the mould of European manners and customs would be disastrous. There must be gradual development and prudent adaptation. Nor must they be required to conform in every respect to European ways, for their own distinctive qualities are capable of rich development.

Though the majority of non-Europeans are still undeveloped, there are many of them well qualified to participate fully in the social, political and economic life of the country; some, because they have a long tradition of civilization behind them, derived from their ancestry in its entirety or along one line of forbears; others because they have risen beyond the cultural level of their people through education.

The problem, therefore, consists in dealing with:

(a) A deep-rooted prejudice on the part of most Europeans against non-Europeans;

(b) On the part of many non-Europeans, resentment and distrust, almost innate in the illiterate and aggravated in the literate through their experiences and reading to such a degree that they can scarcely conceive that Europeans might want to help them to higher attainments;

(c) A group of non-European people in various stages of cultural development, of which the majority is still totally unprepared for full participation in social and political life patterned after what are commonly called Western Standards.

(d) Divisions and animosity between various non-European groups.

The solution to this vexed problem of human relationship can be sought only in prudent and careful planning and in the practice of charity and justice. . . .

Justice demands that we give every man his due. It is a virtue that prompts us to recognise the rights of others and forbids us to hinder their legitimate exercise. There are rights that flow from the very nature and constitution of man, whatever the inequalities in the natural and social spheres. Such rights are fundamental and inviolable, and include the right to life, dignity, sustenance, worship, to the integrity, use and normal development of faculties, to work and the fruit of work, to private ownership of property, to sojourn and movement, to marriage and the procreation and education of children, to association with one's fellowmen. . . .

If South African conditions are considered in the light of what has been said, one arrives at the following conclusion:

(a) Discrimination based exclusively on grounds of colour is an offence against the right of non-Europeans to their natural dignity as human persons.

(b) Though most of the basic rights of non-Europeans are in theory respected, conditions arising out of discriminatory legislation (such as laws restricting employment), social conventions and inefficient administration, seriously impair the exercise of these fundamental rights. The disruption of family life is a case in point.

(c) Justice demands that non-Europeans be permitted to evolve gradually towards full participation in the political, economic and cultural life of the country.

(d) This evolution cannot come about without earnest endeavours on the part of non-Europeans to prepare themselves for the duties connected with the rights they hope to enjoy.

These are the principles that must govern any Christian solution to the racial problem. Charity and justice must supply the driving force, prudence will be the guide. What has been said remains in the realm of principle; it is for men versed and specialised in different branches of study and technique to apply these principles to difficult and complicated situations. It will be no easy task. It can be made lighter by the prayers, goodwill and co-operation of all who earnestly desire to see justice and peace reign in this country, and who sincerely believe that it is a Christian duty to love one's neighbour as oneself.

1957: STATEMENT ON APARTHEID

By 1957 the bishops had come to realise that the National Party would not be voted out of office, and that the apartheid policies had come to stay. Under the prime ministership (1948–1954) of D. F. Malan the National Party began to implement complete apartheid between white and black in the social, residential, industrial, and political fields. Many leading party members, including Afri-

kaans church leaders, also wanted complete territorial apartheid between whites and Africans. J. G. Strydom (prime minister 1954–1958) made it clear that in the 'European areas' there should be white domination or baasskap, *not just white leadership. Political institutions of blacks must be in their own areas, where they would exercise political rights under the 'guardianship' of whites. Between 1948 and 1957 much legislation enforcing these policies was passed: this included the Bantu Education Act which provided for different educational systems for whites and blacks, the prohibition of inter-racial marriage and social contact, and separate residential areas.*

In this statement the bishops condemn apartheid as 'intrinsically evil' because it aims to preserve white supremacy at the expense of black rights. By the same token the statement opposes 'separate development'. It makes a strong moral appeal to whites, and is reformist in tone.

In 1952 the Catholic bishops of South Africa issued a statement on race relations which emphasised the evil of colour discrimination and the injustices which flow from it. This statement maintained that non-Europeans in South Africa had a strict right in justice to evolve towards full participation in the political, economic and cultural life of the country. It pointed out, however, that this evolution could not take place unless the people concerned made their own vigorous contribution towards fitting themselves for the exercise of full citizenship.

Five years have gone by since this statement was issued. During that time there has been no change of direction in South Africa's racial policy. Rather, the old policy of segregation, responsible in large measure for the social pattern of the country, has under the name of apartheid received clearer definition and more precise application. Apartheid is officially held to be the only possible formula for South Africa's mixed society. Integration is considered unthinkable and partition into separate states impracticable.

The basic principle of apartheid is the preservation of what is called white civilisation. This is identified with white supremacy, which means the enjoyment by white men only of full political, social, economic and cultural rights. Persons of other race must be satisfied with what the white man judges can be conceded to them without endangering his privileged position. White supremacy is an absolute. It overrides justice. It transcends the teaching of Christ. It is a purpose dwarfing every other purpose, an end justifying any means.

Apartheid is sometimes described as separate development, a term which suggests that under apartheid different races are given the opportunity of pursuing their respective and distinctive social evolutions. It is argued that only in this manner will these races be doing the will of God, lending themselves to the fulfilment of His providential designs. The contention sounds plausible as long as we overlook an important qualification, namely, that separate development is subordinate to white supremacy. The white man makes himself the agent of God's will and the interpreter of His providence in assigning the range and determining the bounds of non-white development. One trembles at the blasphemy of thus attributing to God the offences against charity and justice that are apartheid's necessary accompaniment. . . .

From this fundamental evil of apartheid flow the innumerable offences against charity and justice that are its inevitable consequences, for men must be hurt and injustice must be done when the practice of discrimination is enthroned as the supreme principle of the welfare of the state, the ultimate law from which all other laws derive.

This condemnation of the principle of apartheid as something intrinsically evil does not imply that perfect equality can be established in South Africa by a stroke of the pen. There is nothing more obvious than the existence of profound differences between sections of our population which make immediate total integration impossible. People cannot share fully in the same political and economic institutions until culturally they have a great deal in common. All social change must be gradual if it is not to be disastrous. Nor is it unjust for a state to make provision in its laws and administration for the differences that do exist. A state must promote the well-being of all its citizens. If some require special protection it must be accorded. It would be unreasonable, therefore, to condemn indiscriminately all South Africa's differential legislation. It would be unfair to disparage the services provided for less advanced sections of the population and the noble and dedicated labours of many public officials on their behalf.

Many who suffer under the sting of apartheid find it hard to accept counsels of moderation. Embittered by insult and frustration, they distrust any policy that involves a gradual change. Revolution not evolution is their slogan. They can see redress only in the sweeping away of every difference and the immediate extension of full civil rights to all. They do not stop to contemplate the confusion that will ensue, the collapse of all public order, the complete dissolution

of society and perhaps their own rapid destruction in the holocaust. This is particularly true of those who find atheistic communism the inspiration of their present striving and their hope
for the future.

A gradual change it must be: gradual, for no other kind of change
is compatible with the maintenance of order, without which there
is no society, no government, no justice, no common good. But a
change must come for otherwise our country faces a disastrous
future. That change could be initiated immediately if the ingenuity
and energy now expended on apartheid were devoted to making
South Africa a happy country for all its citizens. The time is short.
The need is urgent. Those penalised by apartheid must be given
concrete evidence of the change before it is too late. This involves
the elaboration of a sensible and just policy enabling any person,
irrespective of race, to qualify for the enjoyment of full civil rights.
To achieve this will undoubtedly take statesmanship of a higher
order for the difficulties are not to be minimised. It is no easy
matter to dispel fears and prejudices and introduce measures so
contrary to the main trends and customs of the past. . . .

To our beloved catholic people of white race, we have a special
word to say. The practice of segregation, though officially not
recognised in our churches, characterises nevertheless many of our
church societies, our schools, seminaries, convents, hospitals and
the social life of our people. In the light of Christ's teaching this
cannot be tolerated for ever. The time has come to pursue more
vigorously the change of heart and practice that the law of Christ
demands. We are hypocrites if we condemn apartheid in South
African society and condone it in our own institutions.

This does not mean that we can easily disregard all differences
of mentality, condition, language and social custom. The church
does not enforce human associations that, because of these differences, can produce no good. She understands that the spiritual
welfare of her children cannot be fostered in a social atmosphere
wholly alien and uncongenial. But the Christian duty remains of
seeking to unite rather than separate, to dissolve differences rather
than perpetuate them. A different colour can be no reason for
separation when culture, custom, social condition and, above all, a
common faith and common love of Christ impel towards unity. . . .

To all white South Africans we direct an earnest plea to consider
carefully what apartheid means: its evil and anti-christian character, the injustice that flows from it, the resentment and bitterness
it arouses, the harvest of disaster that it must produce in the country

we all love so much. We cannot fail to express our admiration for the splendid work done in many quarters to lessen prejudice, promote understanding and unity and help South Africa along that path of harmony and co-operation which is the only one dictated by wisdom and justice. On the other hand we deeply regret that it is still thought necessary to add to the volume of restrictive and oppressive legislation in order to reduce contact between various groups to an inhuman and unnatural minimum.

1960: PASTORAL LETTER

The late 1950s was a time of increasing political tension in South Africa. H. J. Verwoerd (prime minister 1957-1966) gave to apartheid a more definite form than it had hitherto possessed. Each ethnic group of blacks was to be regarded as a national unit, and to be allocated to a specific land area, where it would have full opportunity for political and other forms of development, culminating in self-rule. Whites were to retain domination in the rest of the country (87% of the land's surface area). The number of blacks in the 'white' areas was to be progressively decreased, and only those needed for their labour would be allowed temporary residence. There would also be a maximum degree of residential, social, and educational separation there. Faced with the prospect of losing their South African citizenship, blacks increased their protests. These culminated in the anti-pass-laws demonstrations of 1959 and 1960.

The document below was issued in 1960, one month before the tragic shootings at Sharpeville in which 67 blacks were killed by police bullets. It has an ominous note. It condemns violence and the migratory labour system; it assumes that race prejudice is the source of the political legislation; it supports a doctrine of human rights; and, for the first time, it advocates a political solution for South Africa—the extension of voting rights to persons who meet certain qualifications.

We are gravely concerned about the future of our country and all its people. . . .

We have already spoken about this question of race relations in our previous statements, published in 1952 and 1957, but the urgency of the matter requires that we speak about it again. This problem must be solved soon, and in the light of Christian principles. Otherwise there is little hope for peace and order, as antagonisms will grow, prejudices harden into intolerances, and frustration lead to outbursts of disorder and violence.

We recognise the legitimacy of political aspirations and of the use of such means to bring benefits to the individual and the community, but we must demand that these be subject to the law of God. We have to 'render to Caesar the things that are Caesar's, but to God the things that are God's.' 'For there is no power but from God and those that are ordained of God.' (Rom. 13, 1) We demand that all peaceful means and methods be tried and tried again, and condemn the unlawful use of force and violence.

The State as the authority charged to achieve the common good has the right to use force to protect the common good, to maintain peace and order, and to 'put down malefactors', but within those limits only.

People are justified in striving for their legitimate rights, but they must use peaceful means. However, a sense of exasperation can lead to outbursts of violence. While we do not condone such acts, we would demand that their root cause in the way of injustices and oppressive measures be removed.

We would remind those who are impatient that they must be on their guard lest they be misled by men who do not desire the real and true good of the people, but only selfish and destructive ends. . . .

All human beings are one. It is the practice to speak of different races, but there is truly only one race, the human race. We are all children of Adam, and we all share the same human nature. We are all made in the image and likeness of God, possessing each of us an immortal soul, with its faculties of mind, and will, and sense, and we have all an eternal destiny. God planned that we should all be united to Him and to one another, in this world, as well as in the next. This unity overrides all differences and makes us one family, all ultimately related to one another. . . .

It is in the light of this unity and dignity that all of man's life on earth must be directed, in whatever phase it may be considered —social, cultural, economic, political. It is the whole man who has this value, and all affairs must be subordinate to man's nature and purpose.

It is true that men gather together in groups with loyalties that arise from the bond of relationship or association, but these too must be subordinate to the great overriding fact of the human person's dignity and his unity with all fellow men. It is true likewise that there are social distinctions and conventions, which have their purpose in the perfection of man and the ordering of society, but they are transitory and changing, and they cannot be allowed to oppose the unity and dignity of which we are speaking.

It is a fact also that man differs from man in the talents he possesses, in the heritage of the past that he carries with him, in the ability that he has to contribute to the common good. All of these must be taken into account in the ordering of social life, but they must be looked upon as imposing greater responsibility upon the more gifted, rather than as simply bringing with them positions of privilege. These inequalities, these accidents of birth and origin, do not and cannot deny the fundamental unity of the human race and all persons who belong to it.

The rights of each man

Nor do these differences render less forceful the fundamental rights which each man possesses. These rights arise precisely from the obligations each man has to fulfil his nature and reach his destiny, and they transcend other claims and desires.

Thus we find that each of us has the following rights:

The right to life.
The right to maintain and develop our physical, intellectual, and moral life, and in particular the right to a religious training and education.
The right to worship God both in private and in public, including the right to engage in religious works of charity.
The right in principle to marriage and the attainment of the purpose of marriage, the right to wedded society and home life.
The right to work as an indispensable means for the maintenance of family life.
The right to a free choice of state of life, and therefore of the priestly and religious life.
The right to a use of material good, subject to its duties and its social limitiations.
(Pope Pius XII: The Rights of Man.)

These fundamental rights include also the right to the proper ordering of the social and communal life, with equality of all before the law, and the rule of law enforced, including the right of trial, with justice being the criterion of legislation. This proper ordering of society requires that, in the sphere of industry and commerce, the labour of each be accorded its proper dignity, that a just wage adequate to the needs of the man and his family be paid, and that the development of the social order should render it possible for each man to secure a portion of private property, and favour higher educational facilities for those children who are intelligent and well disposed.

We recognise that in the conduct of public affairs the State has the right to impose restrictions on its members for the common good, but we deplore the tendency to multiply restrictions until they constitute an intolerable and exasperative burden, amounting almost to complete suppression of the right of free movement, and seriously affecting the right to work and earn a living.

Likewise the just social order condemns the migratory labour system, and demands that the family be allowed to fulfil its proper function with the husband and father joined to his wife and children in a genuine home life.

The same Christian conception seeks the promotion of a practical social spirit in the neighbourhood, the district and over the whole nation, thus bringing about a cessation of hostility between classes and interests, between groups and loyalties. Only in this society can the human person experience that feeling of truly human solidarity and Christian brotherhood which should be his. . . .

National groups may well exist within a community, and they have their legitimate claims, but they must be subordinate to the good of the whole community. They arise from reasons of history and custom, but they are not unchangeable, and in the course of time they alter or even disappear through merging into other groups that must be left to the Providence of God, who certainly rules the destiny of nations as well as of men. Much as the loyalty felt to one's own group draws one to work for it and its advantages, yet this loyalty must yield priority to a greater loyalty, loyalty to God's will, loyalty to the transcendent unity of all men.

New vision of society

For good rather than bad, the differing sections of our country are economically interdependent. This interdependence must be strengthened and not lessened, or abolished, for this economic solidarity is but a concrete expression of Christian love.

There are many persons of goodwill in the South African community who realise that the basis of a solution is to be found in the transcending of the colour-bar, and in the treating of their fellowmen as human persons, essentially the same as themselves.

There are many restrictions which could be done away with, much prejudice to be overcome, much fear to be allayed. This can only be gained through a new vision of society, one in which charity and justice are paramount, in which the Gospel is the foundation of life.

There are many fears and frustrations that beset our country. There is the fear on the part of some that they will be swamped politically and economically, and this has resulted in legislation which has deprived others of an effective voice in the councils of government. While we concede that it would be wrong to allow those with a more advanced culture to be deprived at this stage of an effective part in the government, and to have their economic status reduced, yet this protection need not and must not operate oppressively on the other sections.

Political participation

In the political field this can be achieved by the operation of a franchise based on justice. It does not follow that the giving of the vote directly to all qualified members of the community will result in the domination of one section over another.

The first point to be made is that colour should not be the criterion; the qualification should be the ability to exercise the vote in a truly responsible manner.

It is universally recognised that conditions must be laid down for participation by citizens in the political life of their country. In a country like South Africa with its special problems it is undoubtedly difficult to arrive at a satisfactory determination of these conditions, but it should not be beyond the ability of men motivated by the spirit of justice and concern for the common good.

As persons emerge from a less developed state, and show that they have these qualifications, they must be admitted to participation. The form that participation takes must be such that it is genuine and effective, and provides an opening for the highest possible participation, that is at the top level as well as at lower levels.

Mere political advantage cannot be the criterion for determining this participation in government. There are higher considerations which must come into play.

Economic opportunities

Similarly, in the economic sphere, while the common good requires that conditions of industry and trade, management, employment and labour should not be suddenly and abruptly disturbed and changed, yet nevertheless, the common good demands that those who have the skill and ability, the sense of application and patience, the desire to advance, should not be deprived of the opportunity of such advancement and progress in their economic position.

In this country there is an economic unity by and large in the sense that all are contributing to the general material well-being. There is a mutual interdependence between different sections. This fact requires in justice the payment of proper wages and the provision of decent living conditions in the form of housing and amenities, but it also demands that the opportunity should be open to all to acquire technical skills, and to dispose of their use without consideration of colour. The equilibrium of production and distribution must, of course, be safeguarded, as well as the advantages already gained by the worker, and the security he has obtained for his economic position protected. Adjustments that may be required through the adoption of this principle should be framed to cushion any ill effects that may arise for those who hold protected positions and, of course, responsibilities with that position. Nevertheless, such protection cannot be allowed to operate solely to maintain a privileged position for them in the economic order.

1962: PASTORAL LETTER

This statement was primarily an announcement of Pope John XXIII's intention to convene the Second Vatican Council. The bishops also used the occasion to re-state their stand on South African social issues.

. . . Since we are a people of diverse racial and national origins, it seems inevitable that human weakness will express itself in colour prejudice and in national misunderstandings. The fact of human frailty should not however constitute an insurmountable barrier to the building up of mutual trust and co-operation, if we remain faithful to the moral principles which are the foundation of Christian tradition 'where Justice joins hands with Charity'.

As a Christian people we dare not remain silent and passive in face of the injustices inflicted on members of the unprivileged racial groups. Colour must never be permitted to offer an excuse or a pretext for injustice. 'We must use every lawful means suggested by our Christian conscience in order to counteract and overcome the injustices pressing down on underprivileged groups through the toleration of a starvation level of wages, of job-reservation, of the evils which flow from compulsory migratory labour, particularly when the people who belong to these groups are denied the elementary right to organise in defence of their legitimate interests.'

Let there be no doubt among us that it is a Christian duty to use every lawful means to bring about a more equitable and harmonious relationship between all the different groups of people who together form our Southern African society. . . .

1964: BANTU LAWS AMENDMENT BILL
STATEMENT TO THE PRESS

The Bantu Laws Amendment Act of 1964 was designed to limit the movement of blacks from the 'bantustans' to white areas. It extended the laws relating to 'influx control', gave the government powers to restrict the movement of blacks and was a key law in the implementation of the apartheid policy.

The Conference of the Catholic Bishops of South Africa deeply regrets that the Government has judged it opportune to proceed with the Bantu Laws Amendment Bill, 1964. Although the Bill contains some provisions which are to the benefit of Africans, as, for instance, the protection given to Africans against malpractices, and the permission for re-entry to prescribed areas, the Bill, as a whole, is an invasion of primary human rights, and the minor concessions it contains are deprived of any real value by the deadweight of restrictions under which they are buried.

The effect of the Bill would be to deprive seven million African citizens of a strict right to residence, movement and employment outside the Bantu areas; that is, in four-fifths of the entire Republic. It would strip the African of his basic freedom in the country of his birth, making him dependant upon the possession of a permit to explain his presence anywhere, and at any time, outside the 'Bantu Homelands'. This is not consonant with any concept of the dignity of the human person.

This Conference fails to see how such a drastic curtailment of rights can be reconciled with natural justice and Christian charity. The Bill is a negation of social morality and Christian thinking, striking, as it does, at the basic Christian institution, the family, through its inflexible restriction of the individual. The Archbishops and Bishops of the Conference feel in conscience bound to join their voices with those of other Churches and Christian bodies in the Republic, in protest against the Bill.

1966: PASTORAL LETTER

This letter reasserts the doctrine of human rights, repeats the bishops' earlier condemnation of the migratory labour system, and criticises the South African practice of sectional rule for the benefit of a minority. Written during the Second Vatican Council, it is an attempt to apply the official declarations of the Council to South Africa.

. . . we find it necessary to reiterate that it is a grave violation of the dignity of the human person to prevent anyone, on grounds of race or nationality, from choosing his own mode of living, to restrict his choice of employment, his right of free movement, his place of residence, his free establishment of a family. If any laws make the exercise of these rights unnecessarily difficult or almost impossible, all legal means should be used to have them changed.

. . . we feel compelled once more to deplore any system of migratory labour involving the enforced separation of husband and father from wife and children over long periods, especially where the situation cannot be regarded as temporary. Such as system is not only unjust, but must result in grave injury as a whole. . . .

We appreciate and praise all that has been done, and is now being done, to raise the standard of living of the less-developed groups in South Africa, particularly in the fields of housing, education, health and social welfare. Striking progress has been made, at great expense, in all these spheres, over the past few years. Much, however, remains for us all to do for the betterment of the lot of the unskilled worker, whose wage is generally far below that necessary for the proper maintenance of a family; for it should not be forgotten that he is not merely a cog in the industrial or commercial machine, but a human being, with human needs and human interests. Here, perhaps, more than anywhere else, justice must be accompanied and supplemented by compassion.

'The [Second Vatican] Council lays stress on reverence for man. . . . Everyone must consider his every neighbour without exception as another self.' With this in view, the Council condemns everything which offends against the dignity of the human person, 'such as sub-human living conditions, arbitrary imprisonment, deportation, slavery, prostitution, the selling of women and children, as well as disgraceful working conditions, where men are treated as mere tools for profit, rather than as free and responsible persons; all these, and others of their like, are infamies indeed. They poison human society, but they do more harm to those who practise them, than to those who suffer from the injury.'

In stressing the essential equality of men, the Council says that it is true that 'all men are not alike from the point of view of varying

physical power and the diversity of intellectual and moral resources.' But, 'with respect to the fundamental rights of the
person, every type of discrimination, whether social or cultural, or
based on sex, race, colour, social condition, language or religion, is
to be overcome and eradicated as contrary to God's intent. For in
truth it must still be regretted that fundamental personal rights are
not yet being universally honoured.' The Council, rightly, does not
unduly stress racial or colour discrimination over other forms; it is
neither more nor less serious than the rest. But in racially pluralistic countries, like South Africa, racial prejudice takes on a crucial
prominence. It is for this reason that this Plenary Session finds it
necessary to reiterate the vigorous condemnation of the Vatican
Council: 'Discrimination is to be eradicated as contrary to God's
intent.'

1972: A CALL TO CONSCIENCE ADDRESSED TO CATHOLICS IN SOUTHERN AFRICA

*This statement marks the beginning of a shift away from the tone
and content of the earlier documents. It shows the influence of
radical concepts on the relationship between religion and politics
introduced to the Second Vatican Council by Latin American
theologians. Instead of listing contraventions to human rights, as
was the practice earlier, it speaks about the need to re-distribute
wealth, the de-humanising effects of South African legislation, and
the Church's responsibility to the poor. It makes recommendations concerning trade union rights, a minimum wage, and other
welfare services. It also makes a strong statement of identification
with the victims of oppressive political legislation.*

Your bishops have addressed you several times on social and inter-
racial justice. They have also repeatedly referred to documents of
the Popes and of the Second Vatican Council on these issues. Re-
grettably there has been little significant response. But we can try
again. We can renew with greater vigour and urgency our efforts to
do our share in creating a just, stable and peaceful Christian society
in our country. . . .

The social situation here gives us serious misgivings. Legislation
and conventions divide even those who are called to live and work
together and to share the same bread in Christ. We are thus prevented from knowing one another. A social gulf separates us as
Christians and humans, causing ignorance of one another, resentment and suspicion. In collaboration with other Christians and all

who are willing to work with us, we must do everything in our power to stop this fragmentation of brotherhood and love.

When we consider specific points in our social system needing reform, one of those most urgently demanding attention concerns the disastrous effects of migratory labour especially on the family. While the system of short term migratory labour may be helpful to young men from rural areas in South Africa to make a start in life, long term migratory labour has disastrous human consequences. The dehumanising effects of prolonged migratory labour can be seen throughout the world, but they are particularly serious here, where about one and a half million men, around half of the main African male labour force of the country, are obliged to live more or less permanently separated from their families. It is the common experience of mankind that such enforced separation leads to the breakdown of family life, and the increase of prostitution. . . . We, therefore, welcome recent indication that more men will be allowed to bring their wives with them to their place of work.

A country claiming to be Christian cannot countenance the humanly destructive effects of this labour system. Nor can it remain indifferent to life in compounds and in hostels, where men and women are denied a full human existence. There can be but one answer to this situation, and that is to work to eradicate the evils of the system. This problem should form an important subject for discussion and action among us. . . .

Opportunity for higher education should not be on grounds of race or economic position. Deep frustration begins with half-education. The African in particular is continually being told that he cannot assume responsible positions without proper education and development, while the necessary opportunities are not sufficiently available to him. To make educational opportunities readily available to some sections of the population, while others are restricted or impeded from them, is to create artificial feelings of superiority and inferiority. . . .

What we have said of education applies also to opportunities in skilled work and public services. It is wrong to deny a person deserved promotion on grounds of race, religion, sex, class or political opinion. Job reservation and lack of opportunity in skilled work are forcing not only adults but more particularly energetic youths to idleness and despair, to gangsterism and violent attitudes.

The Church has a serious duty to champion the right of the masses to a living wage. It is urgently necessary in our country that a minimum wage enabling families to live above the poverty datum line be secured for all workers for whom it is not laid down at present. Employers can do much to improve the workers' lot. Government regulations can be helpful. But it is universally recognised that the best means of securing a living wage and suitable working conditions is the registered trade union with the legally recognised right to negotiate, which unhappily is denied the African worker in particular . . .

In many ways the poorest members of our mixed population are the least protected. There is no unemployment insurance required by law for those who earn least. Pensions are below the subsistence level. There is a lack of care for the aged, the deprived and the handicapped. There is a serious and critical shortage of housing. Recreational and cultural facilities that would make life more human and tolerable are inadequate. Resettlement camps have shown how people are uprooted and moved in a heartless manner. Policing in townships and hostels and on trains urgently needs improvement. The innocent and poor have little protection against violence, exaction of bribes, abuse of the hire purchase system and similar practices. In addition to all this, 'pass laws' inflict on them a most grave and quite unnecessary burden.

There is in all this a deplorable failure to protect ordinary human rights, and a carelessness and indifference about needs, that conflicts with the spirit of Christianity.

In a democratic society the franchise is indispensable to any discussion of human rights. South Africa depends on Africans, Asians and Coloureds for 75% of its labour force, yet it denies full citizenship and franchise to them.

Whatever may happen in the homelands, common justice requires that South Africa face up to the question of granting citizen rights to all who in practice reside permanently in the Republic and have no other country.

We are deeply troubled by the memory of many people who have been detained, banned, silenced or restricted, without public trial, or who have become the object of suspicion and harassment because of their Christian concern for neighbours of a different race. All that we know of many of them is their struggle and protest on behalf of the voiceless who suffer under discriminatory legislation and way of life, and this deserves our sympathy and praise. It is also our duty to express our concern for the welfare of political detainees. We support those who believe a judge to be the proper authority to determine the humanity of detention conditions.

1974: BISHOP P. F. J. BUTELEZI: BLACK CONSCIOUSNESS AND HUMAN RIGHTS

After the formation of the interdenominational University Christ-ian Movement (UCM) in 1968 there was intense activity on black university campuses to define the position of blacks in a racially oppressive South African society. This resulted in the formation of the black South African Student Organisation (SASO) under the leadership of Steve Biko. UCM and SASO used ideas derived from the civil rights movement in the United States to work out a 'black theology' under the 'black consciousness' programme, relevant to the condition of blacks in South Africa.

Between 1968 and 1974 Southern Africa was in a state of flux. The political awareness of South African blacks was heightened by a number of developments: In 1973 there were nation-wide strikes in South Africa, and the starting of the guerila war of liberation in Rhodesia; and in 1974 Mozambique and Angola won their inde-pendence from Portugal. The bishops were forced to take note of the black consciousness phenomenon, and in 1974 Bishop Butelezi (now Archbishop of Bloemfontein) issued this statement.

. . . A new question has arisen recently with the appearance of the Black Consciousness movement. Despairing of being accepted as equal citizens many blacks are now withdrawing from attempts to meet whites in discussion of their problems and sufferings. They are deciding to 'go it alone', to declare their rights and take their future into their own hands. Some people are saying that this is the colour-bar in reverse, another form of racism and division of people, not by what they truly are but by their colour. They say Christians should have no part in anything that divides the chil-dren of God. . . .

In the Christian community there should be a great freedom about political and social action. We agree on faith, but we can dis-agree about the means of promoting social justice. The Christian community should not take sides here. If one man thinks he can do more for his people by working with whites, and another thinks he can do more in separate black organisations, each should be allowed his freedom. We should have the wisdom of the ancient Gamaliel who said: 'If this plan or this undertaking is of men, it will fail; but if it is of God you will not be able to overthrow it.' I am not writing to recommend or condemn one or other way of working, but to answer the scruples some people have about the Black Consciousness movement being Christian. Different movements may work equally for the same good end.

Black Consciousness seems to be such a movement. Blacks have begged, petitioned and demanded to be accepted as full persons and citizens. This has been refused and is being refused. Humiliating laws impose a separate, secondary and inferior position on them. The same is happening in other countries, if not by law by social conventions. It has raised a giant question for the black man, and started this movement, which is now linked up in various countries.

This question is: Is there something wrong with being black? What is the divine plan, the purpose of God in making some people black and their being conquered and used by others? Is being black a curse or a gift? The Black Consciousness movement has decided that black humanity is a gift like any other humanity, that the black man's history has given him experience that others have not, and that he now has something to give.

This movement may do something for the whole world, showing that those people who are most rejected are human persons, and with gifts to give others. It may be a defence of the poor and oppressed in any part of the world. This can be a truly Christian purpose. In the eyes of God, as Jesus taught us, what is important about human beings is not that they are clever, or rich, or powerful, or gone far ahead in progress, but that they are persons made in his image, capable of loving God and others, responsible to God for their own souls and their own lives.

Through demanding recognition and citizen rights the Black Consciousness movement can serve God. It is the teaching of the Church that human rights are built into man by God. In fact unless you believe these rights to be given by an authority beyond man's, and to make every human person somehow sacred, protected by a law of God, you have no sure foundation for them. These rights are given by God not only to assure a better and happier life now, but because without them it is difficult for a man to be a true man, to serve God and others, and to live up to his human dignity. . . .

There are those who say that to speak like this is not like the Gospel, where Jesus taught humility and patience, not resistance to evil, but turning the other cheek. It is our own cheek we should turn, not that of our children or our fellow men dependent on our assistance. For them we should struggle for justice, fulfilling another word of Our Lord, that if you help the poor, the prisoner, the sick or the homeless, you are serving him. Jesus died for opposing an exclusive law in which his people did not want others to have the same advantages as them, and whose leaders, while professing to be religious, 'ground the faces of the poor'. To this he opposed a freedom of faith making all equally children of God, and a universal brotherhood of men.

If Black Consciousness were to be exclusive and deny the humanity of the white man, or if it taught hatred, then it would be wrong. But if it defends all humanity in defending the most misused of humanity, intends to allow everyone his rights, and only works in separation to re-establish those who have been most disinherited, then it may be doing a service to God and all men.

1977: THE CATHOLIC BISHOPS' CONFERENCE

In 1976 a group of Soweto schoolchildren demonstrated against the enforced use in black schools of the Afrikaans language, which they saw as the language of the oppressor. A confrontation with the police resulted in shooting and the death of some children. During the ensuing months a wave of retaliatory violence engulfed the country. Over 500 people lost their lives.

Protests against the Afrikaans language soon gave rise to demands for the removal of 'Bantu Education', which many young blacks saw as an educational system designed to keep them in a subordinate position in society. The mood of South African blacks had changed: no longer were they willing to accept passively their inferior position in South Africa.

In their post-Soweto statement the bishops made their strongest ever judgement on the political situation. The majority of South African blacks are seen not merely to be poor (as in earlier documents) but 'oppressed'; the gospel is a means of 'human liberation'; the government's law enforcement methods are criticised; and the ideas of black consciousness are supported. In addition the bishops were aware of the escalation of the guerrilla war on South Africa's borders and the crisis of conscience of many white Catholics who were reluctant to fight in defence of South Africa's racial order. Their statement on conscientious objection is a plea that these people be accorded rights of non-participation in the war effort.

We recall that the disturbances began in Soweto with a demonstration on the part of the youth against a system of education which the students regarded as narrowing and limiting rather than developing their education.

The disturbances represent a wider frustration of black youth unwilling to grow into a society in which they can have no say as to the manner in which they are governed; cannot even have ordinary worker organisations to defend their right to a living wage; cannot be sure of having the right to a house and home near where they must work when they marry; are declared by the system in the Republic unfit for citizenship on grounds of colour only, without question of ability or qualification; and if they protest are suppressed with the unnecessary and horrifying violence we have recently witnessed.

Realising that South Africa has entered a critical phase in the rejection by the majority of its people of a social and political system of oppression, we add our corporate voice as leaders of the Catholic Church in this country to the cry for a radical revision of the system.

People starved of freedom, deprived of their just rights and humiliated in their personal and corporate dignity will not rest until a proper balance of justice is achieved.

We affirm that in this we are on the side of the oppressed and, as we have committed ourselves to working within our Church for a clearer expression of solidarity with the poor and deprived, so we commit ourselves equally to working for peace through justice in fraternal collaboration with all other churches, agencies and persons dedicated to this cause.

We again profess our conviction, so often repeated, that the only solution of our racial tensions consists in conceding full citizen and human rights to all persons in the Republic, not by choice on the false grounds of colour, but on the grounds of the common humanity of all men, taught by our Lord Jesus Christ.

In the struggle that has reached new intensity since June 1976 we are especially perturbed by what appear to be reliable reports of police brutality. Be realise that a situation of violence breeds atrocities on both sides, but we are speaking of seemingly systematic beatings and unjustifiable shootings during disturbances and of cold-blooded torture of detained persons.

With these reports coming in as the accompaniment of confirmed accounts of the many deaths of persons in detention, we cannot but harbour the gravest misgivings about police action and behaviour.

We call for an investigation and resolve to collaborate with others intent on bringing the truth to light and we protest in the strongest possible terms against the intention of the Government to provide legal indemnity for the police and other security personnel who may have been guilty of unprovoked and disproportionate violence.

It is clear that the Black people of the Republic have passed the point of no return, and no temporary suppression by violence, only a just sharing of citizenship, can give hope of any safety for the children, Black or White, now growing up in the Republic, and prevent the horrors of civil war in the future.

This is only to say that the Christian commandment of love must be fulfilled, and if it is fulfilled we can trust in God to give the grace of friendship and peace in social life.

. . . we commit ourselves to the following programme:

There follows a list of recommended changes in the social life of the Church to do with the eliminating of the 'apartheid mentality', the adequate distribution of church personnel and resources among all groups, and the integration of the Church's institutions.

. . . To be mindful of the Church's duty to minister to Christ where he most suffers in society and therefore to make more strenuous efforts to direct special attention to the growing numbers of un-employed, to industrial workers in general and migrant workers in particular, to worker organisations, to the thousands of squatters living on the periphery of large cities, to political prisoners, detain-ees, banned people and their dependants, and to other distressed and displaced groups discovered; and to provide as far as possible for the care of these groups and the creation of communities among them by specially appointed priests, religious and lay workers. . . .

. . . To give practical expression to the conviction that the Church's mission includes work for complete human liberation and to the teaching of *Evangelii Nuntiandi* that evangelisation includes trans-forming the concrete structures that oppress people; and in the light of this, to strive that the Church be seen in solidarity with all those who work for the promotion of human dignity and the legi-timate aspirations of oppressed people; on the side, therefore, of Black Consciousness, in regard both to those who promote it and those who suffer for it. . . .

. . . To take into account the singular situation and resultant ten-sions of the Church in South Africa, where 80% of the laity are Black and 80% of the clergy White, and to investigate as a matter of extreme urgency the feasibility of a Pastoral Consultation in which lay people, religious and priests, in large majority Black, may participate with the bishops, in arriving at policy on Church life and Apostolate but not on doctrinal and canonical matters. . . .

On conscientious objection

In the armed struggle that is developing on our borders and could easily spread internally, a grievous situation arises for all who are concerned about the use of violence. On the one side the conviction grows in a significant sector of the oppressed majority that only violence will bring liberation. On the other hand, the minority in power sees itself threatened by indiscriminate violence supported by international Communism.

In these agonising circumstances we can only promise with God's help to give leadership in a Christian examination of this tragic situation. We intend to publish reflections from time to time as incentives to Christian prayer, thought and commitment, and we hope to be able to do this with the representatives of other Christian churches and organisations. In the meantime we have resolved to say something about conscientious objection.

According to the teaching of the Second Vatican Council, 'it seems just that laws should make humane provision for the case of conscientious objectors who refuse to carry arms, provided they accept some other form of community service' (Constitution: *The Church in the modern world*, No. 79).

In order to understand the issue of conscientious objection, a careful distinction should be made between universal conscientious objection (the pacifist) and selective conscientious objection (e.g. on the grounds that a particular war is unjust); between combatant military service (carrying arms) and non-combatant military service (e.g. in the medical corps); and between military service (combatant or non-combatant) and national service (which could include services to the community, like social welfare, education, housing).

In South Africa the Defence Force Act [section 67 (3)]

(a)   makes no provision for any conscientious objector (universal or selective) to do non-military national service;

(b)   provides for universal conscientious objectors (those who belong to pacifist church denominations) to do non-combatant military service;

(c)   makes no provisions for selective conscientious objectors even to do non-combatant military service.

Such provisions are made in some way or another by almost every other non-communist country in the world which has conscription.

It should also be noted that objectors are sometimes accommodated, despite the lack of legal provisions for it, by being given non-combatant tasks but never by being given non-military national service.

Consequently in South Africa the selective objector and the universal objector refusing to do non-combatant military service are liable to a fine and/or imprisonment [Section 126, 127 (c)].

In this matter of conscientious objection we defend the right of every individual to follow his own conscience, the right therefore to conscientious objection both on the grounds of universal pacifism and on the grounds that he seriously believes a war to be unjust. In this, as in every other matter, the individual is obliged to make a moral judgement in terms of the facts at his disposal after trying to ascertain these facts to the best of his ability. While we recognise that the conscientious objector will have to suffer the consequences of his own decision and the penalties imposed by the State, we uphold his right to do this and we urge the State to make provision for alternative forms of non-military national service as is done in other countries in the world.

1982: REPORT ON NAMIBIA

In May 1982 the bishops issued a report on the conflict in Namibia between the South West African People's Organisation (Swapo) and the South African army. The following extracts show a new willingness on the part of the bishops to speak directly of political matters, often to the point where they strongly dissociate themselves from the policies of the South African government in Namibia.

The document accuses both the South African army and Swapo of committing atrocities against the civilian population, but states that a large part of the population considers the South African army to be an 'occupying' one; it questions South Africa's continued military and political presence in Namibia; it finds that Swapo would easily win a free and fair election and that this would be accepted with equanimity by the christian community; it doubts the South African government's accusation that Swapo is marxist- or communist-inspired; finally, it calls for a cease-fire and the establishment of a state of peace in which Namibia can achieve its independence.

. . . The impression we got of the attitude of most black Namibians to the present regime is that they consider it a device to ensure South African control of Namibia and the imposition of a structure and policy dictated by South Africa. It is blatantly geared to apartheid,

which is cordially detested by the great majority of the population, although among the Hereros and the Tswanas there may be
some significant appreciation of the separateness it offers. . . .

It was the almost unanimous opinion of those to whom we spoke
that the great majority of the people do not want the South Afri-
can-imposed constitution. They do not want the ethnic divisions
enshrined in this constitution. They want a unified and united
country. To this end they want free and fair elections under United
Nations supervision and are prepared to accept whatever government emerges from such elections. . . .

Proclamation AG149 of the Administrator General, published
on 17 October 1980, contains a proclamation of the State President of South Africa extending conscription to Namibia without
distinction of race. We encountered in Windhoek a group of
people, mainly 'Coloured', bitterly opposing this. It horrified them
to think that their young men would be forced to carry out the
same task as the South African security forces and to participate in
what would now become a civil war against the very people they
believed were fighting an anti-colonial war of liberation. . . .

In the greater part of Namibia, South Africa maintains its hold
over the country by means of ordinary police and security police.
In the operational area there is a complex of army units, police,
security police, special constables and home guards under the control of the army. Many are recruited from the local population.

Service in the army, the police or the home guard means some
kind of income in a situation of widespread unemployment. Head-
men, collaborating with the regime, have to be protected by home
guards. The whole complex of security forces in the operational
area is designated by the Ovambo word *omakakunya*. We found it
hard to determine the literal meaning of the word but its implications are by no means flattering − 'bloodsuckers', 'bonepickers'
and so on. Not all units may be guilty of atrocities but the local
population is inclined to lump all security forces together under
one common label. . . .

That detention and interrogation in any part of the country are
accompanied by beating, torture, spare diet and solitary confine-
ment is accepted as common knowledge. We found this attitude
among most church representatives we met and among many
others as well.

Reports of what occurs in the operational area indicate that it is
commonly accepted that in searching out Swapo guerrillas the
security forces stop at nothing to force information out of people.

They break into homes, beat up residents, shoot people, steal and kill cattle and often pillage stores and tearooms. . . .

Concerning reprisals, it was put to us that it is not the policy of Swapo to intimidate because it is a guerrilla army dependent on the goodwill of the people. But if Swapo learns that someone is collaborating with the security forces it issues a warning. If the collaboration is seen to continue it strikes. It has been known to prevent the burial of its victims to make sure that the neighbourhood gets the message.

On the other hand we were told that the security forces parade the bodies of killed Swapo guerrillas by driving around with the bodies dangling from army vehicles. . . .

As the events [of torture under interrogation] described above are accepted as characteristic among people in the operational area it is easy to understand their attitude when they say that they do not fear the Swapo guerrillas but the South African security forces. These forces are looked upon generally throughout Namibia as 'an army of occupation'. . . .

We discussed Swapo with practically all the people we met and gained the impression that support for Swapo is massive and that it would be easily victorious in any free and fair election held under United Nations supervision. . . .

The great propaganda weapon against Swapo by South Africa is the accusation that it is a marxist movement. We constantly asked what people thought about this. We were told time and time again that Swapo is essentially a national liberation movement, that, when it first opted for the armed struggle, it turned to Western nations for arms and only because supplies were refused by the West did it go to the Warsaw Pact countries. . . .

Church groups like the Council of Churches in Namibia and the entourage of the Lutheran bishops of Ovambo-Okavango said that they had no evidence that Swapo was marxist. On the contrary, they knew great numbers of Swapo guerrillas who are believing and practising Christians, young people who read their Bibles and say their prayers and are most resolute in maintaining contact with their churches. Church services are held in Swapo camps. . . . It was maintained that if there were marxist tendencies in Swapo they would be held in check by the christian faith so widely upheld and cherished by Swapo members.

A representative of the Democratic Turnhalle Alliance [a political party made up of an alliance of leaders of various ethnic groups, and holding the balance of power in the government] did not share this optimism about Swapo. He pointed out that its leaders were constantly visiting East Berlin and Moscow and must be influenced. He mentioned that it had been reported that in Bonn the question had been clearly put, 'Are you a communist?' The reply had been, 'Not yet.' Moreover, Swapo was working hand in hand with the MPLA in Angola which maintained that 'God is dead.'

The group that visited Namibia felt that there was some cause for misgiving in that Sam Nujoma [Swapo leader] refused to indicate what form of government Swapo would establish in Namibia. . . . He replied to questions relating to this point by saying that once the country was liberated the people must decide. . . .

Whatever the marxist tendencies of Swapo it seems to be a movement with powerful popular support, inspiring little apprehension in the majority of christians in Namibia and looked upon as a certainty to win any election. . . .

As is usually the case in situations of conflict, the pictures presented on one side by the South African government and on the other by the churches in Namibia and by persons interviewed by the representatives of the Southern African Catholic Bishops' Conference are so different that they scarcely seem to refer to the same issue. . . .

South Africa, in the eyes of the [South African] Prime Minister, is an unselfish benefactor of the Namibian people and its great protector against violent domination by Swapo, which . . . he sees as marxist as the forces that have taken over in Angola and Mozambique. . . .

In contrast with the picture presented by the South African authorities, South Africa, in the eyes of church personnel and of other Namibians that our representatives interviewed, is the blameworthy party. It is South Africa, they maintain, that all along has been the main cause of the conflict; first by refusing to give up its control of the country when the United Nations terminated the mandate and the International Court gave an advisory opinion justifying this action; secondly, by maintaining its armed forces in the country and by trying to impose a political pattern on Namibia based on apartheid and ensuring its subordination to South African interests; thirdly, by withdrawing from the Geneva negotiations of January 1981. . . .

In concluding our report on the Namibian conflict we do not feel it necessary to analyse and evaluate in detail arguments and statements put forward on both sides. In broad outline it is clear enough to us that there is a universal consensus, with South Africa

virtually the only dissenting voice, that South Africa has no right
to be in Namibia. To dismiss as biased or irrelevant the decision of
the United Nations and the opinion of the International Court of
Justice is to discard everything, however imperfect, which has
been slowly built up in mankind's agonising search for institutions
designed to promote and safeguard peace.

It also seems clear to us that the great majority of Namibians
have one overriding desire, and that is the implementation of UN
Security Council Resolution 435, resulting in a cease-fire, the
withdrawal of South African Security forces and the holding of
elections under United Nations auspices. They are quite prepared
to live with whatever government emerges from these elections, be
it Swapo or any other party or combination of parties. As has already been mentioned, it is a widely held opinion in Namibia that
Swapo is first and foremost a national liberation movement, and
that its marxist associations are due to the support it has received
from eastern block countries. It is also strongly held that the West
could become the predominant outside influence of an independent Namibia if it adopted a friendly and helpful attitude.

We conclude this report with an appeal for understanding, for a
creative, humane and christian effort on the part of South Africa
to conclude a just and peaceful settlement, and for sustained and
fervent prayer that, with the help of God, this will be achieved.

Aspects of the Namibian situation that we have presented,
though known in certain church circles, are so different from what
is usually publicised in South Africa that they are bound to come
as a shock to many. From what we have gathered from reliable representatives of several churches in Namibia, especially the Lutheran, Anglican, African Methodist Episcopal and Catholic churches,
also from the Council of Churches in Namibia and from our own
observations, we firmly believe that the picture we have presented
is a true reflection of the realities of that country as they appear in
the eyes of the great majority of the people. We make this statement in the hope that it will touch the conscience of many in South
Africa, especially those who share our belief in Christ and have
some say in the conduct of peace negotiations. South Africa owes
it to the people of Namibia and, for that matter, to its own people
to demonstrate a willing, just and generous spirit in speeding up
these negotiations and bringing them to a happy conclusion.

We call upon all who are believers in God to engage in fervent
prayer for this intention; for a rapid achievement of a cease-fire,
putting an end to the killing and suffering; for the withdrawal of

South Africa from a situation of violence that appears totally unacceptable to us; and for the establishment of a state of peace and reconciliation in which Namibia can achieve its independence and with the help of friendly states, including please God South Africa, can take its rightful place among the free nations of the world.

SELECT BIBLIOGRAPHY

Brady, J. E. *Princes of his people: the story of our bishops, 1800–1951* (Maseru, Mazenod Institute, 1962)

Collins, Colin B. *Catholic Bantu Education* (Pretoria, the author, 1957)

Higgins, Edward. *Predikant and priest: some calvinistic and catholic role profiles of the religious functionary in South Africa: a comment and review of two empirical studies* (Grahamstown, Institute of Social and Economic Research, Rhodes University, 1972)

Hinwood, Edward Victor. *Race: the reflection of a theologian* (Rome, 1964)

Hurley, Denis E. *The ideal of Catholic education* (Durban, Catholic Schools' Association, 1953)

— *Catholic views on Christian National Education* (Port Elizabeth, Education Department of the Catholic Bishops' Conference, 1960)

— *Apartheid: a crisis of the christian conscience* (Johannesburg, SAIRR, 1964)

— *A time for faith: the 1965 presidential address* (Johannesburg, SAIRR, 1965)

— *Catholics and ecumenism: prospects and problems* (Grahamstown, Rhodes University, 1966)

— *Facing the facts: the South African Institute of Race Relations* (Johannesburg, SAIRR, 1966)

— *Human dignity and race relations: the 1966 presidential address* (Johannesburg, SAIRR, 1966)

— *State and church: an approach to political action by christians* (London, 1966)

* This list of books supplements those found after each essay. A fuller bibliography on the Catholic church in South Africa is provided by Paul Meyer in *The Roman Catholic church in South Africa: a select bibliography* (Cape Town, University of Cape Town Libraries, 1979).

Kiernan, James. *Fragmented priest* (Durban, 1971)

Kolbe Association of South Africa. *Winter School, Mariannhill, 1951, 1952* (Mariannhill, Kolbe Association, 1953)

— *Summer School, Pretoria, 1957* (Mariannhill, Kolbe Association, 1957)

— *The Church and Ecumenism: papers delivered during the Christian Unity Week* (Pretoria, Kolbe Association, 1966)

Murray, Andrew H. and Versfeld, Martin. *The church's guide to politics* (Lovedale, Christian Council of South Africa, 1943)

National Catholic Federation of Students Conference. *Moral conflict in South Africa, papers presented at the NCFS conference July 1963* (Johannesburg, NCFS, 1963)

Nolan, Albert. *Jesus before christianity* (Cape Town, 1976)

Synnott, Finbar. *Catholics and the colour problem* (Maseru, Mazenod Institute, 1952)

— *Waar staan die Katolieke kerk in sake rasseverhoudings in Suid-Afrika?* (Pretoria, South African Catholic Bishops' Conference, 1976)